PRAGUE

ARCHITECTURE · HISTORY · ART

PHILIP'S

PRAGUE

ARCHITECTURE · HISTORY · ART

STEPHEN BROOK

PHOTOGRAPHY BY JOE CORNISH

GEORGE
PHILIP

To my father

TITLE PAGE *Crowded against a riverscape of water, bridge and willow is the dense jumble of Prague's churches and palaces, towers and domes, which has remained virtually unaltered for a century or more.*

First published in 1992 by George Philip Limited,
59 Grosvenor Street, London W1X 9DA

Text © Stephen Brook 1992
Photographs © Joe Cornish 1992
Maps © George Philip Limited 1992

British Library Cataloguing in Publication Data

Brook, Stephen, *1947–*
    Prague: architecture, history, art.
    I. Title
    914.37120443

ISBN 0540012572

Page design by Kathy Gummer
Maps by John Gilkes
Typeset by Tradespools Ltd
Printed in Hong Kong

Contents

....

Preface 7
Introduction 9

1
Hradčany 33
THE CASTLE *to* THE LOBKOVIC PALACE

....

2
The Castle District 59
CASTLE SQUARE *to* THE STRAHOV MONASTERY

....

3
Malá Strana 75
MALOSTRANSKE NÁMĚSTÍ *to* THE VALDŠTEJN GARDENS

....

4
Staré Město 97
CHARLES BRIDGE *to* ST JAMES'S CHURCH

....

5
The Old Town Square 123
THE TÝN CHURCH *to* THE OBECNÍ DŮM

....

6
Nové Město 145
WENCESLAS SQUARE *to* CHARLES SQUARE

....

7
Outside the city 165
THE LAPIDARIUM *to* THE MUNICIPAL MUSEUM

....

Appendices 178
CHRONOLOGY OF EVENTS 178 RULERS 179
ARTISTS AND PATRONS 180 OPENING TIMES 182

Glossary 183
Further Reading 186
Index 187

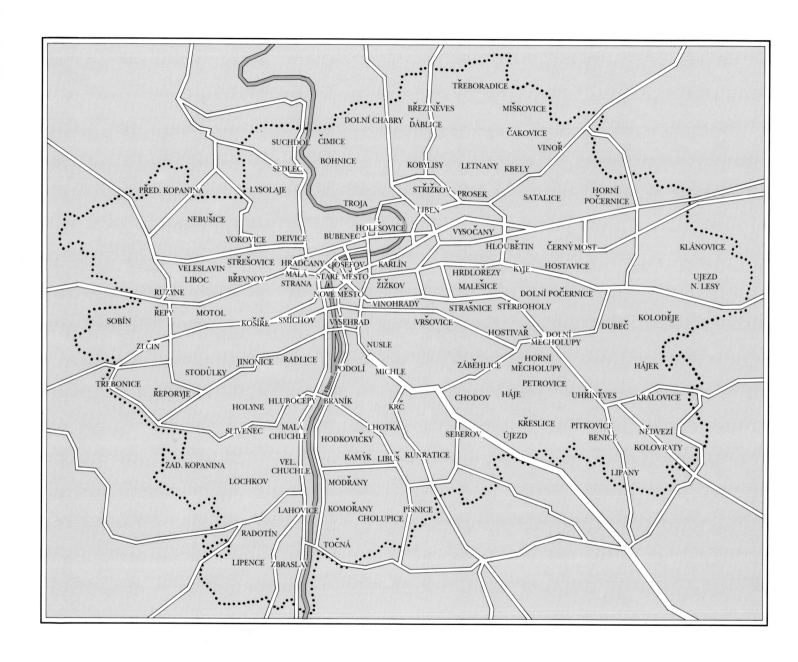

Preface

....

Prague evolved from a number of settlements, like Hradčany, as well as specific instances of urban planning, such as Nové Město, and every quarter has its own specific character and ambiance. Thus, in each of the seven itineraries in this book, the houses, palaces, churches, museums and squares share a common history and location. The historic core of Prague is compact enough to cover quite easily on foot, but is better served by public transport than many other cities, so none of the itineraries is particularly arduous or long. I have also suggested coffee houses, bars, or restaurants along the way.

Although all the major tourist attractions, and the buildings and museums of the greatest interest, are covered in the seven routes, no book can hope to be totally inclusive, and the itineraries are not meant to act as a straitjacket. Prague is a perfect city, once you have become acquainted with its layout and history, for laying aside guide books and wandering freely. Scarcely a single street is without interest, as many baroque gems, or art nouveau apartment houses or shops, can be encountered down side streets and in small shady squares. I am always astonished by how easily most tourists are contented with the principal sights of the city. The Old Town Square, the Castle, the Charles Bridge, these are invariably packed with visitors at all times of the year, but a hundred metres away even more delectable squares and churches and palaces remain unvisited. I find them particularly magical at night, when areas such as Mala Strana are virtually deserted and it takes only the lightest use of the imagination to transport you back into the seventeenth century.

OPPOSITE PRAGUE

Introduction

....

Compared to many other European cities, Prague is not especially ancient. Yet it rapidly evolved into one of the most culturally complex cities of Europe, with a variety of influences feeding like tributaries into its life and consciousness. It began as a Slav fortress, and soon became an international city in every sense; in the Renaissance too, it was immensely sophisticated, a centre of learning and culture with few rivals in Europe. The early seventeenth century saw a standardization of sorts when Habsburg rule became consolidated and somewhat petrified; with the Habsburgs came not only a dominant German culture but the Counter-Reformation. In the nineteenth century Czech nationalism challenged the prevailing German culture, and the rivalry between the two ended only with World War II, when German influences were all but obliterated.

Consequently it is dangerous to generalize about Prague, for its complexities defeat any glib attempts to categorize the city. When travel brochures proclaim the glories of Prague as a baroque city, the acclaim is at the expense of all the other phases of its history, most of which are still visible. There are romanesque houses, a gothic cathedral, renaissance mansions, rococo town houses and vast institutional buildings in a grandiose historicist nineteenth-century style, even some distinguished art nouveau and cubist buildings – all alongside the city's baroque glories.

The great fortune of Prague is that so much of the earlier phases of its building history has survived intact. There are a number of reasons for this. One of the most important is that it is one of the few major European cities that was virtually untouched by aerial bombardment in World War II. Plenty of bombs fell on the outskirts, but very few touched the city centre. After the war the Communist government embarked on enormous housing projects in the suburbs and continued to industrialize the countryside, but it spared the centre of Prague any major redevelopment schemes. Patrick Leigh Fermor, in his *A Time of Gifts*, recalls pre-war Prague and remarks: 'The higher the buildings climbed, the more

OPPOSITE *The Catholic Church flourished in Habsburg Prague, as the positioning of the immense Archbishop's Palace, just a few paces from the entrance to the castle, makes evident.*

9

ABOVE *Statues with rippling muscles groan beneath the weight of the balcony of a patrician mansion on Lazarská.*

OPPOSITE *Flying buttresses leap out from the choir of St Vitus's Cathedral, making a more graceful impression than the stylistic hodgepodge of the Great Tower alongside it.*

densely the woods enfolded the ancient town.' And although modern suburban building has replaced many of these woods, you still do not have to travel far from the centre of the city before finding yourself among the Bohemian forests.

Of course, not only were many of the buildings left intact, they were also severely neglected. There was no incentive for flat-dwellers to repair the exterior of their buildings, which were owned by the state or municipality, itself an indolent landlord when it came to the upkeep of the thousands of blocks under its care. Only in those parts of the city frequented by tourists – the castle, the Old Town Square – were there elaborate attempts to restore and maintain the architectural heritage, and the results are highly successful.

All this will change in the 1990s. Property laws will restore ownership to previous landlords, who in return will be obliged to maintain the fabric of their buildings. Licences have been granted to foreign companies to redevelop entire sections of the city such as Karlín, but on the condition that the neglect of decades is repaired by the foreign investors who stand to profit so handsomely from their enterprise. The character of Prague is likely to alter as radically as it did during previous phases of urban redevelopment, such as the slum clearance in Josefov at the end of the nineteenth century. What form the city will take by the year 2000 is impossible to guess. One can, I believe, be reasonably confident that Prague will not allow its architectural heritage to be squandered. It is a city that is high on anybody's list of the loveliest cities of Europe, and that is a resource no sensible regime can afford to lose or dilute.

The founders of Prague could hardly have envisioned how rapid the development of the fledgling city would be. Legend has it that Princess Libuše stood on the rock at Vyšehrad overlooking the River Vltava, about a hundred miles north of the far more important Danube, and foresaw the greatness of the city that was about to be established. She married a ploughman (*přemysl*) at work on a house near the city-to-be and thus founded the first dynasty of Bohemian rulers. A handy legend for the self-esteem of the city, but not one that can be substantiated. Nonetheless, the decision to convert this riverside trade route from a collection of hamlets into a capital city was, it appears, a deliberate one, and once Prague had been founded its growth, and growth in its importance, was swift.

The area now occupied by central Prague had been inhabited for centuries, possibly millennia, before its founding as a city in the ninth century. Various Slavic tribes had settled in Bohemia and Moravia, and the strategic importance of what was to become Prague was not overlooked. But factions were small and warlike, and only with the victory of the Přemyslid clan – said to derive their name from the no doubt mythical ploughmen of the Libuše legend – was any continuity brought to this part of Bohemia. The Přemyslids, under their first chronicled leader Bořivoj, developed two hilly sites on opposite sides of the river: modern-day Hradčany, the castle, and the rocky outcrop of Vyšehrad. Both were fortresses, but over the centuries Vyšehrad began to lose its importance, while by the early twelfth century Hradčany acquired a significance that Vyšehrad could never again rival.

It may not be based on the finest architectural models, but the dome of the Obecní Dům is an extravagant adaptation of art nouveau motifs.

By the tenth century the Přemyslid rulers, entertaining dynastic ambitions that were to be fulfilled, found their regime increasingly legitimized. Bohemia became part of the Holy Roman Empire, with borders stretching far to the east. A bishopric was founded in Prague in 973, during the reign of Boleslav II. Churches were built, including a rotunda on what was to be the site of St Vitus's Cathedral. The first monastery in Bohemia was founded a few miles from the city at Břevnov in 993.

Prague expanded swiftly, especially on to the bank of the river opposite the castle. The Old Town was established rapidly as the city's importance as a trading centre increased, and the street plans laid out in the early Middle Ages have survived to the present day with few modifications. Merchants from other countries were encouraged to settle in the city and German merchants, in particular, would later be encouraged by being granted special privileges. The eleventh century witnessed the strengthening of the fortifications of the castle, which by 1140 had supplanted the stronghold of Vyšehrad completely. At the same time the Strahov Monastery was founded outside the city walls, as well as numerous other ecclesiastical establishments on both sides of the river. In 1158, Vladislav II was upgraded from ducal to regal status, and became the first king of Bohemia under the title of Vladislav I.

Malá Strana, the Lesser Town, which occupied the slopes between the castle and the river, was founded by King Přemysl Ottakar II in 1257. He was also responsible for completing the Judith Bridge that linked the two banks of the Vltava. Gradually the different quarters of the city – Hradčany, the Old Town (Staré Město), the Lesser Quarter (Malá Strana) – were granted their own administrations with their own walls and town halls. The city, despite its tripartite character, was growing in importance, and so was the kingdom of Bohemia, which was no longer a Slav backwater. By the thirteenth century Bohemian power was being exercised as far away as Italy.

With the murder of Wenceslas III, a child who only occupied the throne for a single year, in 1306, the Přemyslid dynasty came to an end. The succession was to prove complicated, with other European princes ruling for brief and often war-torn periods. By 1310 John of Luxemburg was in command, with the consent of the local aristocracy, the Bohemian Estates. Luxemburg married Bohemia in the form of the Přemyslid princess Elizabeth, and John kept the throne until 1346.

With the accession of his son Charles I, better known under his imperial title of Charles IV, Prague's first period of indisputable glory began. Charles was 31 when he ascended the throne, and, like his father, he had been exposed to international influences. He had travelled widely and was ambitious for his city. After his election as Holy Roman Emperor in 1355, Prague became an imperial capital and Charles was determined it should look and act like one too.

His achievements during his reign of just over 30 years were extraordinary by any standards. He used his connections with Pope Clement IV to upgrade Prague from a bishopric to an archbishopric. Once this had been achieved he lost no time in importing French masons and architects to begin the reconstruction of St Vitus's Basilica on a magnificent scale as a cathedral. Charles founded the first university in central Europe in 1348. He added another quarter to the three existing districts of the city: the New Town (Nové Město). In doing so, Charles did more than point vaguely towards empty land and suggest that the city be expanded in that direction. The New Town was the most meticulously planned urban creation of the Middle Ages: all aspects of its design, construction and organization were tightly regulated, and huge squares, which still survive, provided marketplaces and open spaces among the busy medieval streets.

Hradčany was walled, and the Hunger Wall, so-called because it was constructed as a kind of public works project, still defines one of its boundaries down the side of Petřin Hill. Just as importantly, Charles replaced the Judith Bridge with the more substantial bridge that bears his name, although it was not completed until after his death. Dozens of churches and monasteries were founded under his patronage, even though an excess of ambition meant that few of them were completed by the time of his death in 1378, and some of them, such as St Mary of the Snows, were never completed at all.

After Charles's death, his son Wenceslas IV, who ruled until 1419, could not sustain the momentum established by his father. He also had to deal with a different kind of threat to his authority as king and emperor, the rise of the Hussite movement, exacerbated by the execution of Jan Hus. Populist preachers, of whom the most notable were Hus and Jan Želivský, attracted a strong following throughout the city, but especially in its poorer sections. The Bethlehem Chapel is the best known of the many churches where Hus, who subsequently became rector of the Charles University, and others proclaimed their message, which was a precursor of that of the Reformation. The king was not unsympathetic to this change of theological tack, but the clergy saw things very differently and perceived, no doubt rightly, that the reformist ideas of the Hussites posed a considerable threat to their authority and vested interests. After Hus ignored an order from the archbishop to desist from preaching, he was excommunicated and later brought before the Council of Constance in 1415 on charges of heresy. Hus had been given a safe conduct, but his judges insisted that his guilt as a heretic outweighed such niceties. In the course of lengthy disputations, Hus stoutly maintained his views, was condemned, and then burned at the stake.

In the historical museums of the city, an almost disproportionate amount of space is devoted to the Hussites. This is less a reflection of their theological contributions than a recognition of and perpetuation of the nationalist elements in their discourse. Reinforced by the essentially nationalist overtones of reformist preachings, the Bohemian nobility as well as the broader populace asserted themselves over the German minority. In 1409 thousands of German students at the university felt compelled to leave the country. By the early fifteenth century there was open conflict between the Hussites and the municipal authorities who sought to restrain their activities. The king kept his distance. After a group of Hussites had been arrested in July 1419 and a demand for their release had been snubbed, Želivský led a band of his supporters to the New Town Hall in Charles Square and stormed the building. Fighting led to the first known instance of what was to become an established procedure in Prague for dealing with uncooperative officials: 'defenestration'. A number of city officers were tossed out of the New Town Hall windows, and were replaced in office by Hussites.

Wenceslas IV took stronger measures against an obstreperous cleric than he did against Jan Hus and his followers. According to legend, John Nepomuk (c. 1350–93) refused an order by the king to disclose a secret revealed to him by the queen within the confessional. For this act of disobedience, the king ordered the priest to be tipped headfirst into the River Vltava. This at least secured John's martyrdom and, in 1729, canonization, and ensured him a permanent place in central European Christian hagiography. There must be dozens of baroque statues of the saint, a patron saint of Bohemia, both inside and outside most of the churches of Prague. He is invariably portrayed wearing a biretta and clutching a crucifix.

A month after the defenestration Wenceslas IV was dead, and the Hussite reformers appeared unstoppable, despite a crusade against them mounted by

OPPOSITE *From Vyšehrad you can look past the institutional buildings of nineteenth-century Prague to the graceful tower of St Apollinaris.*

Pope Martin V. The ecclesiastical authorities were expelled, and the Hussites appropriated their estates. Although the Hussites triumphed, it was at the expense, at least in the short term, of their principal city. Decades of revolt and conflict had hardly benefited the urban economy. Stability was only restored with the election of George of Poděbrady as the new king of Bohemia in 1458, despite papal opposition to the elevation. Gradually the city regained its prosperity, and George, like Charles IV, embarked on an ambitious building programme that saw the completion of the Týn church and the towers of the Charles Bridge.

After George's death in 1471, the Jagellon family ruled Bohemia for half a century. The Jagellons were Poles, and thus Bohemian lands were linked to both Poland and Hungary. The first Jagellon king, Vladislav, ended the reformist domination of Prague by allowing the Catholics to return to the city, which only led to renewed conflict and, inevitably, to another bout of defenestration, this time from the Old Town Hall. Vladislav, and his architect Benedikt Ried, were to make an indelible impression on the castle with the astonishing hall that still bears the king's name. Vladislav died in 1516 and was succeeded by his son Ludvik, who maintained his father's policies and enlarged the palace Vladislav had built at the castle.

Ludvik reigned for only ten years, and after his death the Bohemian Estates elected a Habsburg as their ruler: Ferdinand I, the brother of the Emperor Charles V. Visitors to Prague acquire a fondness for Ferdinand as the builder of the Belvedere, his exquisite summer palace, and one of the greatest Italianate renaissance buildings outside Italy itself. But, as an Austrian Catholic, he was not to be an outstandingly popular ruler, and found himself in growing opposition to the Protestant nobles who had been responsible for his accession to the throne. When the Estates were plainly reluctant to support the king in his wars against other Protestant powers, Ferdinand lost patience and suppressed with considerable ruthlessness the vestiges of the Hussite movement, and thus the Bohemian nobility, within his kingdom. The Counter-Reformation had begun in earnest when in 1556 the king, newly elected Emperor, summoned the agents of Catholic revival to Prague; by the time it was completed the Protestant institutions of Prague were obliterated.

From a nationalist point of view this Habsburg triumph was not a happy period of Czech history. Culturally, however, it was a different story. Ferdinand and his successor, Maximilian II, were autocratic but they were not barbarians, and the next Habsburg ruler of Bohemia, Rudolf II, was an outstandingly cultivated man. Like Charles IV centuries earlier, he established his imperial residence in Prague. Thus during Rudolf's reign from 1576 to 1611 the headquarters of the Habsburg empire were here. Nor was this merely of administrative significance. Rudolf attracted to Prague countless artists and architects, doctors and scientists. The very fine picture gallery in the castle is essentially the private collection of Rudolf II. This was also the era of the alchemists, who thrived under the emperor's patronage, and of astronomers such as the Dane Tycho Brahe (1546–1601), who is buried in the Týn church, and Johannes Kepler

OPPOSITE *The broad cupolas of the remarkable Karlov church contribute to the skyline a vaguely Byzantine shapeliness not found elsewhere in the city.*

(1571–1630). It was Kepler who established the three laws of planetary motion, thus laying the foundations of modern cosmology.

Mysticism pervaded the city in the late sixteenth century alongside the pursuit of more conventional scientific research. Rudolf was obsessed by alchemy and astrology, so that magicians such as John Dee (1527–1608), the English physician and magus once favoured by the Elizabethan court, found a safe haven in Bohemia, where his practice of the black arts intrigued a gullible nobility. Dee was playing a dangerous game, since, among other claims, he asserted that he had engaged in intercourse with angels, not the kind of thing likely to endear him to ecclesiastical authorities, despite a degree of protection offered by the emperor. Both Dee and another hermeticist, Edward Kelley, made a speedy departure from Prague in 1586.

The large and mostly prosperous Jewish population of the city – estimated by the English traveller John Taylor in 1630 as about 60,000 in number – was also infected by this craze, which in their case took a cabbalistic turn. The most famous rabbi of renaissance Prague was Jehuda Liwa ben Bezabel, better known as Rabbi Löw. He used, it was said, his mystical arts to create a being known as the Golem, fashioned from mud and clay and invested with life by the incantation of religious formulae. The Golem had been referred to in medieval cabbalistic literature, but no attempt to bring such a creature into existence had been made before Rabbi Löw's magical practices. Commentators often write about the Golem as though it had actually existed, so, at the risk of being a killjoy, I must stress that the whole story is no more than a legend, and the great and scholarly rabbi was only connected with it long after the events it describes had taken place.

Rudolf's reign was not to be free of trouble and conflict, for the Protestant Bohemian Estates began to assert themselves once more, and were sufficiently powerful to be able to persuade the Catholic emperor to issue in 1609 a document known as the Letter of Majesty, which guaranteed freedom of religious expression almost two centuries before the more celebrated proclamation along the same lines by the Habsburg Emperor Joseph II. This sweetness and light were to be short-lived. Rudolf was forced to abdicate in 1611 and Prague was soon to be embroiled in the appallingly destructive Thirty Years War. The war was precipitated by the action taken by Protestant citizens, who defenestrated Catholic imperial counsellors from the windows of Prague Castle on 23 May 1618.

In his book on *Austria*, J.G. Kohl in 1843 gave a vivid account of the defenestration. The counsellors, frightened by the proposal of the Protestant noblemen that they be ejected from the window, pleaded to be put on trial instead. But:

> William of Lobkowitz did not stop to make any such reflections. He seized Martinitz by both his hands. Four other nobles lifted the trembling governor from the ground, bore him to the nearest window, and without ceremony pitched him out. It is said that the assembly stood for several moments in dead silence, terrified apparently by what they had themselves done . . . The first to interrupt

this silence was the Count of Thurn. 'Gentlemen,' he exclaimed, 'there's another of them,' pointing at the same time to Slavata; who was immediately seized, and dealt with in the same way as his colleague. Master Philip Platter, the private secretary, was also ejected in the same unceremonious way as his masters... Not the least remarkable part of the little political drama was the fact that not one of the three gentlemen, who so unwillingly showed their agility, suffered any serious inconvenience from the compulsory leap, though the window through which they made their exit, was at least 60 feet from the ground.

The counsellors were able to escape from the city in disguise.

It is usually maintained that the defenestration prompted the outbreak of the Thirty Years War, although it is simplistic to suggest that there was a direct causal connection. But the action did inaugurate an uprising of the Estates. The war brought Swedish troops into the heart of the city, and some of the damage they inflicted is still visible on the fabric of the city, especially on the Charles Bridge towers at Malá Strana and Staré Město.

Battle lines were hardened further after the throne passed to Ferdinand II, who was determined to take no nonsense from the Bohemian Estates. When the Estates resolved to replace the Habsburg with the Elector of the Palatinate, Frederick V, Ferdinand brought his armies from Vienna to Prague, their numbers swollen by the troops of Maximilian of Bavaria, the head of the Catholic League. (Among Maximilian's troops was a private by the name of Descartes, who would later distinguish himself in more intellectual spheres.) On the slopes of White Mountain, just outside the city, a crucial battle took place on 8 November 1620. The army of the Estates was routed in a matter of hours, Frederick fled to the Netherlands the following day, and Ferdinand returned to Prague in triumph.

Nor was he disposed to show the rebellious Protestants much mercy. Twenty-seven leading members of the Czech and German nobility were executed in the Old Town Square, and Protestant leaders were expelled. The Letter of Majesty was a dead letter, and Catholicism became the sole permitted religion. According to Kohl, an eloquent but not necessarily accurate historian,

> whoever refused to embrace Catholicism was declared incompetent to exercise any corporate trade, and was generally deprived of his property into the bargain, and expelled from the country. So far was the system of persecution carried, that the Protestant poor and sick were turned out of the hospitals, and orders were given that none but Catholics should in future be admitted there.

Bohemia was reduced to colonial status as Ferdinand moved his court to Vienna. Like many other autocrats, the emperor, who ruled until 1637, did bring a measure of stability to his Czech domains. He and his successors also brought heavy taxation and a growing Germanic and Catholic influence. Under the Habsburgs there was both a flight of Protestant families from the city, and the construction of splendid palaces and gardens by the Catholic nobility. By the end of the seventeenth century some of the superb baroque churches of the city were

Every piece of statuary on the Charles Bridge – here an ensemble depicting St Francis Xavier – enjoys as a backdrop the broad waters of the River Vltava.

rising from their foundations, and Jesuit colleges were establishing not only a religious but an educational orthodoxy over the land. Prague became involved in the Habsburg wars of the eighteenth century, and was occupied at various times by foreign troops.

During the latter part of the seventeenth century and throughout the eighteenth, Prague played host to a number of artists, sculptors in particular, who developed the baroque style of Bohemia. It is to them that we owe so much of the texture of the city. Some of their work can be examined at close quarters in Prague's museums, but most of it is scattered throughout the city, on bridges and churches, statues and monuments. Architects such as the Dientzenhofer family thrived in baroque Prague, and their distinction, like that of the major sculptors, is by no means parochial, for their work ranks with the finest baroque achievements of central and northern Europe. Some of the first artists to come from abroad to embellish the city arrived before the heyday of the baroque: sculptors such as the Dutchman Adriaen de Vries (1546–1626), whose most notable contribution to Prague may be seen in the Valdštejn Palace gardens.

De Vries would be considered a mannerist sculptor, but Karel Škréta (1610–74), a native artist, was firmly in the baroque camp, and after studying for a number of years in Italy, brought Italian pictorial values back to Prague. His near contemporary, Jan Bendl, who died in 1680, was probably the first of the superb carvers who enriched the city. Ottavio Mosto (1659–1701) was Italian, but spent his last six years in Prague and made a very distinctive if sometimes controversial contribution with his rather florid carvings. To me, more interesting than either Škréta or another Italian-trained painter, Jan Krystof Liška, is Peter Brandl (1686–1735), who as court artist contributed dozens of altarpieces to the baroque churches of the city, and whose secular paintings, many of which can be seen in St George's Convent, reach a high level of achievement. Unlike Brandl's, Jan Kupecký's superbly accomplished paintings are rarely encountered within the churches of the city but are generously displayed at St George's Convent, where the nation's finest collection of Bohemian art is housed. Václav Reiner (1689–1743) is a more frequently encountered artist, whose fluent brushwork decorates many a ceiling of church and palace.

By the beginning of the eighteenth century Prague must have been packed with sculptors. Matthias Jäckel produced some enormous statues among those that posture on the façades of the city's churches, but the two names to conjure with are those of Brokoff and Braun. There were two Brokoffs of importance, Jan and his son Ferdinand Maximilian (1688–1731), who contributed an abundance of statues to the city, though unfortunately most of them are devoted to the revered local saint, St John Nepomuk. Matthias Braun (1684–1738) was born in the Tyrol, but arrived in Bohemia in his twenties after studying in Italy. Braun is probably the greatest of the baroque sculptors of Prague, his work being wonderfully fluid and expressive. Carvings by both the younger Brokoff and Matthias Braun may be inspected at close quarters on the Charles Bridge, and, in the case of Braun, in the church of St Clement in the Old Town, as well as in numerous

Nowhere in Prague will you find a greater wealth of sgraffito design than on the facade of the Schwarzenberg Palace in the Castle Square.

other churches. Both artists established workshops, just as their great medieval predecessor Peter Parler had done, and sometimes carvings attributed to these masters may well be the products of their pupils and followers.

Many of the architects active in baroque Prague were imported from France or Italy – I am thinking of Jean Baptiste Mathey, Giovanni Santini, and Giovanni Alliprandi, among others – and they were responsible for many of the palaces in Malá Strana, as well as a number of churches. One name stands out, however: Dientzenhofer. Christoph Dientzenhofer (1655–1722) came from a Bavarian clan of architects. He was succeeded by his even more gifted son, Kilián Ignác (1689–1751), who designed some of the most striking churches of Prague, such as

St Nicholas in Malá Strana, various churches in the New Town, and the monastery church at Břevnov. What I particularly admire about the Dientzenhofers is their sculptural quality, the sweep and bravura with which their façades are moulded. Baroque decorative artists are thick on the ground in Prague, but no one could rival this family for boldness and invention. By any European standards, their works are masterpieces of the Baroque.

Baroque, as the eighteenth century ran its course, became increasingly stylized and standardized, but a fresh impetus was given to the style in the latter part of the century by the development of Rococo. It was an essentially decorative rather than sculptural style, but it is hard not to succumb to the sheer prettiness of the best rococo work in Prague, especially façades by Johann Joseph Wirch, and by an artist who thrived just before the heyday of Rococo, Ferdinand Maximilian Kaňka, whose façades and interiors are widely encountered in the city.

The Habsburgs were Austrians, and Bohemia was only one of their many domains. They loved administration and bureaucracy, and those great networks, spread throughout their lands, inevitably brought a measure of uniformity. Maria Theresia put an end to the separate Bohemian Chancellery in 1749 and the kingdom was ruled from Vienna. In 1784 the discrete municipal administrations of the various quarters of Prague were abolished, and the city was unified for the first time. German was the language of administration and education, and the continuing richness of German culture as well as its imposition on the populace brought about a decline in the importance of the indigenous Czech culture. During the Hussite revolution, Czech culture had come of age, and Czech-language printing houses had thrived. The language was not suppressed under the Habsburgs, but it was supplanted by German as the language of the professional classes.

The torpor of Habsburg rule was not to continue indefinitely, as, like most cities of Europe, Prague was ignited by the spirit of 1848. With the failure of the revolutions in Europe to dislodge the Habsburgs or temper the mostly benign autocracy of their rule, Czech nationalist fervour was again relegated to the back burner, especially since the German-speaking population continued to wield the economic power within Bohemia. But it was now unavoidably on the agenda, just as it was among the dozens of other national groups under Habsburg domination. During the protracted reign of Emperor Franz Josef I, accommodations had to be made with various groups and his control gradually weakened. With his death in 1916 the game was up, and his successor Karl, the last Habsburg to rule, proved highly ineffectual and was forced from power in 1918.

This, together with the end of World War I and the resurgence of nationalist claims throughout eastern Europe, paved the way for the establishment of the Czech republic in October 1918. Tomáš Masaryk, already enjoying the status of elder statesman, was elected the country's first president a month later. During this inter-war period the country prospered. Sophisticated and industrialized, it was able to compete economically with the other new, and some of the old, nations of Europe.

The calendar by Josef Mánes located beneath the astronomical clock on the Town Hall Tower is more decorative than useful.

Tension between the Czech and German populations of the capital may have subsided, but new tensions replaced it. The Slovaks have never felt comfortable within the Czechoslovak federation, and the inclusion of the Sudeten Germans within the new borders was to have disastrous consequences. With German culture giving way to the now dominant Czech culture allied to nationalism, the Sudeten Germans were prone to regard themselves as a second-class minority, and demagogues such as Konrad Heinlein encouraged them in this view. It was not difficult for Hitler to exploit this discontent among the German minority within Czechoslovakia. This led to the Munich Agreement of 30 September 1938, and in March 1939 to the invasion of the country by German forces. Bohemia and Moravia became a German protectorate, but Slovakia, which showed distinct pro-Nazi sympathies, was treated more favourably.

Once the war was over, independence was restored but not for long. After liberation by Soviet troops, there was considerable goodwill within the country towards the Russian-inspired Communists, who swiftly manipulated their way into a position of control. Until 1948 a coalition also including socialists and social democrats ruled the country, but Communist control of vital institutions such as the police and the divisions in the opposition meant that it was only a matter of time before the Communists took over. By 1948 Czechoslovakia was firmly within the Eastern bloc, and in the grip of Stalinist leaders such as Klement Gottwald. The old tradition of defenestration may have been revived in March 1948 to dispose of the sole non-Communist member of the Gottwald cabinet, Tomáš Masaryk's son Jan, who 'fell' from a window in the Černín Palace.

*From Kampa Island there is a beautiful
view across the Vltava onto the
eastern embankment and the slightly
gaudy Smetana Museum.*

Four decades of Communist rule, which was inseparable from economic colonization by the Soviet Union, impoverished the country. A culturally and politically sophisticated people were kept under tight reign. Show trials and executions terrorized the country during the 1950s, and the courageous attempt in the late 1960s to soften the ideological rigour of the centralized autocratic Communist system led to the Russian invasion of 1968 and the reimposition of a Stalinist-style regime.

Even in the late 1980s the Communists ruled with a firm hand, although their ideology was widely recognized to be bankrupt, and the system survived only by rewarding those who were loyal to the power structure and punishing those who were not. Tomáš Masaryk, virtually a father figure to generations of Czechs, was a non-person in the museums and libraries. German-language authors, especially those with a potentially subversive message such as Franz Kafka, remained absent from the bookshops and school curricula. A mindless uniformity prevailed, with all independence of thought driven underground, where, perilously, it flourished. With the rise to power of the reform-minded Mikhail Gorbachev in the Soviet Union, the days of the old regime in Czechoslovakia were numbered, and the collapse of the East German system sealed the fate of its Czech counterpart. When push came to shove, there was no one left, apart from a few time-servers and a handful of blinkered ideologues, who was prepared to defend it, and in November 1989 the Velvet Revolution achieved its bloodless triumph. A man of complete integrity, Václav Havel, became president, and a free market economy was instituted.

The consequences for the capital city are incalculable. After 40 years of neglect there are, as mentioned earlier, strong possibilities that many buildings of architectural importance and beauty will at last be restored. But the damage to the city in recent decades has not been restricted to its fabric. Czechoslovakia's major writers, painters and performing artists mostly found themselves unable to function freely within the autocratic state, and either left the country or operated underground, where their influence was bound to be limited. Theatre directors managed to be fairly innovative, but the works of playwrights such as Havel with texts uncomfortable to dictators and political manipulators were not performed. Even non-political writers who had offended against the regime by taking a prominent role in the Prague Spring of 1968 or by signing Charter 77 found themselves in artistic limbo, compelled either to leave the country or to resort, dangerously, to samizdat. The opera house, more often than not, was a joke, with good singers stumbling about in appalling productions. Only the music festival mounted in Prague each spring was of a high standard, largely because it was able to attract international performers. No doubt Prague will revitalize its long-dormant artistic traditions, which could not flourish in a context devoid of liberty, and the city will regain its reputation as a major cultural centre in Europe.

The economic and, perhaps, political uncertainty of the newly self-liberated country should not deter anyone thinking of visiting Prague. There are very few traffic-clogged streets, and the city can be comfortably travelled on foot.

Indeed, there are few major European cities easier to explore than Prague. As one would expect in a city where car ownership is far from universal, public transport is extremely reliable. Large stretches of Malá Strana and the Old Town have been converted into pedestrian zones, and those portions still open to traffic tend to be narrow and bedevilled by one-way systems. If you are staying in one of the major hotels on Wenceslas Square, it is possible, if you secure one of the special permits from your hotel, to leave your car on the square. Othewise, you are better off leaving your car outside the city centre and using it as little as possible.

It does not take more than half an hour to walk from one end of old Prague to the other, so in fine weather it is often easier and more pleasant to use your feet than public transport. Feet can be supplemented by three kinds of public transportation: metro, tram, and bus. There are three metro lines, of which A is probably the most useful, linking Malá Strana with the Old Town and New Town. Trams are slightly less frequent than the metro, but still a very useful way of getting around. Bus lines tend to begin where the metro lines end, and mostly serve suburban districts. Be sure to buy an up-to-date street map, which should mark all tram and bus routes, as many of the routes indicated on older maps have been altered. Moreover, many station names have been changed. Florenc replaces Sokolovská; Vyšehrad replaces Gottwaldova; and Anděl replaces Moskevská – to mention only the most important changes.

Tickets are available from machines at the entrance to every station, and it is wise to keep a small supply on you, as such machines are not always available near tram or bus stops. You can also buy 24-hour tickets, worth doing if you intend to use the system more than eight times in that period. Your ticket must be stamped on entering whichever system you are using. In Prague, public transportation operates on an honour system, but plain-clothes inspectors do rove about and are empowered to impose on-the-spot fines if you are travelling without a ticket.

As you wander about the city, you will find that the house numbering system is somewhat confusing. Most buildings have two numbers, an old and a new. If two figures are cited in the text as a house number, the figure in brackets, usually with three digits, will be the old number, or, as some guide books refer to it, the descriptive number.

The language can be a problem. In the 1920s E.I. Robson, in his book *A Wayfarer in Czecho-Slovakia*, ruefully recalled:

> Having studied languages all my life, even to the point of making from them a meagre bread-and-butter, I attacked Czech with a light heart and took its initial difficulties with a frolic welcome. But as I got farther, I wallowed deeper, and was obliged at length to give it up. I fear this will be the fate of many others.

This certainly reflects my own experience. Quite apart from the need to acquire a new vocabulary, another major problem is posed by the complexities of Czech pronunciation. The language can be difficult to pronounce – some words seem composed entirely of consonants, indeed some words such as *trh* are composed entirely of consonants – and difficult to understand. For me the greatest difficulty is that Czech, like most Slav languages, is heavily inflected, which means that the same word will appear in different forms according to the grammatical role it is playing.

Most guide books provide a small working vocabulary which, however, it is worth learning, if only as a means of being polite and of distinguishing pork from chicken on a menu. In most hotels and restaurants frequented by tourists, the staff will speak some English and better German, but many Czechs speak only their own language. Most Czechs studied Russian as a compulsory second language in school (until 1989), but they are loath to speak the language and often deny any knowledge of it. Since the revolution everyone wants to learn English, so communication will become easier from year to year.

Given the long German heritage of Bohemia, it is not always easy to know how to refer to Czech historical figures and artists. Some are best known by Czech names, other by German names, and occasionally by English names. I have made no attempt to be consistent about this, and have usually adopted the name most likely to be familiar to English-speaking readers. Thus, there seems little point referring to King Václav or King Karel, and I have used the English names Wenceslas and Charles. I see little to be gained in using the Czech label Sv Jindřich in place of St Henry, and have not done so. On the other hand, it seems sensible to use Czech topographical names rather than to anglicize them. Thus, instead of Castle Square, I have tended to use Hradčanské náměstí, since it can do no harm for potential visitors to Prague to accustom themselves to the street signs and place names they will encounter. On the other hand, it seems perverse to keep referring to the Karlův instead of the very well-known Charles Bridge. During the Habsburg era many Bohemian families adopted Germanic forms for their names, but since 1918 and 1948 it has become more usual for Czech versions of those names to be used. Although there are exceptions to this rule, I have tended to respect the Czech adaptations, referring to Valdštejn rather than Waldstein and to Lobkovic rather than Lobkowitz.

Tourism has been complicated in some respects by the revolution, as the status of a number of museums has become doubtful. The dismantling of the centralized state apparatus that took effect in 1991 means that many properties confiscated after 1948 will be returned to their former owners, who will then be responsible for their upkeep. This could affect, for example, the museum of musical instruments and the museum of literature, both of which are presently housed in former church property. The Mozart Museum in the Villa Bertramka could also be affected. Other museums have been closed, and good riddance. They were devoted to Stalinist propaganda, and nobody ever went to them except school parties under compulsion and devotees of the ghoulish such as myself.

After the revolution the government recognized what every black market currency dealer had always known: that the official rate of exchange was a farce. It promptly brought the Czech crown into line with the prevailing black market rate, which was, after all, the realistic rate. In most cases this increased the purchasing power of the Western visitor about fourfold. Tourists will still be approached by black market operators and invited to change money, but I advise strongly against doing so. The black market rate is likely to be only slightly higher than the official rate, so the dealers are making most of their income out of defrauding those who use their services. Many a tourist, after a hurried negotiation in a doorway, has returned to his hotel to discover that half the wad of crown bills consists of blank sheets of paper. Given the very favourable exchange rate, the only motive for using the black market is excessive greed, and if you are cheated you will have only yourself to blame.

Eating out in Prague can prove something of a disappointment. If you play safe and eat in one of the large hotels, you will enjoy the convenience of waiters who almost certainly speak English and can advise you about certain dishes. You will also be charged a good deal for your meal, although by Western standards it will still strike you as a bargain. But although standards are improving, the quality may still be mediocre.

Another possibility is to eat at one of the well-known restaurants such as the Valdštejnská hospoda, the Three Ostriches (U tří pštrosů) or U Malířů. Unfortunately every other discerning visitor has the same idea, and you are almost certain to find the restaurant fully booked if you arrive on spec. During the tourist season, which is almost year-round thanks to easy access to Prague from southern Germany and Austria, these well-known restaurants are likely to be booked days, even weeks, in advance. Their prices, while expensive by Prague standards, are reasonable, and in such places you will dine in comfort and have a good selection of dishes and local wines.

These voluptuous figures above a doorway on Široká are typical of the lushly fanciful redevelopments that took place in Josefov a century ago.

Other restaurants that are not quite as well known can offer comparable food and service. I've eaten well at, for example, U Kolovrata, a wine bar in Malá Strana, and at Vikárka next to St Vitus's Cathedral, where in winter you may find wild boar on the menu. But it is wise not to come to Prague with great gastronomic expectations. Even in the more luxurious places, such as the Klášterní Vinárna on Národní, the food can exhibit a numbing sameness. You will find identical garnishes on soups and meats, *pommes frites* as a standard accompaniment, and an inability to cook a decent sauce. Pork is the most common meat, and is often better than the more expensive beef, which is frequently overcooked, a fate that rarely overcomes the pork. Soups are good everywhere, even though some of the bits floating in them can seem a bit suspect in the cheaper places. Fish is risky, and likely to be a piece of overcooked and very bony carp. Trout is available at some restaurants and is probably a safer bet. Fresh vegetables are almost unheard of, although stewed vegetables such as cabbage and spinach are reliable. Many dishes are garnished with *oblahu*, an assortment of cold tinned vegetable salads and shredded raw onions and cabbage. It is usually awful.

There are local customs which it is well to be aware of. It is common practice, even in some of the smarter restaurants, and certainly in the cheaper ones, to share tables if the place is crowded. Do not be put off if the Czech at whose table

These lovely bronzes by Adriaen de Vries in the Valdštejn gardens may be copies of originals removed to Sweden long ago, but the gardens would be impoverished without them.

you propose to sit appears grudging. This is not Italy, or Greece. I always welcome interlopers to my table with a friendly wave and smile, to introduce a little civility into public communications. They'll sit there anyway, so you may as well be accommodating. You will also be expected, except in small or very informal restaurants without appropriate facilities, to leave your coat at the cloakroom. This is also true of most cafés. There may or may not be a charge for this but it does no harm to hand a crown to the crone. There will be another crone guarding the lavatories, and she too will expect a crown. Lavatory paper must also be bought from the attendant, as stalls are not equipped with it. Tipping is not the norm, though waiters will half-expect to be allowed to keep small change. If you have received particularly good or helpful service, by all means leave a tip of about five per cent; anything above ten per cent is likely to be regarded as throwing your money around.

You may also experience some difficulty, except in the centre of town, in finding places open for dinner. Many cheaper restaurants cater to the busy lunchtime office trade, and close in the evenings. Others serve a limited range of food or stop serving it quite early in the evening. Prices are higher after about 5 o'clock, except in the smart restaurants where the prices are high all the time.

Office workers and students cannot afford to eat regularly in the smarter restaurants and wine bars. They frequent plain restaurants, which often are open only at lunchtime, or beer halls that serve food. There is nothing wrong with these places, as long as you don't mind sharing a table and don't object to people smoking cigarettes 2 feet away from your plate. The food will be uniform – a pork chop with dumplings and sauerkraut is the most frequently encountered dish – but tasty and filling. Begin with soup, and don't even think of ordering dessert. One of the waiters will circulate with trays of beer and, if you signal, deposit one by your elbow, and mark your tab. The beer is excellent everywhere, especially the dark beer from Braník or the home brew of U Fleků. At such places, soup, main course, and a beer or two should cost about 40 crowns at lunchtime, whereas more formal restaurants are likely to cost 120–150 crowns, or even more.

If you don't wish to stop for a proper meal, there are innumerable snack bars throughout Prague. Some are marked Bufet; others are attached to butcher's shops; others are street stalls selling rather greasy kolbasy sausages with mustard and bread for under ten crowns. At bufets you will find a variety of salads, often potato-based, open sandwiches, and pastries. Because of the turnover the food is fresh and tasty, if not exactly refined. Bufets will also wrap food for you to take away. Formal cafés are not plentiful in Prague, but cukrárnas are, and they are much the same thing, serving coffee and pastries, except that you may have to eat and drink at counters rather than at tables. The quality of pastries and cakes varies from dull to excellent.

Coffee tends to be gritty and lacking in flavour, but espresso machines are increasingly common and worth keeping an eye out for, even though aficionados of the French and Italian versions will find the Prague 'espresso' rather weak. Czechs often favour what they call Turkish coffee, which is sludgy and doesn't have the intensity of its oriental model. Czechs also have quite a sweet tooth, and so in addition to the numerous cukrárnas you will find street stalls selling waffles and ice-cream (*zmrzlina*), which is often very good.

Before the revolution, cheating was a way of life, and cheating tourists was second nature. I used to grow very impatient with being short-changed, being brought dishes other than those I had ordered, being told only the most expensive dishes and wines were left on a menu, and so forth. The situation is greatly improved, but you can still encounter, as I have done, waiters who, after twenty years on the job, don't seem to have learned to add up correctly and whose errors invariably work to the customer's disadvantage, and shopkeepers who, knowing that you can't read the price tags on goods stacked on the shelves behind the counter, improvise totals to their advantage. This kind of behaviour is the exception rather than the rule, but it doesn't hurt to be on your guard.

A favourite trick of waiters is to refuse to give you a menu on the grounds that it's in Czech, which indeed it is. This allows them to offer you in your own language a few dishes from which you make your selection; having placed yourself entirely in the hands of your waiter, your bill is likewise at his mercy. The more grand and prestigious the restaurant, the more likely you are to be cheated. I always ask to see a menu and then ask the waiter to translate parts I don't understand. In cheaper restaurants and beer halls where foreign visitors are uncommon, I often point at the most appetizing-looking dish on a neighbouring table, and order the same. Some travellers may feel that since the sums involved are relatively small, the convenience of never having to learn to decipher a Czech menu is worth the risk of occasionally being cheated. I take a different view.

On Na Příkopě is the useful Prague Information Service, which provides information on walking and sightseeing tours and interpreters. Next door is the Čedok travel service, from where you can book rail and air tickets. Although travel by bus and rail within the former Eastern bloc is still very inexpensive, journeys into Western Europe must be paid for in hard currency. Although you would expect international rail tickets and sleeper reservations to be made at the central railway station, transactions which involve hard currency must be made from the Čedok office on Na Příkopě. Allow an hour for queueing and negotiation. Air travel is easier, since most major airlines have an office in town.

Prague will obviously change rapidly over the coming years, as the neglect of buildings is swept away. Western money and influence are already making their presence felt, but hopefully Prague will emerge with its beauty and character enhanced rather than impaired.

1
Hradčany

....

For a thousand years, the castle has dominated Prague. Perched high above the Vltava, it has functioned as fortress, cathedral, royal palace, administrative headquarters, and, since 1918, presidential palace. Within its walls remain traces of every period of the city's history, making it the obvious place at which to begin a visit to the city.

The easiest way to get to the castle is to take the metro to Malostranská, cross the sculpture garden adjoining the station, cross Valdštejnská and then turn left up the Old Castle Steps, which will bring you directly, after a long climb, to the eastern gate. However, I would recommend an alternative route, both because it saves wear and tear on the feet and because it allows you to visit the Belvedere without making a separate expedition there from the castle. From Malostranská take tram 22 one stop to Belvedere. You can also take this tram from Charles Square or the National Theatre if more convenient.

The BELVEDERE, or Royal Summer Palace, is the finest example of Italian renaissance architecture in Prague. It was commissioned by the Habsburg emperor Ferdinand I as a summer palace, and the designer was Paolo della Stella. The glory of the building is the tall graceful loggia that surrounds it (1535–41); the upper levels were added between 1557 and 1563 by the court architect Bonifaz Wohlmut. The roof resembles an upturned boat and its green copper skin can be seen from all over Malá Strana. The pedestals on which the columns stand and the spandrels between the arches are adorned with reliefs, mostly representing mythological scenes. But there is also a charming relief showing Ferdinand presenting his wife Anna Jagellon with a flower (a copy in the Historical Museum in the Lobkovic Palace (pp. 56–7) permits closer inspection of this panel). The pavilion is often used for exhibitions.

The gardens, now open to the public, are also very lovely, and their finest feature is the so-called Singing Fountain built from 1564 to 1568, a very elegant design by Francesco Terzio, cast by Tomáš Jaroš in 1564. Adjoining the

OPPOSITE *The Belvedere: with its graceful arcades and elegant gardens, this summer palace of the Habsburg rulers is the loveliest renaissance structure in Bohemia.*

The celebrated sixteenth-century Ball Games Court, with its lavish sgraffito decoration, has been meticulously restored after it was savaged by a fire.

Belvedere are the Royal Gardens. These are usually closed to the public, but can be glimpsed by following the main road after leaving the Belvedere and turning left. These gardens were designed in 1534 by Giovanni Spazio, but they were much altered and enlarged in the centuries that followed. If you can get into the gardens, you will be able to enjoy superb views of the north side of the castle, especially of the defensive towers that are otherwise difficult to see: the round Dalibor tower of 1492 to 1494 beneath the tall square Black Tower at the east end, and the former jail of the White Tower. From the gates you can also see a remarkable structure, the Ball Games Court, a sumptuous round-arched building erected by Bonifaz Wohlmut between 1567 and 1569, decorated with beautiful, delicate renaissance sgraffiti. Not long ago the building was completely restored after a major fire.

Continue along the Marianské hradby, then turn left at the tram stop. The large building on the right is the Riding School built in the 1690s by Jean Baptiste Mathey. The interior has been completely gutted and redesigned so that the building can be used for exhibitions, which frequently relate to modern Czech art. Continue across the bridge. A few centuries ago this bridge used to be covered, and the gully it crosses was the castle deer park. The ditch also had a military function, as it provided a natural defence against attack from the north.

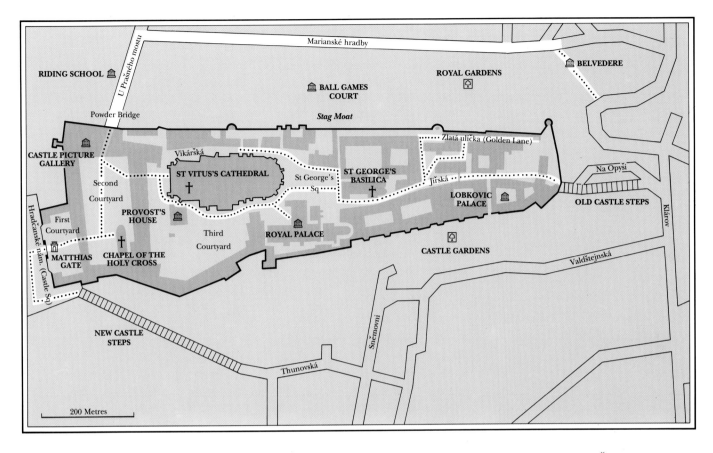

You will enter the second courtyard of the castle. Take either of the archways on the right to the first courtyard and then go through the iron gates into Hradčanské náměstí, Castle Square.

From the ramparts you are rewarded with a magnificent view of the entire city, with the churches and palaces of Malá Strana cascading below, and beyond them the glint of the river; to the left are the towers of the Týn church, and as your gaze passes slowly to the right you will see the Charles Bridge, the golden roof of the National Theatre, the expanses of Petřín hill, and on the far right the spires of the Strahov monastery. If they are open you can also stroll through the south castle gardens, which are entered from the top of the New Castle Steps near the ramparts.

The CASTLE began life in the ninth century as a fortress of the Přemysl clan. They chose this site because it allowed them to control the trade routes that passed along the valley. Its importance was consolidated in 973 when the bishop of the new diocese of Prague chose the fortress as his residence. Proper fortifications were built in the mid eleventh century during the reign of Břetislav I, fortifications that approximately defined the area occupied by the castle to the present day. The castle was gradually expanded until a catastrophic fire in 1303 destroyed much of it. When Prague became the seat of an archbishopric in 1344,

KEY TO MAP SYMBOLS

- 🏛 Monuments
- † Churches
- ▯ Columns and statues
- 🏛 Houses, palaces and museums
- ⬒ Parks and gardens
- ✡ Synagogues/Jewish cemeteries

Charles IV set about rebuilding the basilica and adding to the castle. But by 1382 the court was no longer based at the castle, as Charles's son Wenceslas IV had moved it to the Old Town across the river, where it remained for a century. After the partial completion of St Vitus's Cathedral, the next important additions were made by kings Vladislav Jagellon and Ludvik Jagellon who built palaces with strong renaissance elements in the late fifteenth and early sixteenth centuries. Subsequent emperors, including Ferdinand I and Rudolf II, both of whom are buried in the cathedral, continued with the renovations, and by now the area to the west of the castle was being expanded as a district of aristocratic palaces.

The castle had been not only a royal residence and site of the cathedral but the base of the Bohemian government and thus of the Bohemian Estates. After the defeat of the Estates at White Mountain in 1620, Habsburg rule was consolidated. The rule, however, was based not in Prague but at the Hofburg in Vienna, where Bohemia was merely one out of dozens of Habsburg domains across Europe. The castle remained an important administrative centre, of course, but its almost symbolic significance had been diminished. The Habsburgs continued with the alterations to the castle's architecture and gave it the appearance it has today. Its pale cappuccino expanses, visible from Malá Strana and the Old Town, were built under Maria Theresia, embracing and in places obscuring the older buildings, such as the cathedral and the basilica of St George and the ranges built by Rudolf II and Maximilian II. These wings were designed by the empress's court architect Nikolaus Pacassi and the actual construction work, which took place from 1756 to 1774, was supervised by Anselmo Lurago. As architecture, it is unexciting, and the endlessly repeated bays become numbing. Because he had to accommodate the existing structures, the design weaves its way around them and has little shape or form of its own.

You enter the first courtyard through a splendid set of gates, with gigantic statuary (or, to be exact, copies of statuary) by Ignác Platzer the Elder, of 1768, making a suitably intimidating impression. Of the older buildings in this courtyard, only the imposing renaissance gate of 1614 survives, slapped against Pacassi's block. Built to glorify Emperor Matthias, it used to be a free-standing monument, overlooking a former moat, and as such it would have provided a better context for Giovanni Maria Philippi's rusticated piers, obelisks and heraldic devices. No matter: it still looks splendid. Within the gateway, broad staircases rise on either side, sweeping up to the state apartments of the palace.

At noon each day there is a changing of the guard in the first courtyard, a performance so endearingly amateurish that not even the participants, including the officers, can take it seriously. The frivolous mood is assisted by the new blue, red and white uniforms of the presidential guard, a creation of the costume designer for the film *Amadeus*. One crisp morning as a thousand visitors, myself included, gazed on, the band thumped in the background and grinning officers yelled their orders, while soldiers giggled, creating a ripple effect that soon infected the entire crowd that had gathered to watch. There is much to be said for a military force with a sense of humour.

Ignác Platzer's huge statues successfully intimidate any intruders tempted to make an unauthorized entrance into the first courtyard of the castle.

Enter the second courtyard, which is entirely enclosed by Pacassi's monotonous ranges, although in places the façade conceals some structures from the previous two centuries. In the centre stands the imposing sandstone fountain of 1686 by Francesco della Torre and Jeroným Kohl. The grand, rather pompous three-tiered design holds its own in this imperial context. Next to it is a well screened by an elaborate wrought-iron grille added in 1702. Hunched in one corner of the courtyard is the CHAPEL OF THE HOLY CROSS, designed by Pacassi in the 1750s but altered in the 1850s. Since 1961 the treasury of St Vitus's Cathedral has been displayed in the chapel, a collection that includes medieval textiles, precious stones, fourteenth-century reliquaries and crosses, monstrances and chalices. At time of writing, the chapel had been closed for extensive renovations, and what form the exhibition will take after its eventual reopening no one seems to know.

In the opposite corner of the courtyard is the entrance to the CASTLE PICTURE GALLERY, which occupies what used to be the stables, built during the reign of Rudolf II. Remnants have also been found here of a ninth-century chapel that must have been the first castle church. In the 1960s these early seventeenth-century stables were converted into a gallery. Appropriately, the first room contains a copy of a bust of Rudolf by Adriaen de Vries, and paintings by Hans von Aachen (including a fine portrait of Emperor Matthias) and Bartholomeus Spranger, who came to Prague from the Low Countries and stayed on under Rudolf's ardent patronage. Until recently the collection included Lucas Cranach the Elder's painting depicting a young woman in the embrace of an old man, with one arm around his neck, the other deep in his purse. This criminal theme proved an unfortunate inspiration, as the painting was stolen in December 1990. Also by Cranach is a brutal painting of Christ being tormented by malevolent musicians, while another man squirts the contents of a large syringe into his eye.

The gallery houses many Italian paintings of the sixteenth and seventeenth centuries, by artists such as the Bassano clan, Pordenone, and Guido Reni, but none of this work is of outstanding quality. More impressive are canvases by Veronese and Tintoretto, although among the latter are some highly questionable attributions. Two of the finest paintings are Titian's beautifully coloured portrait of a young woman (1512–15) and Rubens's large and highly complex *Assembly of the Olympian Gods* (c. 1602).

Another room contains portraits by Jan Kupecký and Peter Brandl, whose work will be seen later in St George's Convent in greater profusion as well as in numerous churches throughout the city. The final room contains portaits of outstandingly ugly members of the Habsburg and other ruling families of the sixteenth and seventeenth centuries.

On leaving the gallery, it is worth taking the first archway out of the courtyard, which brings you into the bastion garden. The large portico on the right is by Pacassi and forms the entrance to the immense ceremonial Spanish Hall, created in 1602 to 1606 by Giovanni Maria Philippi, the designer of the Matthias Gate. Unfortunately it is not possible to visit the hall. Return to the second courtyard and walk through the passage into the third courtyard. It passes on the right the entrance to the offices of the president of the republic. The president's official residence has been the castle since 1918, thus reviving the complex's historic role as the seat of government. At right angles to this entrance are a few surviving blocks of romanesque masonry.

The third courtyard is dominated by St Vitus's Cathedral. To the right is the PROVOST'S HOUSE, with its mid seventeenth-century façade composed of bands of lozenges and other panels between the storeys. The house itself is much older, and stood here during the romanesque period, when it was the bishop's palace. In a corner niche of the house is an early baroque statue of St Wenceslas by Jan Bendl. Nearby stands a sore thumb of a granite obelisk erected by J. Plečnik in 1928 as a memorial to World War I, distracting attention from the remarkable fourteenth-century statue of St George and the Dragon cast by the brothers George and Martin of Cluj. This version is a copy of the original, which I shall have more to say about when we encounter it in St George's Convent.

The first church of ST VITUS, a rotunda, was founded by Duke Wenceslas in 929. It was replaced by a romanesque basilica in the late eleventh century under Spytihněv and Vratislav II. When Prague became an archbishopric in 1344, Charles IV conceived the idea of replacing the church with something on a grander scale. The first architect to be involved in his scheme was Matthias of Arras, imported from France, and some of the radiating chapels of the choir completed by Matthias naturally echoed the styles of French churches. Matthias died in 1352 and was succeeded as principal architect by Peter Parler in 1356. Parler was an architect and mason from Swabia who became the dominant architectural

OPPOSITE *A constant parade of visitors to the castle is utterly dwarfed beneath the Great Tower and the spires of St Vitus's Cathedral.*

figure of late fourteenth-century Prague, making an impact on the city that still marks its physical appearance and character. He was responsible for the superb choir, which was completed in 1385. After his death in 1399 his sons and nephews continued his work. They began the magnificent Great Tower in 1396, but they had to leave it unfinished in 1406. Construction ground to a halt during the Hussite wars, and in the 1420s, during the Hussite occupation of the castle, considerable damage was done to St Vitus's.

Work resumed only in the early sixteenth century, when the nave pillars and the north tower were begun during the reign of Vladislav Jagellon. Bonifaz Wohlmut, the court architect, capped the Great Tower with a renaissance design in 1562, and it was only given its final form in 1770 by Pacassi. The tower is about 100 metres high and holds the Sigismund Bell, cast in 1549, the largest bell in Bohemia. As if the Hussite rampages weren't enough, the rebellious Estates also sacked the cathedral in 1619. In his *Austria*, J.G. Kohl writes graphically about Frederick the Great of Prussia and his attack on Prague in 1757:

> on the 6th, 7th, 8th, and 9th [June], the town was complimented with 7144 bombs, 14,821 balls, and 111 carcases, of which the majority were aimed at the cathedral. During those four days the building was thirty times on fire ... The roof was perforated by no less than 215 balls ... Scarcely one of the many splendid tombs remained uninjured.

Only in the 1870s was a serious effort made to finish the cathedral. Even so, that building programme took over half a century to complete.

Given that the west front is a relatively modern structure, it is remarkably successful, blending smoothly with the gothic sections. The bronze doors, which narrate the history of the building, and the carved tympanum are all highly competent. Indeed the only jarring note on the exterior is Wohlmut's addition to the tower. Walk past the Provost's House to the Great Tower. Along the south wall of the cathedral you will see excavations of the romanesque chapel that once stood here; and if you look up to the left, you can also see unmistakable romanesque windows at the back of the Provost's House, showing that it is indeed far older than it appears. On the other side of the courtyard is another entrance to the president's offices, a large portal with statuary by Ignác Platzer. During the last days of 1989, the new president of Czechoslovakia, Václav Havel, appeared on the balcony over this portal to greet wildly enthusiastic crowds.

Attached to the Great Tower is the large and elegant south porch, the Golden Gate, constructed by Peter Parler. Above the central bay are faded mosaics of 1371, composed by Venetian artists, depicting Charles IV and Elisabeth of Pomerania, both kneeling, and above them a Christ in Majesty; over the bays on either side is a mosaic of the Last Judgment, composed, like the other mosaics, out of Bohemian glass. The craftsmen responsible for this ravishing work were Italian, but the conception and design were Bohemian. The mosaics and furnishings inside the porch are modern. The immense window above the gate was

The pedestals of empty statue niches and elegant rib vaulting shelter the south portal of St Vitus's Cathedral.

added in 1908 by Kamil Hilbert, but it blends well with Parler's gothic designs. Above the window is sweeping blind tracery, plunging and rising across the balustrade. At the same level as Hilbert's window a beautiful early seventeenth-century grille is set into the tower.

The choir is splendid, with a maze of flying buttresses, pinnacles and crockets. In wet weather water gushes from the leaping gargoyles jutting out at every angle from the pinnacles, and in winter daggers of ice are suspended from their jaws. The view of the east end of the cathedral is particularly exhilarating, as buttresses arch up from the sheer walls of traceried stone to support the lofty choir with its steeply pitched roof.

Return to the west front and enter the church. The immediate impression is thoroughly harmonious, both because of the absence of baroque clutter and because the modern parts of St Vitus's continued the principles laid down five centuries earlier. Above the arcades, a gallery runs the length of the cathedral, and immediately behind its balustrade huge windows, in nave and choir, rise to the height of the roof, which is spanned by rib vaults and has numerous bosses. A

curious feature of these windows is the smaller window set within each at a slight angle, providing a somewhat jolting rhythm. Along the gallery, but hardly ever visible from ground level, is a series of fourteenth-century busts from the Parler workshop, portraying members of the royal family, some of the artists who worked on the cathedral, several archbishops, as well as Matthias of Arras and Peter Parler himself. Since these are probably among the earliest portrait busts in medieval Europe, it is regrettable that there is no access to the gallery. Photographs suggest that the quality of the carving is very high indeed.

The crossing is dominated by large gilt statues on the piers. In the north transept is Wohlmut's renaissance two-tier organ gallery of 1557 to 1561, which, like his cap of the Great Tower, is completely at odds with the gothic style of St Vitus's. But Wohlmut was working at a time when he no longer had access to a gothic vocabulary, so one can't be too censorious. Until 1924 this organ gallery was installed at the west end, where it might have been less obtrusive. The organ itself is housed within a lofty baroque case of 1757.

Beneath the choir gallery are painted coats of arms of all the lands in the possession of Ferdinand I by the mid sixteenth century. In the centre of the choir, behind a beautiful and varied wrought-iron grille completed in 1589 by J. Schmidthammer and others, is the immense imperial mausoleum, three tombs wide. It was executed by the Dutch sculptor Alexander Collin between 1571 and 1589. A figure of Christ triumphing over Death in the form of a skull beneath his foot stands at the far end of the tomb, while angels are posted on guard on all sides. Three effigies – Ferdinand I in the centre, flanked by his wife Anna Jagellon and his son Maximilan II – lie on the top, but unfortunately, unless you are very tall, it's hard to see more than the imperial boots. Around the sides of the marble mausoleum are the coats of arms of the members of the Bohemian royal family who lie buried in the vault below. The whole monument, while of the greatest magnificence, is somewhat glacial.

Return to the west end of the cathedral to take a closer look at the side chapels, beginning on the north side. The first chapel contains a late gothic altarpiece, the main panel depicting the enthroned Madonna. In the second chapel is another late gothic painting, a triptych in a modern frame. Monumental heraldic tomb slabs line the walls, as they do in many other chapels. There is no ancient stained glass in the cathedral, and much of the modern glass is of indifferent quality, although little of it is positively unpleasant. Of some interest, however, is the window in the third chapel, which has painted glass by Alfons Mucha, as richly coloured as a child's story book. The fourth chapel is the Old Treasury, with a modern gothic extravaganza framing the spiral staircase leading up to the gallery. Walk past the organ gallery, with its finely carved wooden doors (the outer ones date from 1630) to the next chapel, that of St Sigismund, which houses a number of renaissance and baroque tombs.

A little further up on the right is the first of a number of ambitious wooden reliefs carved by Caspar Bechteller in 1623. This panel portrays the city in about 1620, just before its baroque transformation. The Charles Bridge (pp. 97–104) is

ABOVE *Alfons Mucha's contribution to the stained glass of the cathedral's side chapels may not be in the purest ecclesiastical spirit, but it would be churlish to object to such a sensuous design.*

OPPOSITE *The lofty arcades and stylish vaulting of the fourteenth-century cathedral choir are more suggestive of northern France than central Europe.*

there but without its statues, and one of the towers of the Týn church (p. 124–6) is incomplete. Bechteller must have been an obsessive carver, as he seems to have recorded every single house and tree he could see. The next panel shows the flight of Frederick V of the Palatinate after his defeat at White Mountain in 1620. Close by is the eloquent bronze statue of the kneeling Cardinal Bedřich Schwarzenberg cast by Josef Myslbek in 1895.

At the head of the north ambulatory is the chapel of St John the Baptist, which contains the tombs of two early Přemyslid rulers: on the left Bořivoj II, who died in 1124, and on the right, with a headless effigy, Břetislav II, who died in 1100. Both tombs were made long after their deaths by the Parler workshop in the 1370s. Within the east apse, which is known as the Lady Chapel, are the tombs of Břetislav I (1034–55) and Spytihněv II (1055–61), both monuments, like those in the preceding chapel, made by the Parler team. Between the Lady Chapel and the high altar is the nineteenth-century tomb of St Vitus, a fairly simple piece of work, easily overlooked, which is odd considering the trouble taken over six centuries to provide a suitable home for these relics.

The next chapel on the right is the Reliquary, or Saxon, Chapel, with the tombs of two important Přemyslid rulers, Ottakar I (d. 1230) on the right, and Ottakar II (d. 1278) on the left. Again, both tombs and their damaged effigies are from the Parler workshop and were executed in the 1370s. There are fragmentary frescoes, possibly fifteenth-century, above the tomb of Ottakar I. If you look up to the choir gallery from here, you can see in the distance some of the celebrated fourteenth-century busts.

Blocking the ambulatory at this point is the lavish silver tomb of St John Nepomuk, who achieved martyrdom in 1393 when King Wenceslas IV ordered him to be thrown into the River Vltava. The tomb was designed by Joseph Emanuel Fischer von Erlach – the son of Johann Bernhard Fischer von Erlach, the greatest master of Viennese baroque architecture – and executed from 1733 to 1736 by silversmith J.J. Würth, who was also Viennese. The saint, holding a crucifix, kneels on top of his tomb, which is supported by angels and enclosed within a complex marble balustrade. On the corners of these balustrades are placed urns of a rococo design so complex that they have become virtually abstract compositions. The entire tomb is canopied, and the fringes of its curtains are held up by four flying angels, also in silver, who are supported by brackets attached to the choir piers and the side chapel walls. The angels, which were donated by Empress Maria Theresia, were designed by Ignác Platzer and wrought by the Prague silversmith I.F. Novák in 1771. I find the whole tomb a most exhilarating composition, even if it is not exactly suffused with the spirit of piety.

There is more silver in St Adalbert's Chapel opposite the tomb, where four half-figures of saints Adalbert, Wenceslas, Vitus, and Cyril were placed in 1698 to 1699 by Rinaldino Ranzoni. On the right is another tomb with the massive marble effigy of a bishop, and on the walls are fifteenth-century frescoes. In the next chapel, the Waldstein Chapel, a monumental tomb slab bears a portrait of Peter Parler. Facing the chapel is the other principal relief panel by Bechteller, narrating how the Calvinist intruders desecrated the cathedral's holy images in 1619. The imperial mausoleum is clearly visible on the left of the panel.

The next bay is the Vladislav Oratory, a gallery with grotesquely carved balustrades and pendants of 1493, probably by Hans Spiess of Frankfurt. In place of tracery there are rough branches, hardly a formula for finesse. The arms on the balustrade represent the numerous lands in the possession of Vladislav Jagellon. On the east side of the oratory, a polychrome figure carved by Matthias Braun in 1723 portraying a miner comes leaping forth, as though keen to join his more expensively dressed neighbours over at the Nepomuk monument. In the next chapel, the Holy Cross Chapel, is the entrance to the royal burial vault. In the chapel itself is an elaborate silver altar and above it a damaged fresco of 1369 depicting the six patron saints of Bohemia. The passage leading to the vault passes some of the excavated foundations of the romanesque church. Within the vault itself, and mostly encased in modern marble and metal tombs, are the bodies of Charles IV (1346–78), George of Poděbrady (1458–71), Wenceslas IV (1378–1419), and a handful of other members of the Bohemian royal family. The pewter sarcophagus at the back contains the remains of Rudolf II (1576–1612).

On emerging from the vault, return to the ambulatory. To the right of the Holy Cross Chapel is the Martinitz Chapel, which contains some renaissance tombs, including that of the imperial counsellor Jaroslav von Martinitz, who died in 1649 after surviving his participation, in the role of victim, in the second defenestration of 1618. Opposite the chapel, placed at an angle against one of the choir piers, is the monument to Count Schlick, who died in 1723. It was designed, like that to St John Nepomuk, by Joseph Emanuel Fischer von Erlach and František Maximilian Kaňka, but executed by Matthias Braun. The bust of the field marshal, placed in a niche within the obelisk rising from the tomb, is a first-rate piece of carving.

The last chapel in the ambulatory is the most glorious: the Wenceslas Chapel, built by Peter Parler from 1362 to 1367. The tomb containing the body of the saint is in the shape of an ark and draped in red and gold cloth. Wenceslas, Duke of Bohemia, came to a grisly end in 929 or 939, when his brother Boleslav the Cruel murdered him in a power struggle. The retrospectively saintly duke was reaching for a door knocker at the time, and a similar knocker is still preserved in the chapel, attached to the door leading to the ambulatory. Unfortunately this particular knocker dates from the thirteenth century, long after the duke was murdered. A silver bust of the saint peers out from his shrine, the base of which is early twentieth-century work that harmonizes with the much older sumptuous decor of the chapel.

This decoration is quite remarkable, as the walls are studded with over 1300 semi-precious stones, mostly jasper and amethyst. Equally sumptuous are the fresco cycles. The lower cycle, portraying scenes from the Passion, is by Master Oswald of Prague, Charles IV's court painter; executed in the 1370s, they are very delicate and often highly expressive. The upper series vividly depicts scenes from the legend of the saint, painted by the Master of the Litoměřice Altar in

A number of Czech churches pay tribute to miners, but this energetic example from the ambulatory of the cathedral is surely one of the best.

about 1505. Above the altar is a polychrome statue of a rather diffident-looking St Wenceslas, carved by Heinrich Parler in 1373, and painted by Master Oswald. To the right of the statue a panel by the Master of the Litoměřice Altar depicts the moment of Wenceslas's murder, his hand stretching out to the door-knocker, while Boleslav pins him down with one knee, a nicely brutal touch. Close to the ambulatory exit is a splendid renaissance bronze candelabrum of 1532 by the Nuremberg carver Hans Vischer, in which the candlestick plays a subsidiary role to the chunky statuary, canopy, and heraldic devices.

From this chapel a doorway leads up to the room where the Bohemian Crown Jewels and regalia are stored, but unfortunately this treasury has been closed to the public since 1978, so the crown of St Wenceslas commissioned by Charles IV in 1347, and a sceptre and orb from the sixteenth century, remain locked in their safes.

The huge window in the south transept is filled with stained glass by Max Švabinský depicting the Last Judgment; installed in 1934, it has impressive intensity of colour, although the design itself is conventional. Return to the west door up the south aisle, where the chapels contain little of interest except for marble tomb slabs.

Leave St Vitus's and walk to the south side of the choir, opposite which you will find the entrance to the ROYAL PALACE. To the left of the entrance hall is the Green Room, where a court used to sit; it is now a bookshop. From here a door leads to what is known as Vladislav's bedroom (it was in fact some kind of chancellery, decorated with splendid vaulting by Hans Spiess and with coats of arms), but there is no public access. Instead you are shown directly into the immense 62-metre-long Vladislav Hall, which was built under Vladislav II Jagellon and designed by Benedikt Ried between 1493 and 1502, either to replace an existing hall or to add an extra storey to buildings erected during the reigns of earlier rulers. Some of these earlier structures can still be seen from the outside.

The glory of the hall, which occupies the entire second floor of the palace and is lit by huge renaissance windows on both sides, is the vaulted ceiling. Some see this as a variation of gothic rib vaulting, but to me the spirit of the place is wholly of the Renaissance, and the tantalizingly half-functional vaulting is decades away from the gothic spirit. Here the ribs don't so much spring as slink forth from the piers along the sides of the walls, and in some places, where the ribs have nowhere useful to go, they simply stop in mid-air.

On the right a passage leads into another renaissance chamber, that of the Bohemian Chancellery. From the room beyond it are views on to the river and the palaces of Malá Strana, a view perhaps not especially relished by the victims of the second defenestration who tumbled from the windows on the left. At the very end of the hall is the late fourteenth-century Chapel of All Saints, built by Peter Parler. It was more or less rebuilt in 1580 after a major fire, and it was then that the chapel was linked to the Vladislav Hall. Václav Reiner contributed a crowded altarpiece in 1732. The organ is enclosed in a deplorable neo-rococo case.

OPPOSITE *Every inch of Peter Parler's Wenceslas Chapel is decorated with frescoes and semi-precious gems in honour of this most celebrated of Bohemian saints.*

On the left side of the hall are a number of doorways. The one nearest the chapel leads into the Hall of the Diet, where the Bohemian Estates used to hold their deliberations. It's a square chamber designed by Benedikt Ried in about 1500, but rebuilt by Bonifaz Wohlmut after a fire half a century later; its vaulting resembles that of the Vladislav Hall. The entrance portal to the hall is bizarre, since its fluted columns are deliberately twisted out of shape, another playful renaissance conceit. Between 1559 and 1563 Wohlmut contributed the renaissance gallery where the recorder of the proceedings used to sit, which fills one corner of the Hall, and on the left are portraits of Joseph II and other Habsburg rulers. The throne is nineteenth-century.

Not far from the entrance to the Hall of the Diet is a double doorway, elegantly pilastered, which gives access to a staircase that leads up to the New Appeal Court (or Chancellery of the Land Rolls) of 1558. The walls and vaults of this room are covered with the coats of arms of the clerks. In an adjoining room the cupboards are stuffed with eighteenth-century volumes that record the land rolls, their spines numbered and painted with flowers, birds and jewels. The main doorway of the Vladislav Hall leads to Ried's famous staircase of about 1500 intended for mounted horsemen on their way to participate in the tournaments held in the hall. This staircase takes you down into St George's Square. On leaving, glance at the door knocker, which, if I am not mistaken, has an erotic theme.

It is worth taking a look at the exterior of the Vladislav Hall, which, with its huge renaissance windows, as old as any in Bohemia, and the pinnacled buttresses between them, is almost as impressive as the interior. Beneath the windows are thirteenth-century arcades built during the time of Přemysl Ottakar II. One used to be able to visit the lower sections of the royal palace, including the subterranean hall built under Soběslav I in the mid twelfth century and the gothic hall built for Charles IV, but for some time these older sections have been closed to visitors. Also accessible no longer is the display of casts made from the Parler busts that line the gallery of the cathedral. One can only hope that eventually these fascinating parts of the palace will be reopened.

Alongside the All Saints Chapel is the entrance to the former Institute of Noblewomen, and indeed the chapel was originally part of that institution. The porch was designed by Pacassi and Anselmo Lurago in 1754. Very little remains of the Rožmberk Palace that was built on this site in 1545.

One side of the square is filled by the façade of St George's Basilica and the entrance to its convent, now a major art gallery. Opposite the royal palace are some extremely ugly nineteenth-century buildings, and to the left of them is the lane called Vikářská, which leads to the Powder Tower (or Mihulka) of 1494. Alongside the tower is the Vikárka restaurant, which is the best place for a meal in Hradčany. The dining rooms are built into the castle walls and also fill the romanesque cellars of the building. Cheaper and more cramped, is the Espreso in St George's Square, which is welcoming and serves good food at modest prices.

The POWDER TOWER is reached across a small bridge that links Vikářská to the sentry walk along the north wall of the castle. There are exhibits on three

ABOVE *The mildly salacious imagery on the bronze door-knocker outside the Vladislav Hall offers some light relief after the regal grandeur within.*

OPPOSITE *Benedikt Ried's astonishingly inventive vaults span and overwhelm the immense spaces of the Vladislav Hall, making even its huge renaissance windows look paltry.*

floors of the tower. On the ground floor are plans and prints relating to the castle's fortifications. On the first floor is an interesting exhibition dealing with alchemy, an art practised with the enthusiastic encouragement of Rudolf II. Kilns, alembics and jars of essential ingredients help to convey the atmosphere of an alchemist's laboratory. Indeed, this tower stands close to the spot where many laboratories were located. Upstairs are displayed items associated with Rudolf's court: jewels, dishes, glassware, paintings and furniture.

The façade of ST GEORGE'S BASILICA dates from the 1670s and gives little indication of the romanesque splendours within. The church has been largely reconstructed, and the western bays of the arcades separating nave and aisles were bricked up long ago. A gallery runs above the arcades for the length of the church. The apse is raised above a crypt and the staircases leading up to the choir are baroque work of 1731. Despite the inevitable jarring notes introduced by any reconstruction and by modern furnishings, the church has retained its noble romanesque proportions. The building took its present form in the 1140s, but parts of the structure are considerably older, dating back to the early tenth century, when it was founded by Vratislav I. Thus it is far older than any part of St Vitus's, including the excavated foundations of the cathedral's romanesque chapels. The presence of a number of carefully placed medieval works of art bestows on the church a museum-like atmosphere, but it is no longer used for religious services. In front of the choir is the large fifteenth-century wooden painted tomb of Vratislav I, who died in about 920, and the wrought-iron grille of about 1730 that surrounds the tomb slab of Duke Boleslav II (the Pious), who died in 999.

The apse retains remnants of early thirteenth-century frescoes, but they are too faded to give much pleasure. From the choir entrance you can just about see St Ludmilla's Chapel, built in the thirteenth century and raised up a floor by Peter Parler's workshop in 1380; behind a tall iron screen are other tombs crafted by the workshop. Ludmilla, St Wenceslas's grandmother, was murdered in 921 and later adopted as one of Bohemia's patron saints. The gothic frescoes in this chapel are far better preserved than the earlier ones in the apse. Tacked on to the south-west corner of the basilica is the Chapel of St John Nepomuk built from 1718 to 1722 with an altarpiece and frescoes by Václav Reiner in the oval cupola.

The NATIONAL GALLERY'S great collection of Bohemian art, which no visitor to Prague should miss, is housed in the Convent of St George, adjoining the basilica. The convent was founded in 973 by Mlada, the sister of Boleslav II; it was rebuilt in the twelfth century and again in the fourteenth century, and it took its final form, apart from the usual baroque alterations, in the mid sixteenth century. The convent was closed down by Joseph II as part of the dissolution of the monasteries in 1782, and it gradually fell into disrepair. The building was restored in the 1950s, with a view to using it as a gallery of Bohemian art.

You enter the cloister and descend to the lower floor, where exhibits are displayed along the corridors and in side rooms. The first major exhibit is the much-mutilated tympanum of before 1346 from the church of St Mary of the Snows in the New Town. The carving in fact consists of two tympana by different artists

OPPOSITE *Only the towers behind the baroque façade of St George's Basilica give any clue that the romanesque church within is one of the oldest structures in all of Prague.*

Bohemian gothic art sometimes mingles the exactitude of naturalism with the transcendence of religious feeling, as in this Resurrection *by the Master of the Třeboň Altarpiece.*

that have been joined together. A large proportion of the exhibits consists of gothic madonnas, from 1300 onwards, both painted panels and statues of the Virgin and Child. Of outstanding interest is the large equestrian bronze statue of St George and the Dragon, the original of the statue that stands outside in the third castle courtyard. Cast in 1373 by the brothers, George and Martin of Cluj, it is of great art-historical importance, since it is the first large free-standing sculpture north of the Alps. The figure of the saint is impossibly slender, but the vigour of the composition and the detail of the armour and the dragon's scales are remarkable. The dragon's tail curled in an almost snake-like way round the horse's leg gives some idea of the artistic subtlety of the conception.

The gallery possesses a cycle of nine paintings by the Master of the Vyšší Brod Altarpiece, produced for the Cistercian monastery in southern Bohemia in the 1350s. The painting is colourful, unpretentious and devotional, with some more characterful panels such as those depicting the Nativity, the Crucifixion and the Resurrection. Some of the panels, including the Crucifixion, are believed to have been painted by other artists in his workshop.

I find it harder to share the widespread enthusiasm for another exhibit: six panels by Master Theodoric and his workshop, which are part of the series of 128 paintings he produced for the chapel at Karlštejn Castle between 1357 and 1365. I find these paintings overblown, fuzzed in their detail, and so puffed up and fleshy that in most cases the painting spills over onto the frame. Unfortunately, the direction in which Theodoric was taking Bohemian art – the so-called 'soft style' – was a far cry from the precision and refinement of feeling of slightly earlier work by other artists.

The ground-floor exhibits begin with more paintings, and with statues from the very end of the fourteenth century and early fifteenth century, some of which show the same baleful tendencies as Theodoric's work. Some of the finest artistry is lavished on wood carvings. There is a badly damaged polychrome limewood Pietà of the early fifteenth century, and a Madonna and very large Child of the same date from the Minorite monastery at Český Krumlov. From slightly later in the century comes a charming panel of the Madonna and Child, with a series of figures painted along the frame.

A number of panels by the Master of the Třeboň Altarpiece are placed in a separate room off the corridor. They formed part of a winged altarpiece of about 1380, but two of the sections, including the central panel, have not survived. The extant panels include the Agony in the Garden, a superb Entombment in which the body of Christ is like a diagonal gash across the surface, and a luminous Resurrection. On the rear of these three panels are figures of saints done by members of the Master's workshop. There is a fine Crucifixion by this great painter in the same room. In another side room is a taut wooden crucifix of the 1420s, and a late fourteenth-century tympanum from the Týn church, which may have been produced by Parler's workshop. The scenes, which seem to be by different hands, are vigorously carved, but sadly the upper section, portraying the Last Judgment, is badly damaged.

Return to the main corridor, where some rather bland fifteenth-century panels are displayed. In contrast, there is a brutal triptych of the Crucifixion (c. 1430) from the Reiningshaus Altar, and a charming Annunciation of the same period by the Master of the Vyšší Brod Altarpiece. The parallel cloister corridor contains more fifteenth-century panels, including a cycle of 1482 by the Master of the Order of the Cross, which once belonged to this order's church on the other side of the Charles Bridge. The imposing polychrome-and-gilt winged Velhartice altarpiece dates from about 1500. From the Master of the

Much of Peter Brandl's best work is consigned to the gloomy side chapels of Prague's baroque churches, but the St George's Convent gallery allows visitors a closer view of his painting, such as this vigorous portrait of Simeon and the infant Jesus.

Litoměřice Altar, who executed many of the frescoes in the Wenceslas Chapel, come charming scenes from the life of the Virgin (*c.* 1505), together with other panels from the Strahov Monastery.

At the foot of the stairs you'll find numerous wooden relief carvings, of the 1520s, by the so-called I.P. Master which are skilfully executed and highly expressive. There are clear allusions to the work of Albrecht Dürer in the iconography and design, and there is also evidence that the carver had studied the work of Andrea Mantegna. Bohemian art had by this time truly become part of the international Renaissance.

Upstairs are numerous mannerist paintings which I can't get excited about: there is a surfeit of work by Karel Škréta, whose altarpieces furnish dozens of Prague churches, and Jan Krystof Liška and Michael Willmann — although the baroque sculptures are much more exciting. There's a copy of a fine bronze, by Adriaen de Vries, of Heracles from the garden of the Valdštejn Palace (pp. 94–5), a naturalistic St Isidor by the early baroque sculptor Jan Bendl (1620–80), and a fine marble bust by the obscure sculptor Jan Jiří Heermann. From Matthias Braun come a Jupiter, Venus, and an overwrought St Jude Thaddeus, all three from the balustrade of the Clam-Gallas Palace in the Old Town, and a swirling angel of 1718. Among the paintings, I would single out the charming flower paintings by Jan Rudolf Bys (1662–1738) and some impressive portraits by Peter Brandl. Ferdinand Maximilian Brokoff is represented by some powerful statues, including one of a Moor holding up a shield.

A painter I had not previously encountered, Jan Kupecký (1667–1740), is thoroughly exhibited here, with some highly sophisticated portraits, notably of his wife, and of the painter Karl Bruni. Don't miss the exquisite series of etchings by Václav Hollar. Since Václav Reiner's frescoes, so abundant in the city's churches and palaces, are not often properly visible from ground level, the presence here of many of his smaller paintings allows one to get acquainted with his style.

On leaving the museum, turn left and left again down Jiřská, the lane that runs along the south side of the basilica. You'll pass the church's south portal, an elegant renaissance design manufactured in Benedikt Ried's workshop in about 1500. The tympanum of St George and the Dragon is a copy of a late gothic work. From Jiřská you also have an excellent view of the two tall romanesque towers of the basilica.

Turn left into Zlatá ulička (Golden Lane). Late in the sixteenth century, members of the royal bodyguard were allowed to construct houses on the sheltered side of the north wall, and here they pursued their second jobs, a long-established East European tradition. Later, these houses, which are extremely modest, became the homes of the poorer residents of Hradčany. Franz Kafka lived at number 22 in 1917, and the Nobel-prize winning poet Jaroslav Seifert lived in a house that has since been demolished. Although they must have been extremely cramped to live in, they undoubtedly present a picturesque appearance; cameras and videos whirr more frequently in Golden Lane than in any other street within the castle compound.

OPPOSITE *It is hard to imagine that Golden Lane, tucked away from the grander courtyards of the Castle and oozing with an almost rustic modesty and charm, was once home to Franz Kafka.*

Return to the beginning of the lane and take the steps back down to Jiřksá. On either side of the sloping street are renaissance mansions such as number 12, and baroque houses such as number 10 (9). Number 4 (6) used to be the palace of the burgrave of the castle, who was the most senior official in Bohemia after the king. In 1963 it became the Czechoslovak Children's House. Over its early eighteenth-century gateway is a small collection of coats of arms from the preceding century. The renaissance mansion and its tower were designed by Giovanni Ventura in 1555. At the other end of Jiřská looms the hefty and somewhat menacing BLACK TOWER, the castle's former eastern gate, originally built by Duke Soběslav I in the twelfth century. The gateway in use today, connecting Jiřská with the Old Castle Steps, is a renaissance structure dating from the late sixteenth century.

Opposite the Children's House is Carlo Lurago's LOBKOVIC PALACE of 1651–68. Its renaissance courtyard, a remnant of the original structure of the 1570s, has some sgraffito decoration. But the main interest of the palace lies in its historical museum upstairs, and a visit will help you understand the background to much of what you will see during a stay in Prague. The first room documents the earliest periods of settlement, and its most exciting exhibit is a moustachioed Celtic head believed to have been carved in the second century BC. From Moravia comes Slav jewellery of the eighth and ninth centuries, including a silver cross from this newly Christianized territory. Also displayed are some early medieval illuminated manuscripts, including a facsimile of an eleventh-century version of the legend of St Wenceslas.

Room 2 deals with the gothic period, and presents objects associated with the Přemysl Ottakar kings, notably the funerary regalia of Ottakar II. Since the crown jewels are usually locked up, it is worth taking a look at the replica of the crown of Charles IV, with its huge emeralds, sapphires and other gems, and his coronation sword. Shown in the same case are the golden orb and sceptre that were probably made for Ferdinand I in the mid sixteenth century. Also on display is the charter establishing Charles University in 1348, with its splendid wax seal. There are many examples of religious statuary and stained glass, and a facsimile of a panel from Karlštejn Castle by Master Theodoric, but I was particularly intrigued by the fourteenth-century copy of the first Czech-language dictionary in existence, by Klaret.

Room 3 concentrates on the Hussite revolution, often in the form of vicious weaponry such as studded flails. From the Bethlehem Chapel in the Old Town comes an early sixteenth century polychrome relief of the Last Supper, a very convincing three-dimensional carving. Room 4 displays domestic and religious artefacts from the Jagellon period.

In rooms 5 and 6 we reach the Habsburg period, and the growth of an urban bourgeoisie and a more sophisticated legal system. Room 7 illustrates Czech culture in the years before White Mountain, the heyday of Czech humanism, with jewelry, scientific instruments, musical instruments, and printed translations of botanical and historical works.

The peaceful courtyard of the Lobkovic Palace offers a tranquil haven after exploring the more crowded streets and lanes within the castle's walls.

Rooms 8 and 9 display Rudolf II's 1609 declaration of religious freedom for the Bohemian Estates. In 1620, after the Estates had been forced to yield to Ferdinand II, the emperor cut out the royal seal, which explains the declaration's damaged condition today. Documents and weaponry illustrate the uprising of the Estates and the catastrophic Battle of the White Mountain.

The exhibition continues on the floor below. Room 10 documents the defeat at White Mountain and such consequences as the executioner's bill for decapitating the leaders of the Czech nobility in 1612 in the Old Town Square. Of more lasting importance were the lists of confiscated properties. A depressing note is struck with the Patent of 1627 by Ferdinand II declaring Roman Catholicism the sole permitted religion.

Room 11 documents the Thirty Years War, and rooms 12 and 13 deal with the late seventeenth and early eighteenth centuries. You'll see baroque church plate on the one hand, and on the other instruments of torture used to keep uppity serfs in their place. The persistence of the Counter-Reformation is illustrated by the inclusion of a book of 1729 listing prohibited Czech books.

There's an aura of slightly greater benevolence in room 14, which follows the rule of Maria Theresia and her reformist son Joseph II. The following two rooms reflect nineteenth-century bourgeois and rural life. The exhibits include musical instruments, textiles, furniture, and playing cards. Room 17 shows the beginnings of the industrial revolution and commercial manufacture, and room 19 documents the growth of Czech nationalism.

I have often bemoaned the fact that important museums in Czechoslovakia, including the main part of the National Museum, assume that their visitors are familiar with the difficult Czech language, and provide no translations whatever, not even into German. This historical museum is a happy exception, and lends visitors catalogues in a number of different languages. The reason why Czech, and indeed Hungarian, museums have been slow to provide translated captions is that there would have been a political compulsion to offer Russian as the second language rather than German, French or English. This no longer applies, of course, and I have been assured that it is planned to provide translations in major museums, but it will take a while yet.

You should also be warned that the Lobkovic Museum is not without its critics. It does too much too fast, resulting in glib generalizations and some displays of questionable value. Nevertheless, I find it useful and recommend it as a way of getting to grips fairly rapidly with the recurrent themes of Czech history.

From the palace, you can either turn right and descend the Old Castle Steps to Malostranksá Metro station, or turn left and return to Hradčanské náměstí, where the next itinerary begins.

2
The Castle District

....

CASTLE SQUARE *to* THE STRAHOV MONASTERY

Only the most important buildings of the kingdom – the cathedral, the royal palace, the formal reception rooms, the ancient basilica and convent of St George, and of course the defensive towers – could be accommodated within the castle precincts. It was thus inevitable that nobles and highly placed clerics whose duties or proclivities kept them close to the royal presence should wish to build their own palaces as close as possible to the castle. Some chose the streets and squares of Malá Strana between the castle and the river, but others constructed their palaces in Hradčany, adjoining the castle itself.

With your back to the castle gates, you can admire at leisure the large expanse of Hradčanské náměstí, Castle Square. It is almost surrounded by large palaces and mansions, yet the square feels admirably spacious, in part because of its location along the top of a ridge, where it can't be overlooked by other buildings. And the marvellous view to the left turns the entire square into a kind of belvedere. Despite its wealth of superb buildings, Prague can sometimes be a difficult city to see, if only because so much of its architectural glory lies behind its florid façades. In Malá Strana in particular, just below Hradčany and its square, many of the great palaces present a somewhat grim face to the world, and it is only when penetrating their portals that one becomes aware of the baroque embellishments of the terraced gardens, and the voluptuous statuary on staircases and balustrades. Equally difficult to see from below are the roofs of old Prague, a wonderful collection of tiled ridges and peaked gables, with dormer windows like snail shells peeking from just above the eaves. From Hradčany this undulating sea of roofs and quirky renaissance gables floats down the hillside, interrupted only by the domes and steeples of the city's churches and towers.

Hradčany consisted of more than the castle, and was a separately defined settlement from about 1320 onwards. It gradually expanded beyond the original confines of this square as far as the Strahov Monastery to the west. Before 1541, when the square was badly devasted by fire, it must have had a very different

OPPOSITE *From the slopes beneath the Strahov Monastery you can look across to the dome of St Nicholas's and, beyond, to the twin towers of the Týn church.*

appearance, with town houses rather than palaces overlooking the plaza. In 1598 Hradčany was given royal status, which it retained until 1784, after which it became simply one of the principal districts of the city.

The square was the original core of Hradčany, and in the Middle Ages would have had a commercial atmosphere, with merchants' houses and markets rather than the concentration of aristocratic and ecclesiastical palaces that one sees today. The first building on the left is the bulky SALM PALACE by F. Pavíček. Built betwen 1800 and 1810, it is not the most graceful of Prague mansions. It is now the Swiss embassy and connected with the neighbouring Schwarzenberg Palace. Opposite it stands a far more distinguished building, the ARCHBISHOP'S PALACE, built in the 1560s and adapted nearly a century later. The buildings that stood here previously were acquired by Ferdinand I and presented by him to the Catholic archbishop after the Hussite wars; thus the palace was initially very much part of the Counter-Reformation campaign. The present façade, by Johann Joseph Wirch, is rococo (1765), with stucco cartouches at either end. Some of the sculpture above the raised pediment, which also has rococo embellishments within it, is the work of Ignác Platzer.

A lane alongside the Archbishop's Palace leads down to the STERNBERG PALACE, which since 1949 has contained the European paintings of the National Gallery. After the Battle of the White Mountain many aristocratic Bohemian families found it prudent to change their names to German ones, and the Sternbergs were no exception. It's difficult to make out the design of the building unless one has access to the sculpture garden, from where there is a fine view of this curious palace. The odd feature is the tall oval drum that rises up from the centre of the garden façade. The architect was Giovanni Alliprandi (1698–1707), one of a number of Italian architects active in Prague in the late seventeenth century. From the galleries there is a fine view of the courtyard, with its stucco ornament and medallions above the second-floor windows.

At the time of writing, the first floor was closed and although some of the paintings normally displayed here were shown elsewhere, there will undoubtedly be considerable rearrangement of the collection. So I will make no attempt here to indicate the location of particular paintings. On the staircase leading up to the second floor, however, is a canvas of the *Triumph of Frederick Gonzaga* by Lorenzo Costa (1522) so enormous that it is unlikely ever to be moved. The collection as a whole is very important, with fine paintings representing almost all the major phases of European art history, from icons to Impressionists. Many of the late gothic paintings, mainly by unidentifiable masters, are of high quality, such as the two contrasting paintings of the beheading of St Barbara (and there's a third elsewhere in the gallery).

Some of the German paintings have a rough energy but are coarse in their detail, but one can't make that criticism of the numerous works by Lucas Cranach the Elder. These include a late painting entitled *Suffer the Little Children to Come unto Me* and shows a rather weary Christ being surrounded by young mothers and their ugly babies; and an exquisite portrait of a young woman

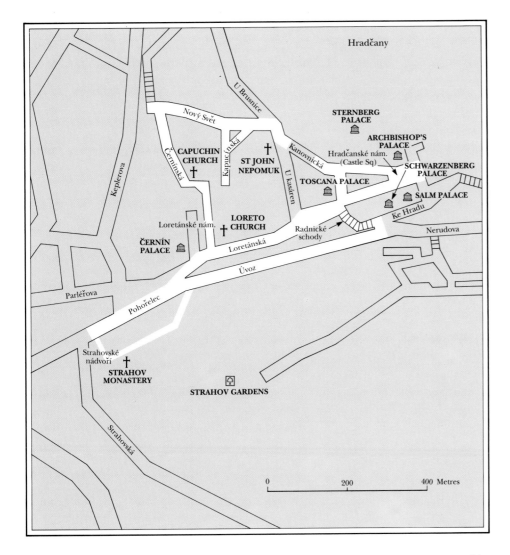

(1538). There are two portraits by Cranach the Younger. Dürer is represented by a large and crowded *Festival of the Rose Garlands* (1506), with meticulously painted plants, jewels and silks. This fascinating painting incorporates not only a self-portrait of the artist, but portraits of Emperor Maximilian I (to the right of the Virgin), Pope Julius II (to the left), and the banker Jakob Fugger. The painting was acquired by Rudolf II soon afterwards and has been in Prague since.

Italian sixteenth-century painting is well represented, but not by very exciting paintings. You'll find a Lorenzo Lotto portrait of a musician, paintings by Palma Vecchio and his great nephew Palma Giovane, by Sebastiano del Piombo and Jacopo Bassano, two Bronzino portraits (one in typically bright colours) of Cosimo de'Medici and Eleonora of Toledo, and a Tintoretto portrait. Later Italian painting includes works by Sebastiano Ricci, a portrait by Giambattista Tiepolo, and a fine townscape of the Thames by Canaletto.

Spanish painting is not a strong point of the collection, but there is a dewy-eyed Christ by El Greco and a striking Goya portrait of 1815 of Don Miguel de Lardizábal. The Dutch and Flemish collection is another matter. It includes Pieter Bruegel the Elder's *Haymaking*, an exquisite still life of tulips by Jan Brueghel the Elder (1608), Van Dyck's *Abraham and Isaac*, Frans Hals's portrait of the haughty Jasper Schade van Westrum (1645), Rembrandt's lush *Scholar in His Study* (1634), landscapes by both Jacob van Ruisdael and his uncle Saloman van Ruysdael, and some remarkable Rubens paintings, including the energetic *Martyrdom of St Thomas* (1638), the portrait of Ambrosio Spinola (1628), and a massive St Augustine (1638).

From more recent centuries there are works by Caspar David Friedrich, Max Liebermann, a large Miró, and bronzes by Henry Moore, Giacomo Manzù, and Georg Kolbe. The two de Chirico paintings are both slight, but there are some striking paintings from the Vienna Secession: Gustav Klimt's garish *Virgin* (1913), and Egon Schiele's *Pregnant Woman and Death* (1911). Also on display are two large paintings by Edvard Munch and many by Oskar Kokoschka, including his portrait of the indolent Albert Ehrenstein (1914) as well as three townscapes of Prague.

Across the courtyard, on the ground floor, are the rest of the late nineteenth-century and twentieth-century paintings and sculptures. This is not an enormous collection, so the fact that it contains good paintings by, among others, Eugène Delacroix, Gustave Courbet, Camille Corot, Honoré Daumier, Edouard Manet, Edgar Degas, Camille Pissarro, André Derain, Claude Monet, Paul Gauguin, and Paul Cézanne, is remarkable. There's a fine Provençal landscape

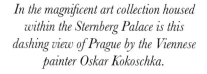

In the magnificent art collection housed within the Sternberg Palace is this dashing view of Prague by the Viennese painter Oskar Kokoschka.

by Vincent van Gogh (1889), a Toulouse-Lautrec of the Moulin Rouge (1892), a pointilliste Seurat of the docks at Honfleur (1886), some chunky landscapes by Maurice Vlaminck, a gorgeous sleepy Provençal scene by Pierre Bonnard (1913), a delightful self-portrait by Henri 'le Douanier' Rousseau (1890), and a Matisse portrait. The Picassos are superb, containing not only some of his statuesque nudes, but wonderfully intense cubist canvases that make a fascinating contrast with the more sedate works in a similar style by Georges Braque in the next room.

As for sculpture, there are major bronzes by Aristide Maillol and Picasso, Degas and Emile Antoine Vourdelle. Auguste Rodin is well represented, and his group includes the huge statue of Honoré de Balzac, John the Baptist (in the palace garden), and a bust of Gustav Mahler. A pair of paintings by Georges Rouault is here, and some whimsical Chagalls, a characteristic Léger, some amiable Utrillos and his mother, Suzanne Valadon's *Flowers*.

On re-emerging into Castle Square, you will find yourself opposite the unmistakable outline of the SCHWARZENBERG PALACE, built by Augustin Vlach for the Lobkovic family from 1545 to 1563. (The Schwarzenbergs only acquired the palace in 1719.) This is an extraordinary building, and not only because of the sgraffito (originally of 1567 but often restored) that covers every inch of its

Facing the Archbishop's Palace on Castle Square is the renaissance bulk of the Schwarzenberg Palace, its surfaces entirely covered with geometric and monochrome sgraffito designs.

surface. The renaissance gables on both the wings are tiered, and the broad eaves are splayed outwards, adding to the imposing bulk of the palace. On the street side the courtyard is enclosed by a high wall, also gabled. Today the Schwarzenberg Palace houses the Military History Museum. Visitors to Vienna may recall that there is another huge Schwarzenberg Palace there, part of which has now been converted into a hotel. The present head of the family, the unassuming Karl von Schwarzenberg, emerged after the Velvet Revolution of November 1989 as a principal foreign policy adviser to President Václav Havel.

Opposite the entrance, within a small park, is a tall pedestal bearing at the top a baroque figure of the Virgin Mary carved by Ferdinand Maximilian Brokoff in 1725. Behind the statue, on the north side of the square, are a number of rather nondescript baroque mansions. Number 11 (61), At the Swan, however, has an appealing late baroque façade. Next door, at numbers 9–10 (62–3) is the Sachsen-Lauenburg house, which now has a façade from the 1730s, with pediments at either end. The architect and sculptor Peter Parler lived in a house on this site in the fourteenth century. To the left, at number 8 (67), is the Martinitz Palace, originally built in the 1570s and rebuilt 60 years later, when it belonged to Jaroslav von Martinitz, one of the imperial counsellors tipped out of the window during the defenestration of 1618 (his tomb is in St Vitus's Cathedral). It has stylish renaissance gables and on the first floor there are extensive sgraffiti of singularly inept draughtsmanship from the late sixteenth century. These decorations were only uncovered in 1971 during the restoration of the palace.

At the end of the square, opposite the castle, is the pompous TOSCANA PALACE, a heavy-handed attempt at a Roman baroque style built by Jean Baptiste Mathey from 1689 to 1691. The one distinguished feature of the palace is the carving on the corner of Loretánská, a lively and vivacious statue of St Michael created in 1693 by Ottavio Mosto. Mosto was an Italian sculptor who spent the last few years of his life working in Prague, dying here in 1701.

In *A Time of Gifts* Patrick Leigh Fermor captured the genial confusion of the city, which is so well represented in this square as well as in the narrow lanes, lined with palaces, that lead down from Hradčany towards the squares of Malá Strana:

> There are renaissance buildings, light arcaded pavilions and loggias on slim Ionic pillars that could have alighted here from Tuscany or Latium, but the palaces on the squares and the citadel and the steep wooded slopes belong to the Habsburg afternoon ... Terraces climb the hillside in a giant staircase and somewhere, above the frosty twigs, juts a folly like a mandarin's hat; it must have been built about the time when *Don Giovanni* was being composed a mile away.

Indeed, it seems easier in Prague than in almost any other European city to make such direct connections with the past; the intervening centuries have left their mark on the city, but the continuum remains, and the renaissance sgraffito of the Schwarzenberg Palace, the Roman grandeur of the Toscana Palace, the more modest baroque façades on the other side of the square, and the gothic spires and baroque domes visible in the distance all coexist effortlessly.

From the square turn right into Loretánská, which opens out into a sort of square. On the left, at number 1 (173), is the former HRADČANY TOWN HALL of 1602 to 1603, ornamented with sgraffito and faded frescoes on the façade. Inside you'll find a pretty galleried courtyard. The building served its purpose during the time when each section of the city had its own independent administration, but after the change in status of 1784 it ceased to be the town hall and has been converted into flats.

Further up on the left at number 7 (176) is the Dietrichstein Palace, a fairly austere structure which in its present form dates from the 1730s. In the centre of Loretánská you will find a very ugly green cast-iron lampstand, constructed in 1867. Perhaps if it were repainted in a less bilious colour it wouldn't seem quite so offensive. At number 9 (177) stands the Hrzán Palace, its gothic core obscured by an eighteenth-century façade. The palace used to be the deanery of St Vitus's Cathedral. A homelier touch is provided by the unpretentious arcaded house at number 17 (103) and the adjacent school at number 19 (104), also arcaded.

You will then emerge into spacious Loretánské náměstí. The pub at number 1 (107) has an elaborate baroque façade, with rococo stucco framing a mediocre painting above the entrance. The renaissance houses along this side of the square are all arcaded. The square is dominated by the colossal ČERNÍN PALACE. The ground floor is heavily buttressed and rusticated, and from these buttresses rise the half-columns that divide the 29 endlessly repetitive bays that extend for an exhausting 150 metres. The place was built from 1669 to 1697 to designs by Francesco Caratti, and Kaňka was responsible for much of the interior design. Its period of glory lasted only one century, and the palace was disposed of in 1779. After serving as a hospital and barracks, it was acquired and restored to something approaching its former glory by the Ministry of Foreign Affairs in 1929. Although the palace cannot be visited, concerts are sometimes held in the splendid gardens. Tacked onto the back, but fortunately not visible from this side, is an extremely dreary modern extension, topped with radio masts and other electronic equipment, the ears of the ministry.

The ramp on the right in front of the palace leads to the LORETO pilgrimage church which was founded as an act of extreme piety by the Blessed Catherine of Lobkovic in 1626. Kilián Ignác Dientzenhofer's façade is completely dominated by the statuary ranged along the balustrade of the forecourt, around the porch and up on the attic. The forecourt statues are copies of originals of 1722 by A. Quittainer; most of the others are by J.F. Kohl. Their dark stone contrasts strongly with the white façade. A tower rises above the entrance, and the belfry contains a famous carillon of 27 bells made by P. Neumann in 1694; just before the hour, it plays prettily.

The entrance leads not into a church, but into a two-storey cloister, of which the upper floor is especially elegant. In the centre of the cloister is the point of the exercise, a reproduction made in 1631 of the Santa Casa from Loreto, itself a reconstruction of the holy family's house, supposedly transported from the Holy Land in the thirteenth century by Franciscan friars. Even this copy of the house reeks of devotion, spreading into each bay of the cloister, which contains either a simple altar or a confessional. In each corner there are chapels, decorated by major baroque artists such as Matthias Jäckel and Peter Brandl. On either side of the Santa Casa are lavish fountains of 1740 by J.M. Biederle, which have recently been replaced by copies.

Inside the Santa Casa are some faded frescoes and a powerful red-and-gold altar screen topped with obelisks. Behind the screen is a niche, entirely silver-plated, in which stands a cedarwood statue of the Virgin Mary; the grille of the screen is also silver-plated. The CHURCH OF THE NATIVITY, which is attached to the cloister, was built by J.G. Aichbauer from 1734 to 1735 and has ceiling frescoes by Václav Reiner of 1736. The church is surprisingly small, and its compactness is reinforced by the relatively low ceiling. The interior is redolent of the Spanish Counter-Reformation and is pretty, if crowded, with lovely gilt baroque balconies, and skilful employment of pink and blue marbles.

A room off the upper storey of the cloister houses the remarkable treasury. On display are the gifts of the faithful and the rich to the Madonna of Loreto. These include some beautiful seventeenth-century Augsburg silver candlesticks; vestments, including pontifical gloves, embroidered with gold thread; bejwelled reliquaries; exquisite seventeenth- and eighteenth-century filigree crosses and caskets; the Wallenstein chalice and monstrance of 1721 studded with amethysts and other precious stones; and, most amazing of all, the monstrance of gilded silver that is studded with 6222 diamonds, some of them of no mean size. The ravishing object, the legacy of Ludmilla Kolowrat, was made by Viennese goldsmiths in 1699, and it is possible that Johann Bernard Fischer von Erlach had a hand in its design.

On leaving the Loreto, look to the right and you will see the gabled roof of the Capuchin church, built in 1600 to 1602, within a walled enclosure that almost conceals the oldest Capuchin monastery in Bohemia. The interior is somewhat boxy, but the baroque furnishings are relatively restrained. On the altar in the north chapel is a much revered image of the Madonna and Child. Next to the church are the gates of the Černín Palace gardens, from where there is a clear view of Caratti's stupendous garden façade, with its two lofty arched recesses.

Follow Černínská alongside the Capuchin church. This descends past pretty old houses to the lane called Nový Svět, an adventurous name, for it means New World. Turn right. Along the cobbled lane are many more such unpretentious houses. On the corner of Kapucínská, number 5 (78) is more imposing than most on Nový Svět, with an irregular seventeenth-century baroque design. On the corner of Kapucínská, beneath a two-storey bay window, is a carving of linked fish. Number 3 (77), now the wine bar U Zlaté Hrušky, has an unsophisticated baroque façade and an ingenious wrought-iron lantern over the door. Nový Svět derives its charm from the almost rustic simplicity of most of the houses, but this should not prevent one from realising that in previous centuries this was the quarter of the poor, within walking distance of employment on Hradčany yet well out of sight in this sunken glade.

OPPOSITE *As a principal rallying point of Bohemian piety, the Loreto church on Hradčany attracts thousands of visitors and pilgrims every week.*

In the early years of this century, Arthur Symons, in his book *Cities*, commented aggressively on what he perceived as the angularity of Prague's architecture, and must have been one of the few observers of the city to have resisted its charm: 'You will find a bastard kind of architecture,' he wrote, 'Renaissance crossed with Slavonic, which has little sense of design and no sense of decoration, except the overlaying of a plain surface with protruding figures.' But some of his other observations seem more appropriate, especially when one is standing among the lanes of the Nový Svět district:

> Nothing is more curious than to contrast this fiery spirit, showing itself in energy of line and angularity of outline, with the gentleness, the soft colour, the placidity of the wide green spaces within the city, and the vast green plains and hillsides in whose midst the city has entrenched itself.

Where Nový Svět runs into Kanovnická, bear right, and you'll soon come to the church of ST JOHN NEPOMUK built by Kilián Ignác Dientzenhofer from 1720 to 1729, a slightly awkward and stubby composition with a broad central tower. Inside there are ceiling frescoes painted in 1727 by the ubiquitous Václav Reiner. On the right at number 7 (73) is the gateway of the former Ursuline convent, founded in 1691. The surviving buildings, also by Dientzenhofer, were erected half a century later around a spacious courtyard, but in the 1780s, during the reign of Joseph II, the convent was dissolved. From here return to Kapucínská, turn left, and walk up the cobbled lane towards Loretánské náměstí.

After the Černín Palace turn right. You'll see a long, low arcaded building with crudely scrolled gables – the Trčka house which dates back to the sixteenth century. The long square ahead is Pohořelec, and it's lined on both sides with many charming baroque houses. The name means 'scene of the fire', a reference to the conflagrations which repeatedly destroyed this former hamlet that used to be on the edge of Hradčany. At the end of the square is a statue of 1752 of St John Nepomuk by T. Hochhaus. In Pohořelec, numbers 4 (151) and 5 (150), both gabled, are especially attractive, and number 5 is of renaissance origin. Just beyond on the left is the Rosina, a modest but very friendly crêpe and waffle bar, a useful place for a snack. I've watched burly Viennese tourists clean the owner out of her stocks of Becherovka, a herbal liqueur that you either love or, as in my own case, loathe. The last house on the right, number 22 (114) is the Kučera Palace with lovely railings, stucco ornament, and thoroughly rococo urns on the balustrade. Dating from the 1760s, it has long been in need of a coat of paint.

The ramp leads to the main gate of the STRAHOV MONASTERY, which remained outside the Hradčany district until the time of Charles IV. Although it doesn't look it, this is an ancient ecclesiastical foundation, a Premonstratensian monastery established in the 1140s by Duke Vladislav II. During the Middle Ages there were about 2000 of the order's monasteries spread across Europe, and Strahov was always one of the richest. The gateway is a conventional baroque structure of 1742 by Anselmo Lurago with three statues by A. Quittainer. Stepping into the courtyard, you'll see the abbey church straight ahead, and in front

OPPOSITE *Once a modest series of workers' dwellings on the far side of Hradčany, the houses of Nový Svět have acquired with age an unpretentious decorative charm.*

of it a seventeenth-century statue of St Norbert, the founder of the order, on a pedestal. On the left is Giovanni Maria Philippi's former church of St Roch built between 1603 and 1612, much altered since and never quite able to make up its mind whether it was going to be a gothic or renaissance design. It is now used for exhibitions. The large building to the right of the church is the famous library.

The church façade, which was originally romanesque, was given the last of its face-lifts in the mid-eighteenth century by Lurago and embellished with more of Quittainer's statuary. Inside, the most striking feature is the long nave with ceiling paintings within rococo panels (by Palliardi). There is an abundance of baroque altars, all much the same, apart from the variations in the columns. The choir furnishings are splendid: pulpit, organ, choir stalls, and railings, all in a rich gilt baroque style. In the body of the church the bench-ends are also richly carved. The principal organ, even more lavish, is in the west gallery. When Mozart visited the monastery in 1787 he improvised on the Strahov organ in the choir, to the delight of the monks, who transcribed his jam session. For eight years, beginning in 1980, the church was closed because of restoration work, but the wait has been worth it. This is now one of the finest interiors in Prague.

The façade of the old abbey library, while also baroque, is in a very different style, far more Italianate. It was designed by Ignác Palliardi and is dated to 1783. In the lunette above the frieze is a medallion portraying Joseph II, who dissolved monasteries throughout the Habsburg domains but spared Strahov. Upstairs there is a small exhibition of rare books, miniature books, and illuminated manuscripts, and in tall glass cabinets a most weird collection of objects. There are shells, butterflies and beetles, which may not be so unusual, together with dried fish and reptiles. More rewarding are the two great libraries. To possess just one of these libraries would have been cause for satisfaction for even the most prosperous of monasteries; to possess two is an astonishing luxury, even though they serve different purposes.

The hall next to the display rooms is the more recent of the two, the Philosophical Library. It's a grand room, 32 metres long and 14 metres high. When the Premonstratensian monastery at Louka in Moravia was dissolved in the 1780s, the monks of Strahov bought its old bookcases and had them installed here in the 1790s. Judging by what we see before us, the library at Louka must have been hugely impressive too. The plans for this library at Strahov had already been drawn up when the opportunity to acquire the Louka furnishings arose, so those plans had to be altered in order to accommodate bookcases of this height and size. Not content with such magnificent furnishings, the monastery then commissioned the septuagenarian Austrian painter Anton Maulbertsch (1724–96) to paint the ceiling. He did do in correspondingly grand fashion, taking as his theme the search for perfection in philosophy.

The Philosophical Library is galleried, which adds to the height and sumptuousness of the hall, as do the very deep window bays. In 1965 a Czech collector donated to the library six Roman busts, which are now placed in the body of the hall. A corridor with more modest bookcases filled with vellum-lined volumes

OPPOSITE *The recently-restored Strahov Monastery church is now in pristine condition and offers one of the most stylistically coherent baroque interiors in the entire city.*

The Strahov Monastery is equipped with two resplendent baroque libraries, of which this, the Philosophical Library, is the grander.

leads to the second and older hall, the Theological Library. Compared to the Philosophical Library, it is low and somewhat cramped, but it has an intimacy lacking in the grander hall. This, surely, is the place one would come to if one simply wanted to sit down and read a book for pleasure.

The bookcases in the Theological Library were made in 1632, although the library to contain them was not completed until 1671 by Giovanni Domenico Orsi. The many globes in the hall date from the seventeenth and eighteenth centuries. The paintings of 1723–7, panels within very lavish stucco frames, are the work of one of the Strahov monks, Siard Nosecký, and he portrayed leading members of his order, himself included. This library contains 16,000 volumes, but Strahov as a whole possesses almost a million volumes, including 5000 manuscripts, of which the most precious is the Strahov Evangelarium, produced in Trier in the tenth century. The reason why the monastery is so well supplied with books is that the libraries of other religious houses dissolved in 1954 were sent here.

On leaving the library walk to the east end of the church, where the baroque building attached to one of the towers gives access to the cloisters, now the home of the Museum of Czech Literature. This museum was established here in the 1950s after the monastery was closed by the Stalinist regime. Although the exhibits are not of overwhelming interest to those not already familiar with Czech literature and music, especially since all the captions are in Czech, the museum is still worth visiting, as it offers glimpses of the old monastic buildings. The reconstructed cloisters retain a few traces of romanesque masonry, but the spirit is baroque. On the other side of the cloister, however, the hall devoted to the achievements of Jan Hus has romanesque walls; there are remains of the four columns that used to support the vault, which has since been replaced. Also off the cloister is the summer refectory, with ceiling frescoes depicting a banquet in heaven, another contribution by Siard Nosecký. Now that the new property laws have come into effect, there is a distinct possibility that the museum, which to some extent had a propaganda role under the Communist regime, will have to find new quarters, but it is too soon to say.

The gate let into the wall on the right leads into a corner of the Strahov gardens on the Petřín hill. To the right, on the summit of the hill, rises the television tower, built in 1891 as a local version of the Eiffel Tower, and straight ahead there is an excellent view of the church of St Nicholas in Malá Strana and the towers of the Týn church; to the left you can see the bridges across the Vltava and the towers of St Vitus's Cathedral. The path bears left and brings you out on Úvoz, a steep lane bordered on one side by the Petřín park and on the other by the backs of houses that line Loretánská. Many of these houses have bay windows so that the occupants too can enjoy the view.

Lower down there are some attractive houses. Number 26 (159) has an early eighteenth-century statue in a corner niche, and number 24 (160), built in 1706, has allegorical busts of Sol and Luna by Jan Brokoff at either end. Next door at number 22 (161), another baroque house, there's a full-blown relief of the Madonna and Child above the portal. Numbers 10–14 (167–5) are modest gabled houses with renaissance outlines, and 6 (169 and 171) is a grand baroque townhouse known as the House at the Golden Star, with a façade from 1728.

At the next corner you can turn left, and beneath the looming Schwarzenberg Palace, mount the ramp up to Hradčanské náměstí. Alternatively you can go straight on to Nerudova to begin the next itinerary.

3
Malá Strana

....

Eight hundred years ago this proud aristocratic corner of Prague was no more than a couple of inconspicuous villages. In 1257, however, King Ottakar II founded what soon became known as the Lesser Town, focused around what is now Malostranské náměstí, midway between river and castle. Charles IV expanded the new settlement, or rather incorporated within it some of the surrounding hamlets and surrounded them with a wall. Malá Strana shows few traces of that medieval past, for a succession of fires, the worst of which took place in 1541, destroyed all the earlier buildings, paving the way for successful merchants and noblemen to build lavish palaces, gardens and churches here. This glorious period of the history of Malá Strana commenced after the defeat at White Mountain, but once Prague had begun to be increasingly marginalized by Vienna's self-glorification as the Habsburg imperial capital, the great aristocratic families found less and less reason to maintain palatial residences here. Joseph II's dissolution of the monasteries in 1782 also adversely affected the many ecclesiastical establishments that had been founded here. Over the years Malá Strana became somewhat seedy, and even today few of the palaces and houses have been given the kind of face-lift bestowed on, for example, the entire Old Town Square on the other side of the river (p. 123).

Many of the streets of Malá Strana are steep, but begin the easy way, from the top. From Hradčanské náměstí, the Castle Square, take the ramp alongside the Salm Palace that will bring you to the point where Úvoz becomes Nerudova, at the boundary between Hradčany and Malá Strana. At the foot of the ramp are statues of St John Nepomuk – it is hard to avoid him in Prague – and St Joseph, both by Ferdinand Maximilian Brokoff.

Nerudova is one of the most picturesque streets in Prague, as film-makers have long known. It is difficult to single out houses for special admiration here, as the street presents a lively baroque ensemble, only slightly marred lower down by some indifferent nineteenth-century blocks. Nerudova is particularly rich in

OPPOSITE *The Valdštejn gardens have everything: flowers, statuary, a loggia, sun and shade, gravel walks, and the large expanse of a lily-festooned pool.*

75

house signs, for a few centuries ago, before house-numbering became the norm, this was the simplest and most obvious way to identify a building. Number 49 (232), for example, has a relief of a swan over the portal, and next door, number 47 (233), the seventeenth-century gabled House of the Two Suns, is easily identified by a relief over the entrance. This house, for many generations the property of goldsmiths, was where the writer Jan Neruda lived from 1845 to 1859, giving his name not only to this street but to the great Chilean poet, Pablo Neruda, who borrowed the Czech's name as his own *nom de plume*. Major alterations were made to the house in the last quarter of the seventeenth century.

Number 43 (235) of 1729 has a less common house sign, in the form of a lobster. A graceful but more conventional baroque statue of an angel stands on a pedestal on the façade of number 35 (239), while number 33 (240), the BRETFELD PALACE, has baroque railings and stucco ornament by Johann Joseph Wirch dating from 1765. The palace was frequented both by the industrious Mozart and the philanderer Casanova on their visits to Prague. At number 23 (219) is a model pharmacy, part of the National Museum, but you can see a more interesting working example in Malé náměstí in the Old Town. On the left is the church of OUR LADY AT THE THEATINES, built between 1691 and 1717 by Jean Baptiste Mathey, one of the few truly dull church façades in Prague. The church adjoins the THUN-HOHENSTEIN PALACE, and between the two buildings a flight of steps (open only during the day) leads up to the top of Thunovská. This is the best spot from which to see the palace's most fascinating feature, the strange renaissance gables at the rear, some decorated with sgraffito. This was built in the 1560s by the lords of Hradec, but only remained in the family until 1602.

Return to Nerudova and the main façade of the baroque extension to the renaissance palace up on Thunovská, built by Giovanni Santini in the 1720s. The much praised gateway is surely one of the supremely vulgar examples of high baroque in the city, and Matthias Braun, who was responsible for the carvings, was clearly responding to the self-importance of the Kolowrats, whose emblem was the eagle. The tops of Braun's huge eagles flapping around the portal have been colonized by pigeons, a just fate. The palace is now the Italian embassy.

The next house, number 18 (213), known as At St John Nepomuk, has traces of unsophisticated sgraffito from the 1550s revealed beneath its lush baroque façade, while number 14 (210), the Valkounsky House, has an even more splendid façade; for many years it was inhabited by its designer, Giovanni Santini. Opposite, at number 5 (256), is the Morzin Palace of 1713–14, also by Santini and decorated with carvings by Ferdinand Maximilian Brokoff of allegorical personifications of Night and Day on either side of the central bay, which is supported by the figures of two hefty Moors, the emblems of the Morzin family; and there are more statues on top of the side bays. Number 12 (210), a house of medieval origin, has a particularly charming sign in the form of three fiddles, a reminder that a family of violin makers, the Edlingers, used to live here. At the end of the street, at number 2, is the excellent beer hall, U Kocoura (At the Cat), less frequented by tourists than many drinking houses in Malá Strana.

ABOVE *House signs within elaborate baroque cartouches were once the simplest way to identify town houses and the trades of their occupants.*

OPPOSITE *It is not hard to see why Nerudova, with its complete array of varying house façades, is regarded by many as the quintessential baroque street of central Europe.*

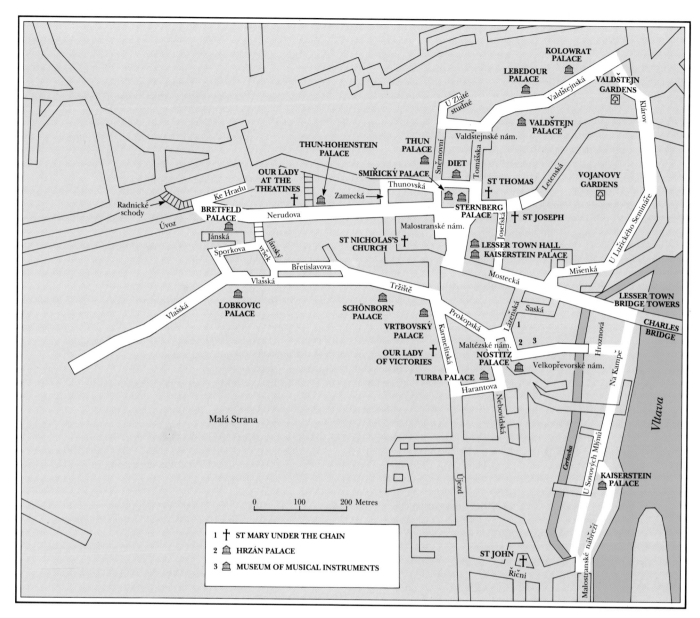

Map legend:

KOLOWRAT PALACE

LEBEDOUR PALACE

VALDŠTEJN GARDENS

Valdštejnská

Klárov

U Zlaté studné

VALDŠTEJN PALACE

THUN-HOHENSTEIN PALACE

THUN PALACE

Valdštejnské nám.

Tomášská

Sněmovní

DIET

Letenská

VOJANOVY GARDENS

OUR LADY AT THE THEATINES

SMIŘICKÝ PALACE

Thunovská

ST THOMAS

Ke Hradu

Zamecká

Nerudova

STERNBERG PALACE

Josefská

† ST JOSEPH

U Lužického Semináře

Radnické schody

BRETFELD PALACE

Malostranské nám.

Úvoz

Jánská

ST NICHOLAS'S CHURCH †

LESSER TOWN HALL

KAISERSTEIN PALACE

Šporkova

Jánský vršek

Břetislavova

Mišenká

Mostecká

Vlašská

Tržiště

LESSER TOWN BRIDGE TOWERS

LOBKOVIC PALACE

SCHÖNBORN PALACE

Prokopská

Lázeňská

Saská

1

CHARLES BRIDGE

Vlašská

VRTBOVSKÝ PALACE

Karmelitská

Maltézské nám.

2 3

Hroznová

Na Kampě

OUR LADY OF VICTORIES †

NOSTITZ PALACE

Velkopřevorské nám.

Vltava

TURBA PALACE

Harantova

Nebovidská

Čertovka

U Sovových Mlýnů

KAISERSTEIN PALACE

Malá Strana

Újezd

0   100   200 Metres

1 † ST MARY UNDER THE CHAIN

2 🏛 HRZÁN PALACE

3 🏛 MUSEUM OF MUSICAL INSTRUMENTS

ST JOHN †

Malostranské nábřeží

Říční

MALÁ STRANA

Here you emerge into the upper part of Malostranské náměstí, the hub of the district since the tenth century, and its principal market-place. The square is divided by the church of St Nicholas, which you can see on the right, and the adjoining Jesuit college. In the centre of this part of the square rises the Trinity Column of 1715, a multi-level design by Giovanni Alliprandi, erected to give thanks for the ending of a plague epidemic. Facing the church and the college is the broad façade of M. Hummel's LIECHTENSTEIN PALACE of 1791; an earlier version belonged to Karl von Liechtenstein, who helped to engineer the execution of the leaders of the 1618 rebellion. Continue into the main square.

Malá Strana can often seem suspiciously quiet, but Malostranské náměstí is never tranquil: trams grind across it, motorists use it as a car park and there is a constant bustle of pedestrian traffic. Under these circumstances it is easy to miss the splendid buildings that overlook the square, especially since few of them are in a particularly good state of repair. The tall arcaded palace on the left, with the polygonal corner turrets, is the SMIŘICKÝ PALACE, built early in the seventeenth century and modified in the 1750s. The defenestration of the imperial counsellors was plotted here in 1618, and implemented the following day. The palace was altered by Joseph Jäger in the 1760s. Just below the Smiřický Palace is the STERNBERG PALACE, which attained its present appearance early in the eighteenth century, and may have been designed by Giovanni Battista Alliprandi. The recessed bays on the left side of the building belonged to another palace that was later joined on to the Sternberg.

On the corner with Tomášská at number 20 (518) is another delapidated mansion, dating from 1585, also with a polygonal corner turret. On the other side of Tomášská is the popular restaurant U Schnellů. The food here is good and sensibly priced, but the waiters are in the main a mirthless bunch. Having watched as German tourists directed stupid jokes in their direction – *Sie sind Schnellů, wir sind langsam!* – I find it hard to blame them. In addition to the standard dishes to be found in any Czech eating place, U Schnellů features what I suppose should be called combination platters, which provide a filling introduction to a wide range of local meats.

At right-angles to the turreted house, number 21 (35), is the arcaded former LESSER TOWN HALL. The original structure was built in the fifteenth century but the present building dates from 1617–22 and was possibly designed by Giovanni Maria Philippi. The façade has firmly delineated and highly stylized symmetrical renaissance ornament, which makes a pleasant change from the baroque extravaganzas of Nerudova. Philippi was also the designer of the splendid Matthias Gate of the castle, so it is not surprising that he should show an equally firm hand here. It was in this building that members of the Bohemian Estates met to draw up a document known as the Czech Confession, later ratified by Emperor Rudolf II; the document asserted religious freedom, but was not to survive the defeat at White Mountain. Today the former town hall is used for cultural purposes, and a well-known jazz club holds concerts here.

Next door at number 22 (36) is a more modest arcaded house of 1720 with a fresco on the first floor, followed by Alliprandi's Kaiserstein Palace built between 1700 and 1720, a handsome and nobly proportioned mansion with elaborately carved window hoods on the two principal storeys, and statues of the four seasons and urns over the attic by Ottavio Mosto. The celebrated opera singer Emmy Destinn lived here from 1907 onwards. Opposite is the well-known coffee house, the Malostranská, which since 1874 has occupied the ground floor of Joseph Jäger's Grömling Palace, built in 1775. The coffee house can't compare in stylishness or comfort to its splendid Viennese precursors, but it's a useful refuge, serving decent coffee and a range of snacks and pastries.

From this lower part of the square there is a good view of the high, complex dome and tower of ST NICHOLAS'S CHURCH. Although by two different architects, the compositions are perfectly harmonious. Kilián Ignác Dientzenhofer's dome of 1736 is more finely detailed, and Anselmo Lurago's tower built nineteen years later more robust and thrusting, but they work well together. Walk alongside the church to the entrance façade in the upper part of the square. You will pass, on the other side of the street, more stuccoed baroque houses, such as number 6 (265), once the property of the architect Palliardi, number 9 (262), designed by Anton Haffenecker, and the renaissance house, At the Golden Lion, at number 10 (261). This row of houses is well stocked with wine bars and restaurants, of which the best known is number 10, U Mecenáše. Another attractive wine tavern on this side of the square is Makarská at number 2 (271). Last time I was there, I spent fifteen minutes waiting for the waiter to make an appearance, and then gave up. Such attitudes are a legacy from the days when all restaurants, whether shabby or grand, were state enterprises oblivious to such concepts as good service. All this is slowly changing, and a blithe lack of interest in the customers is less frequently encountered. It should be remembered that waiters in Prague are not students supplementing university grants, but a cadre of professionals who, by means nefarious as well as legal, are often among the richest Czechs.

Let us return to more elevated matters, and contemplate Christoph Dientzenhofer's façade for St Nicholas's. Designed and built between 1704 and 1711, it is curvacious and sweeping, an eloquent conception that exploits the full sculptural rather than mere decorative possibilities of baroque. Indeed the statues by J.F. Kohl and Ignác Platzer seem of minor importance when placed against so rich and convincing a background. I cannot be so complimentary about the adjoining Jesuit College, with its utterly uninspired late eighteenth-century design.

The superb interior of the church is quite different from that of most other baroque churches in Prague. The fluidity of the façade is reflected inside, with gently curving balustrades in the galleries above the side bays, which themselves are topped with a kind of flattened ogee in pink marble, with rococo cartouches at the tops of the arch. The west gallery undulates wonderfully, and carries an organ that Mozart used to play. It is the width of the church that is so impressive, opening out further into the clearly illuminated crossing beneath the dome. The piers along the nave are topped conventionally enough by gilt pilasters, yet continue to rise, terminating in vast flat-topped moulded horizontal cornices of pink marble broad enough for a family to stand on three-deep. *Trompe-l'oeil* painting continues the architectural motifs yet higher until they blend into Johann Lukas Kracker's bombastic ceiling frescoes of 1761 to 1770, glorifying St Nicholas. The choir, by Kilián Ignác Dientzenhofer, differs from his father's nave: built between 1737 and 1751, it is denser, more compact in style, with closely bunched paired pillars and balconies crowded with figures.

If the overall architectural scheme is magnificent, so is the detail. The tall statues of 1752 to 1755 lining the nave are by Ignác Platzer the Elder, and I assume he was also responsible for the rococo fantasies on the piers at either end of the

OPPOSITE *One of the grandest of Prague's baroque churches, St Nicholas's is a masterpiece by the wonderfully gifted Dientzenhofers, father and son.*

nave. In the first chapel of the north aisle is an altarpiece of the Crucifixion, in warm colours, by Karel Škréta dated 1646. This chapel has a galleried cupola, busily frescoed. Ignác Raab was responsible for many of the other, less distinguished, altar paintings in the church. The pulpit is massive, rising from a giant shell, a standard rococo motif; the statuary here, by Richard and Peter Prachner, dates to 1765. Above the sounding board St John the Baptist is about to lose his head.

Only when standing beneath the dome is it possible to appreciate fully its height of 70 metres. The incoherent frescoes were painted by Franz Xaver Palko in 1751. Platzer's gigantic wooden statues of 1769, like those in the nave, simulate white marble, but are more heavy-handed here, presumably to be sure of making an impression in this broad open space. On the north side of the crossing, beneath a huge painting of the Visitation by Kracker, is a tiny statue of the Virgin brought here from Belgium and believed to have miraculous powers.

In the corner of the square closest to the entrance to St Nicholas's you'll find a passage leading beneath the Hartig Palace at number 12 (designed by Alliprandi and completed by Kaňka) which brings you out into Tržiště (Market Street). Just up the street on the left is the SCHÖNBORN PALACE, which preserves its carved wooden doors. This huge yet rather meanly embellished palace is now the United States embassy. It was built by Carlo Lurago in the seventeenth century, but the present workaday façade, of 1718, is the work of Giovanni Battista Alliprandi or Giovanni Santini. The palace has no real courtyard, but opens out immediately onto the famous seventeenth-century gardens, which are terraced up a large part of the Petřín hill where vineyards were once planted. From the ramparts of the castle you can often see the American flag fluttering from the pavilion at the top of the garden.

At this point Tržiště divides into three. The lane on the right twists past the not very prepossessing backs of various houses and emerges opposite the Thun-Hohenstein Palace on Nerudova. The central lane, Břetislavova, has long been impassable because of building works, but it emerges close to Vlašská, the lane on the left which you should now follow. On the left, at number 9 (355) there is a flower relief over the door and a pretty courtyard that adjoins terraced gardens. Next to this early eighteenth-century house, an alley leads to the American library. On the right, number 2 (364) has a relief of scales over the door, and number 5 (361) has a pleasant courtyard. Vlašská opens up into a little square with some attractive houses, such as 26 (331) and 28 (332). The low building at the top of the square with frescoes and a turret is the Italian hospital, and behind the building is an engaging arcaded cloister. This little complex, including the former seventeenth-century church, is now used for cultural activities by the Italian embassy.

Opposite stands the LOBKOVIC PALACE, now the German embassy. It has an immensely tall portal and a pediment seven bays wide filled with heraldic devices and military emblems. The palace was probably designed by Alliprandi from 1702 to 1705, but altered by Ignác Palliardi in 1769. This street façade is too

Foreign embassies occupy many of Malá Strana's grandest palaces, and these finely carved wooden doors offer entrance to the Schönborn Palace, now the American embassy.

overwhelming, but the garden façades, partly accessible from a side door further up the street, are on a less Olympian scale. One can just about make out the monumental garden gates at the rear of the palace, topped with large urns and statues. The gardens, which were originally laid out in 1703 but given their present shape at the very end of the century, adjoin the Petřín hill park. It was here that in the autumn of 1989 thousands of East Europeans climbed into the grounds of the embassy and thus began the mass exodus to Germany that inaugurated the collapse of the East German regime, swiftly followed by all the other oppressive regimes of eastern Europe.

The large buildings further up Vlašská are now a hospital, but I recommend wandering into the small park and playground opposite, from which there is a sensational view up to the palaces of Hradčany and the castle. You can also see the garden façade of the Lobkovic Palace quite well from here.

Return down Vlašská and opposite the Lobkovic Palace go left up Šporkova alongside the Italian hospital. It emerges into a small square with two baroque mansions, 12 (321), now a school, and 10 (320), the House at the Holy Trinity. Turn right and Šporkova soon turns into Jánská. On the left at number 2 (315) is a house with modern sgraffito. This quiet corner of Malá Strana is charming and little frequented. Turn right down Jánská and left down Břetislavova (if it has been reopened) which leads to Tržiště; passing the neoclassical Břetislav Palace on the right; it is being very thoroughly restored.

At the foot of Tržiště turn right into Karmelitská. Enter the first house on the right, number 25 (373), the VRTBOVSKÝ PALACE (1631), for many years the home of the artist Mikoláš Aleš, who decorated a number of façades in the Old Town in the late nineteenth century. On entering the house there is nothing to indicate that behind it is one of the loveliest spots in the whole of Prague. The courtyard leads to the exquisite Vrtba gardens, designed by Kaňka in the 1720s along a series of steep terraces. At present they are closed for restoration, but should provide delightful views across Malá Strana when they are reopened.

Karmelitská is lined with large town houses of many periods. On the left, just down the lane Prokopská, number 10 is a house with two polychrome house signs, a leaping horse and a Madonna and Child. There is a fine baroque house at number 6 (295) and a mansion at number 3 (265) built on the site of the former church of St Procopius. Among the more attractive mansions on Karmelitská are 17 (378), 18 (379) – the Thun-Hohenstein Palace of 1714, and subsequently a hotel – and 14 (382), the Sporck Palace. Number 17, the Petřín House, stands on the site of the former Malá Strana hospital, but was rebuilt as a palace in 1704. On the right you'll soon come to the broad, rather grim façade of Giovanni Maria Philippi's church of OUR LADY OF VICTORIES (1611–13), closely modelled on Roman baroque churches. This façade is among the earliest baroque architecture in Prague, and it relies on the massive deployment of motifs such as scrolls, lunettes and pediments to build up a monumental pyramid. Philippi, who also designed the Lesser Town Hall and the Matthias Gate at the castle, is surely one of the least appreciated of the great architects who flocked to Prague in the seventeenth century.

The interior of this Carmelite church, which is currently under restoration, is aisle-less, lit by lunettes that are partly obscured by large baroque altars in black and gold with spiral columns, a motif also used on the high altar and pulpit. Many of the paintings are by Peter Brandl. The pulpit is a sternly handsome piece of 1679. Half-way down the nave on the right is the Spanish wax doll known as the Prague Infant Jesus, set within a rococo glass cabinet made by the local goldsmith J. Pakeni in 1741. Prayer cards are available in about ten languages, including Japanese, and votive tablets, from as far away as Peru, record thanks

OPPOSITE *Two powerful fourteenth-century towers dominate the façade of the church of St Mary under the Chain and give no clue to the fact that the interior is now, as so often in Prague, in the baroque style.*

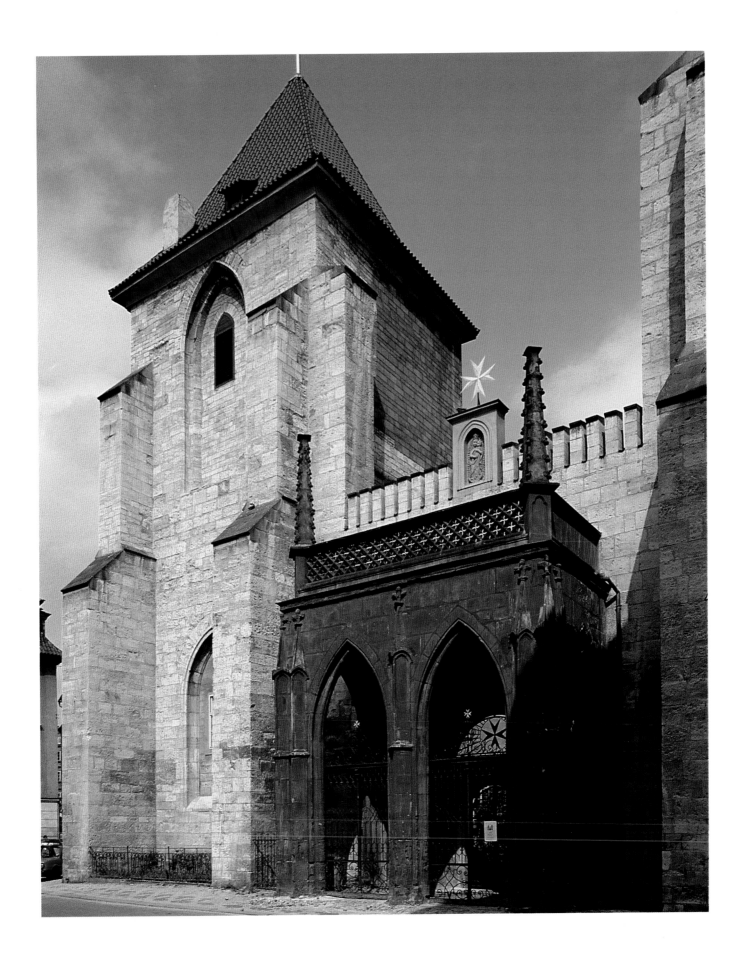

from supplicants. The little figure was brought to Bohemia in the mid sixteenth century by a lady of the pious Lobkovic family and presented to the church in 1628. The Carmelite monks who once inhabited the adjoining monastery are buried in catacombs beneath the church; it is said that their corpses are nicely preserved, but the vaults are not open to the public.

At the end of Karmelitská is the ungainly State Central Archives building, an unrecognizable former monastery. Just before this building turn left down Harantova, which leads to Maltézské náměstí, a square dominated by the early baroque NOSTITZ PALACE, now partly occupied by the Dutch embassy. The façade, possibly designed by Francesco Caratti in 1660, has obviously been modified over the years, but it retains the paired windows that are a holdover from a style grounded in the Renaissance. The lovely portal, highly sculptural and prettily gilt, was a later addition in about 1765 by Anton Haffenecker. On the balustrade on top of the building are copies of statues added in 1720 by Ferdinand Maximilian Brokoff. The palace was famed for its library of 15,000 volumes, which is still housed here. There was a time when the palace gardens covered much of Kampa Island (p. 89–90).

At number 3 (474) is a green house with a relief of a serpent. Continue into the main part of the square. Number 6 (477) is Joseph Jäger's lovely TURBA PALACE (1767), a rococo gem in dusty pink and cream. Unusually, most of the ornament is placed in outer bays, while the central portal is modest. Opposite is the city's music conservatory for blind children, and when wandering through this part of town you often hear unrelated musical instruments sounding forth from open windows. Next to the palace is another pretty rococo house by Jäger at number 7 (479), and beyond, at number 8 (480), is a seventeenth-century building which was Prague's first post office.

At the end of the square is Brokoff's vigorous three-sided statue of St John the Baptist (1715), possibly erected, like the Trinity Column in Malostranské náměstí, to celebrate the end of the plague. On the other side of the square is the fashionable seventeenth-century tavern U Malířů (At the Painter's), which I found disagreeable some years ago, but may be less snooty nowadays. Walk a few paces down Lázeňská to what's left of the Maltese church, ST MARY UNDER THE CHAIN, principally two squat, heavily buttressed, yet shapely west towers, completed in 1389, with a gothic porch between them. The porch leads into a forecourt and on the right are the vestiges of the romanesque arcades of the original church, the oldest ecclesiastical foundation in Malá Strana, dating back to 1169. In those days it occupied a vital strategic position close to the bridgehead of the Judith Bridge.

Carlo Lurago's baroque interior of 1660 is delightful, and it is a pity that the church is so infrequently open. All the ceilings are enriched with white stucco, and dispersed between the gleaming baroque altars are numerous renaissance tomb slabs, some of them with superbly carved effigies in relief. By the entrance, in the north aisle, is another relief of the same period depicting a man in a ruff kneeling before a crucifix. Also in the north aisle are a Pietà, and a Madonna and

With a house overlooking the expanses of Kampa Island, a broad balcony over the entrance seems a necessity more than a luxury.

Child of some antiquity. J. P. Venda's pulpit is a gorgeous piece in gold and green, and flanking the high altar, with its painting by Karel Škréta of the Assumption, are immense and magnificent candelabra.

To the left of the church, along Lázeňská, are a number of graceful baroque mansions. Number 11 (285) used to be a hotel, At the Golden Unicorn, and a plaque records Beethoven's stay here in 1796. Mozart too stayed here, seven years earlier. Number 9 (289), the Sternegg Palace, is also attractive, and number 4 (287), the superbly proportioned former Maltese convent of 1728 by T. Haffenecker, is now an institute for oriental studies. Adjoining this building is the site of the former At the Baths Hotel; a plaque records that the French writer and statesman Chateaubriand stayed here in 1833, as did Peter the Great 150 years earlier. On the other side of the church at number 2 is the former palace of the Grand Priory of the Order of the Knights of Malta, now the MUSEUM OF MUSICAL INSTRUMENTS, with a lovely portal. The priory was built in the 1720s by Bartolomeo Scotti, and the carvings, including those on the handsome stone staircase, are by Matthias Braun and his workshop. In the courtyard, where concerts are given in summer, can be seen faint vestiges of the monastery that stood on this site until 1420.

Within the museum, the keyboard instruments – which date back to the seventeenth century, and include a portable organ, the piano on which Franz Liszt played in Prague in 1846, and various instruments with painted cases – are displayed in a salon with lavishly decorated door and window frames. The museum used to own some superb Amati violins and violas, but a few weeks before I last visited the museum six of them had been stolen, and I found myself

looking at the sorry sight of empty display cases with forced locks. Some other early violins were not taken, but the loss is still a grievous one. There is a delightful collection of mandolins and lutes and zithers, many with mother-of-pearl inlay; the oldest item is a lute made in Bologna in 1520.

Arranged together in one room is a fine collection of Bohemian string instruments, a number of them from eighteenth-century craftsmen, including rarities such as a viola pomposa and a violetta. Among the wind instruments there are basset horns – very odd-looking – and a Hungarian tarogató, which was new to me. The most precious exhibit in this part of the collection is the wind band from the Rožmberské chapel, a unique group of sixteenth-century instruments. Another curiosity is the experimental *viertelton* piano, capable of playing quarter-tones on its three keyboards. It was made by August Förster earlier this century, but unfortunately there is hardly any music written for the instrument.

All this information may soon need to be revised, since the order has expressed a wish to avail itself of the new property laws by reclaiming its old priory. The collection will almost certainly have to be moved, but nobody, at time of writing, knows where or when. This is not the only museum which might be affected by this particular result of the revolution.

Follow the lane into Velkopřevorské náměstí, a tree-filled and tranquil square, one side of which is dominated by the Buquoy Palace, built in 1736 by an unknown architect, though both Ferdinand Hrzán and František Maximilian Kaňka are cited as possible candidates. It is a rather uninspired design, not helped by the stumpy towers at either end. To the right, and adjoining it, is the Little Buquoy Palace, which dates from 1598. It is a boxy mansion with stylistically unrelated gables on the two sides visible from the square. Both of these palaces belong to the French embassy.

Opposite them stands another façade of the Grand Priory, after which this square is named, and at the end of the square at number 1, is the Hrzán Palace or Mettych of Čečov House. Built in 1617, it has renaissance gables and a most peculiar gateway with a column poking up from the centre of a broken tympanum. Continue across the little bridge onto Kampa Island, and bear right past a pretty nineteenth-century villa into Hroznová, which in turn leads into the little square of U Sovových Mlýnů. On the left side of this square is the irregular façade of the renaissance house called At the Golden Grape. Straight ahead, the baroque portal belongs to the Kaiserstein (or Liechtenstein) Palace, although the rest of the building is nineteenth-century.

Bear right into the park on the island. Until the sixteenth century the island was reserved for vines and gardens, which were later joined up to provide the area now filled by the park. In the Middle Ages a mill-race separated Kampa more decisively from the shore than the trickle of the Čertovka does today. Tourist brochures make great claims for this branch-line of the Vltava, seeing this corner of Prague as Venetian in its charm. That clearly isn't so, but nevertheless it is a pleasant spot, full of mothers wheeling baby buggies to the children's playgrounds in the park. This is surely a better use for the space than having it as

OPPOSITE *The baroque cupolas of the Malá Strana churches are a more satisfying spectacle than the unrelenting bays of Pacassi's remodelling of the castle façade at the top of the slope.*

the exclusive preserve of a handful of aristocratic families who occupied the Nostitz and other palaces. The park was created in 1940.

As you enter the park you'll see on the right a late eighteenth-century villa that was the former home of Josef Dobrovský (1753–1829), the Czech scholar and nationalist, whose bust stands outside the house. Within the park, follow the banks of the Čertovka, a duck-cluttered stream that bisects the gardens. Further along you will come to one of the old millwheels, dating from the time when the Knights of Malta operated a mill here. Continue a short distance, then turn right onto Říční, where you will see the small gothic church of ST JOHN set within the galleried courtyard of 1662 of a former hospital. A church has existed here since 1142 as the parish church of the village outside the Malá Strana walls; it was incorporated into the Lesser Town in 1360. After the church was closed by Joseph II in 1784 it entered a new and less dignified period as a laundry, but was made over to the Hussite church in 1935.

Return through the park along the Vltava side. Half-way along, an arch on the right leads to the embankment, so it is possible to walk along the riverbank itself in the other direction. But keep going through the park, past the Kaiserstein Palace, and continue into Na Kampě, an oval plaza with many old houses that once served as Prague's pottery market. At the far end the square is blocked by the Charles Bridge (pp. 97–104). On entering the square you'll see that number 1 (496) is dated 1664 on the lintel, and this is also the likely date of the relief over the door of a fox clutching some branches in its jaw. Number 13 (510) has a rococo façade, possibly by Joseph Jäger, and the Czech composer Martinů (1890–1959) lived at No 11 (512) while a student.

Walk under the bridge and bear left towards the Lesser Town Bridge Towers. Pass beneath the towers and you'll be in Mostecká, which frames a fine view of St Nicholas's at the end of the street. Above the modern shopfronts on Mostecká are innumerable baroque houses, mostly with gables peeking above the cornice, and all varying slightly in design, making the street, like Nerudova, a lively baroque ensemble. Number 5 (282) is charming, despite its delapidated condition. The finest building is at number 15 (277), the KAUNIC PALACE built by Anton Schmidt from 1773 to 1775, heavily stuccoed and with differently shaped windows on each storey. The sculptures over the attic are from Ignác Platzer's workshop. The palace now houses the Yugoslav embassy.

Turn right down the street opposite the palace, Josefská, a street that contains rather oppressive nineteenth-century buildings until you see on the right the recessed church of ST JOSEPH, which has a most remarkable baroque façade of 1686 to 1692 by Abraham Parigi. Both the semi-rusticated half-pillars and the hefty cornices are heavily moulded. The central bay consists of tier upon tier of oddly shaped windows, and above them, on the gable, is a statue of St Joseph, sculpted in 1691 by Matthias Jäckel, adopting a very agitated pose. Jäckel is responsible for all the sculptures.

The interior, for which Jean Baptiste Mathey and Abraham Parigi were mostly responsible, is surprisingly intimate, even though the entire space is vaulted by an oval cupola. The altars are well-proportioned baroque work. On the high altar is a painting of the Holy Family by Peter Brandl, who was also responsible for the painting of St Theresa on the right. The bench ends are covered with joyful rococo carved arabesques.

Just beyond the church is the OETTINGEN PALACE of 1724, a reconstruction of an older palace by Kaňka, and straight ahead lies the south flank of the church of ST THOMAS. The west façade of this church is astonishing. The lower half of the central bay billows out, while the upper part dips back. Between the two a massive pediment is ruptured as though the centre has been blasted out to make room for the west window. This is all Kilián Ignác Dientzenhofer's work from the 1720s, although the tower is of medieval origin. Before Dientzenhofer rebuilt it, there was a basilica of 1265 on this spot. On the north side of the church, accessible from beside the tower, is a tall, cool cloister enclosing a few trees. At the east end of the cloister are two renaissance doorways dated to 1596 which used to lead to part of the original gothic friary.

Inside the church, the tall nave is barrel-vaulted with two-arched galleries over the bays of the aisles. The creamy tones of the interior show up well the vividly coloured ceiling frescoes by Václav Reiner. At ground level the design is less satisfactory, with too many heavy, dull baroque altars in every bay. The choir has a wealth of elaborate ironwork that screens the balconies overlooking it. At the top of the high altar are copies of Rubens's paintings, *St Augustine* and *The Martyrdom of St Thomas* from the Sternberg Palace gallery (pp. 60–63). The pews are splendidly carved, and in the first chapel in the north aisle there is a rustic polychrome Pietà, probably from the eighteenth century. Behind the church on Letenská is the famous beer hall of St Thomas's, but it is very touristy. During the high season it can be a waste of time even trying to stop here for a beer, as the entire hall is reserved in advance for coach parties. If you can get in, you'll find that the beer, which comes from the Braník brewery, is very good.

Return to Letenská. Turn right, then right again into Tomášská. Just after U Schnellů at number 4 (26) is a renowned baroque house, with a façade built by Kilián Ignác Dientzenhofer in 1726. Above the entrance is an unusually elaborate house sign, a splendid version of St Hubert's vision of the stag, carved by Ferdinand Maximilian Brokoff in 1726. There are a number of other houses of similar date along Tomášská, such as 15 and 12, but they are mostly in rather shabby condition.

Across the street from At the Golden Stag is Thunovská. It climbs quite steeply towards a tall sixteenth-century house with a renaissance gable at number 16 (181). A turning on the right then forms the approach to the Thun Palace, which has a weak neo-gothic façade of 1850. The palace, which is now the British embassy, is far larger than it looks, and most of it dates from the early eighteenth century. The embassy has pleasant grounds, only accessible to those with invitations to official garden parties held here. Before the British acquired the palace, it enjoyed a moment of glory when in November 1918 a meeting held here put an end to all future claims of the Habsburgs to the throne of Bohemia.

Return down Thunovská to the corner and turn left into Sněmovní, where on the left you will pass J.A. Lurago's unexciting Kolowrat House of 1707. The huge neoclassical building on the right is the former DIET. Although the core of the palace is considerably older, in its present form it dates from 1801. After 1918 it became the home of the National Assembly, and in 1968 the headquarters of the Czech National Council. The houses opposite are far more ingratiating. Number 5 (175) is the Lažanský Palace, a mansion of 1712 with a wealth of stucco decoration. Next door at number 7 (174) is the early eighteenth-century Černín Palace by Kaňka, and number 9 (173) also has a lovely baroque façade.

Sněmovní opens out onto a little square. Cross it and you'll soon come to At the Golden Swan, a quirkily gabled renaissance house of 1589 with a swan carved over the door. The window above simply looks onto the wall on the other side of the small courtyard. If you turn the corner just beyond this house you'll come to the entrance of U zlaté studny, a famous restaurant with outdoor terraces. But for years it has been closed and there are no signs as yet of an imminent reopening.

Return to the little square and turn left, and you will shortly emerge into Valdštejnské náměstí, one side of which is filled with the magnificent VALDŠTEJN PALACE (1624–30). It was designed by three Italian architects on the site of no fewer than 26 earlier houses and three gardens. Indeed, there is a light caressing rhythm to the façade as the tightly grouped regular windows ripple along. It ought to be monotonous but it isn't, largely thanks to the three portals that break up the surface. In style they are more renaissance than baroque, especially in the scrolls and obelisks carved in relief above the gateways.

The palace was commissioned by General von Wallenstein, Ferdinand II's commander during the Thirty Years War. Wallenstein had already established himself as one of the most successful military leaders of his time. Yet not content with the titles and riches conferred on him by Ferdinand, he also sought the crown of Bohemia. His schemes were detected, however, and aware of the great danger he was in, Wallenstein fled to a castle close to the Bavarian border. Ferdinand sent English mercenaries to deal with the general, and they piked him to death.

Wallenstein shared Rudolf II's fascination with the mysteries of alchemy and astrology, and a section of the palace was devoted to researches into these arcane matters. Also like Rudolf, Wallenstein took a keen interest in more conventional scientific research, and after the death of the emperor in 1611 he offered his patronage to the astronomer Johannes Kepler. The general enjoys posthumous fame, of course, as the subject of Friedrich Schiller's play *Wallenstein*, and the general's heirs continued to live in the palace until 1945.

Before his undoing, Wallenstein had completed his palace, which was unrivalled, except by the castle, for its amenities: it came complete with 700 servants, its own riding school, grotto, and other appurtenances, such as the most sumptuous gardens in Malá Strana, which we shall visit later. Unfortunately the great hall of the palace, which is most lavishly decorated, is only open during the summer months. Most of the palace is now occupied by the Ministry of Culture.

OPPOSITE *In a city filled with garden pavilions and loggias, the Sala Terrena in the Valdštejn gardens is certainly the most noble and profligate example.*

There's scarcely a corner of the old city that is not watched over by a protective statue – in this instance St Peter on the corner of Misenská.

To the right of the palace is a house called U tři Čápů, The Three Storks, but better known as the chic restaurant Valdštejnská hospoda. This is where the St Thomas's brewery used to stand. Opposite the Valdštejn Palace is the inexpressive eighteenth-century Auersperk Palace of 1751, while across the street from it, at number 3 (162), is the LEDEBOUR PALACE, which follows the slight curve of the street. Ignác Palliardi was the architect of this palace, after 1787, and it too is known for its gardens, which were not landscaped like those of the Valdštejn, but terraced up the side of the castle hill. The gardens are older than the house and were designed by Alliprandi and Santini in the 1720s.

If you walk a short distance down Valdštejnská, you'll come to the cosy U Kolovrata wine bar, where the wine, unlike that served in many Prague restaurants, is reasonably priced. Just beyond on the left is a gap beween palaces. The next palace along is the KOLOWRAT PALACE, which has gardens adjacent to Ledebour's. From this lane you can see how the terraces climb the hill, with balustrades, summer houses and pergolas providing garden furniture on the grandest scale. The Kolowrat gardens (correctly but infrequently known as the Černín gardens) are not quite as old as the Ledebour's, and date from 1785, when they were laid out by Ignác Palliardi. These terraces have been closed for years, supposedly because they are undergoing major renovation and reconstruction. There is no longer any clear distinction between the formerly separate gardens of the various palaces, as they have been joined up. The excessively quaint-looking mansion at the end of this lane is the Little Černín Palace, built in the 1770s but disastrously rebuilt in 1952.

The Kolowrat Palace, built by Palliardi after 1784, is cheerfully decorated with stucco, and two splendid wrought-iron lanterns droop over the portal. Like the Valdštejn Palace, it is now part of the Ministry of Culture. There is also an attractive courtyard. Next on the left is the pleasant if unmemorable Fürstenberg Palace (1743–7), now the Polish embassy, set among landscaped English-style gardens. From here there is an excellent view of the terraced gardens of the preceding palaces. The next palace, number 6 (152) is now the Belgian embassy, and in the garden behind is the Indian embassy. If you are after impressive surroundings in the course of a diplomatic career, then Prague is the city to come to.

Turn right into the archway at 1 Valdštejnskà and across the sculpture garden. On the right are the buildings of the former riding school of the Valdštejn Palace, now used for exhibitions. Continue past the metro and the tram stop to Letenská, and turn right. Number 10 is the entrance to the VALDŠTEJN GARDENS. The area is not enormous, yet these gardens are varied in style and spirit. There are formal spaces, statue-lined gravel walks, the pool and fountain, the superb loggia called the Sala Terrena, and for less organized moments, a chestnut grove and an aviary. Peacocks add a splash of colourful exoticism. Apart from the tranquillity of the garden itself, except when it's invaded by coach parties, the major draw here is the Sala Terrena.

Great claims are made for the pure Italian renaissance quality and style of the Belvedere on Hradčany (pp. 33–4), and it is a lovely and serene building.

But this lofty loggia of 1624 to 1627 by Giovanni Pieroni is surely its equal, in it-self the size of a palace, yet no more than a beautifully decorated and sheltered place in which to take a stroll. The bronzes lining the avenue in front of the loggia are twentieth-century copies of works by Adriaen de Vries which were completed in 1627, the year after his death. The originals were grabbed in 1648 by Swedish soldiers during the Thirty Years War and the Swedes are hanging on to them, as they still adorn Drottningholm Palace.

On leaving the garden, walk back down Letenská, then turn right into U Lužického Semináře. Follow the road as it bears right, and soon on the right you'll come to the VOJANOVY GARDENS. These are not as grand as the Valdštejn gardens, but in spring they are awash with tulips and magnolias, and there are dozens of benches on which to rest and soak up some sunshine. From the gardens, turn right and continue down the street, which opens into a little square, with attractive houses on the left – numbers 12–24 (92–100). They are mostly baroque, but 12 is clearly renaissance. On the corner of Mišenská number 13 is a former seminary and now a library. Turn right down Mišenská. On the right is another row of old houses – numbers 8–12 (66–68). Number 10 (67) has a fresco of a lamb as its house sign, and 12 (66) has a statue of St Joseph on the corner.

You are now a few paces away from the Lesser Town Bridge Towers and Charles Bridge, where the next itinerary begins. As you approach the towers, you'll pass on the left the house known as the Three Ostriches, identifiable both by the modern iron sign over the door and by the fresco on this theme on the façade over the entrance. Its original owner pursued the unlikely trade of selling ostrich feathers, but in late sixteenth-century Bohemia these were hot access-ories. The house was built in 1597, but the painted decorations by Daniel Alexius of Květná date from 1606. Fifty years later an additional gabled storey was added to the house. It is alleged that the first coffee house in the city was established here in 1714 by the Armenian Deodatus Damajan. What is certain is that the famous restaurant here has been established for centuries, although the conversion of the house into a luxury hotel is more recent.

4
Staré Město

....

CHARLES BRIDGE *to* ST JAMES'S CHURCH

Malá Strana is linked to Staré Město, the Old Town, by one of the most spectacular bridges in Europe, an elaborate thread that unites the city. In this city of towers and statues, even the bridge bristles with both. This part of Prague was probably first settled in the tenth century, but did not achieve independent status as a town until 1230, and another century went by before the citizens were granted the right to establish their own town hall. By then the Old Town was beginning a period of great prosperity and expansion, and the street layout has scarcely been altered since that time. The street level, on the other hand, had to be raised because of persistent flooding, and the foundations of houses in the Old Town often contain romanesque walls and vaults which survived intact as the houses above them were rebuilt.

Take the metro to Malostranská, and walk down U lužického semináře to the towers that guard this side of the bridge, or walk down Mostecká to the bridgehead from Malostranské náměstí. The two towers, which are linked by a gothic archway of about 1400, are of uneven size. Despite its renaissance gables and fenestration of 1591, the lower tower is the older of the two and dates from the late twelfth century. It once formed part of the defences of the Judith Bridge that was originally built here in the twelfth century. Much of the sgraffito decoration that once adorned the side of the tower facing the bridge has been damaged. The taller tower, with its gothic blind tracery and empty statue niches and needle-like corner turrets was built in 1464 during the reign of George of Poděbrady. On the façade facing the bridge, the arches of both the passageway and the gothic tower are supported on corbels depicting a lion, a griffin and grotesque heads.

The CHARLES BRIDGE has always been a favourite promenade, for Czechs and tourists alike. The views onto both sides of the city, constantly changing with every step one takes, are irresistible, an orgy of spires, palaces and domes. In this one spot, the glorious architectural confusions of the city – medieval, renaissance, baroque – all cohere into a dazzling whole as Prague, divided by the majestic

OPPOSITE *The view onto Malá Strana from the Charles Bridge encapsulates the singular beauty of Prague, a city in which the styles of different periods blend rather than clash.*

Vltava, sprawls and rises before your eyes. In summer a soft gentle light rests over the city, but the view in winter can be equally stunning. Looking up to the castle at dusk on a cold day, with the lights of the castle offices and embassies in the palaces dimly twinkling and the crispness of the air giving a rare crystalline definition to the imposing urban panorama before you, can be a magical experience.

The bridge itself is a medieval masterpiece, begun under Charles IV in 1357 (although not completed until 1402) to replace the earlier Judith Bridge, which was destroyed by floods in 1342. It is over 500 metres long and has a span of sixteen arches. For 500 years it remained the only bridge linking the two halves of the city. Its construction was supervised by Peter Parler, who was also responsible for the fine tower at the Old Town end of the bridge.

The sides of the bridge are usually occupied by pedlars of various kinds. You can buy Bohemian crystal, framed old photographs, and paintings and sketches of the city. You can also be fleeced by gamblers, if you are rash enough to accept their invitation to spot which thimble a little ball is resting under. About a year after the revolution of 1989, second-hand Red Army uniforms were on sale, and the greatcoats and fur hats do indeed provide suitable protection against the rigours of a central European winter. Entrepreneurship of all kinds finds expression on the bridge, and one crisp morning I found two girls, neither of whom could have been more than twelve years old, piping popular songs of the 1960s as an inducement to passersby to toss crowns into their hat.

Walk across Charles Bridge towards the Old Town and revel in the bridge's most striking feature, the series of statues and sculpted groups, all with religious associations, that line both sides. They were originally sponsored, as it were, by the nobility, ecclesiastical orders and faculties of the university. The statues were designed by a number of artists from the early seventeenth century to the early twentieth century. Most of the nineteenth-century statues, commissioned to replace statues destroyed in successive floods, are of disappointing quality but this is more than made up for by the superb craftsmanship of the best baroque work on the bridge. The marriage of the gothic bridge with its baroque ornament is so successful that one is scarcely aware of any clash of styles. There is nothing else like it in central Europe.

The first group on the left depicts saints Cosmas and Damian, placed on either side of Christ bearing the Cross. This is the work of J.O. Mayer and dates from 1709. Opposite stands a dull, conventionalized mid nineteenth-century representation of St Wenceslas by J.K. Böhm. The next pair, erected in 1714, is by the great baroque sculptor Ferdinand Maximilian Brokoff. On the left is St Vitus, the patron saint of the bridge, unfazed by the snakes and lions climbing the rocky peak on which he stands. Opposite is the more complex group of saints John of Matha, Felix of Valois, and Ivo. Here too the figures are supplemented by wild beasts, snakes and a handsome, very hairy stag with a golden cross between its antlers. Guarding three manacled prisoners in a dungeon below is the figure of a pot-bellied Turk holding behind his back a ferociously barbed whip. This group is an allusion to the freeing by St John of Matha of prisoners taken and held for

On the gothic tower guarding the Charles Bridge from the Malá Strana side, a griffin curled on a corbel snarls down.

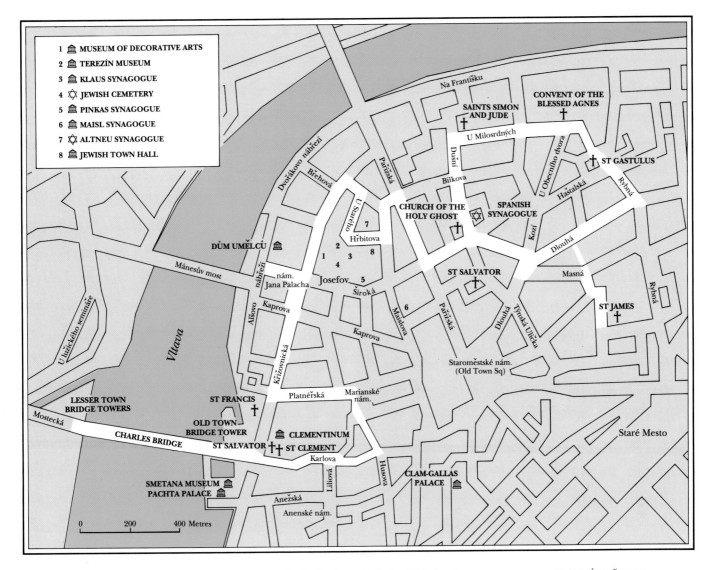

Map legend:
1 🏛 MUSEUM OF DECORATIVE ARTS
2 🏛 TEREZÍN MUSEUM
3 🏛 KLAUS SYNAGOGUE
4 ✡ JEWISH CEMETERY
5 🏛 PINKAS SYNAGOGUE
6 🏛 MAISL SYNAGOGUE
7 ✡ ALTNEU SYNAGOGUE
8 🏛 JEWISH TOWN HALL

STARÉ MĚSTO

ransom by Moslem forces. John, a Provençal cleric, founded the Trinitarian order, which was dedicated to the freeing of captives, and died in 1213.

The next figure on the right, St Adalbert, is a copy of a statue of 1709 by Brokoff. Opposite stands the only marble figure on the bridge, that of St Philip Benizi sculpted by M.B. Mandl in 1714. The statue on the left is of St Cajetan, again by Brokoff and cast in 1709; the saint is shown standing in front of an obelisk encrusted with clouds and putti. Cajetan faces one of the finest groups on the bridge, Matthias Braun's St Luitgard, of a year later, depicted as the blind saint is about to kiss the wounds of the crucified Christ. Braun's carving marks the brilliant debut of this baroque master, and note how skilfully he has used the sky in the composition; it can be glimpsed from various angles – through Christ's legs, beneath his arm as he bends towards the saint who is tenderly supporting him, as

From the Charles Bridge, a quintessential Prague roofscape of gothic turrets, baroque cupolas, and neoclassical pediments.

well as between the outstretched arms of the angels – and this device gives the group a dramatic richness and complexity that could not have been achieved had the carvings been viewed only at ground level. (Because of deterioration caused by air pollution, this group will within the next few years be replaced by a copy.)

The next pair of statues are copies of early eighteenth-century work by Johann Friedrich Kohl. Then, on the right, we come to an imposing pair of 1712 by Brokoff: saints Vincent Ferrer and Procopius. The pedestal is equally elaborate, with a relief carving of the dead awakening from their graves, as well as carvings of a swaggering Turk and other figures. Behind this group, rising from one of the buttresses of the bridge, is the Roland Column, a staid nineteenth-century reworking of an earlier column and statue. The column was originally built to establish the claim of the Old Town to the bridge itself and to the river bank along Malá Strana. The sixteenth-century statue of Roland, which was replaced in 1884, is now in the Lapidarium of the National Museum (pp. 165–9).

Continuing towards the Old Town, the next statue on the left is the gentle, curving figure of St Anthony of Padua by Mayer, which dates from 1707. From this point you can enjoy one of the most splendid of the views on to the Old Town, and in the distance on the right, the raised roof of the National Theatre (p. 151–2). The next statue on the left is a fine bronze of 1683 depicting St John Nepomuk by the Viennese sculptor Matthias Rauchmüller and by Jan Brokoff. On the pedestal a relief portrays Nepomuk at the moment of his martyrdom, being tipped headfirst into the Vltava. Opposite this bronze is the group of saints Ludmilla and Wenceslas, a fluid work of 1730 from the workshop of Matthias Braun, with typically lavish attention to complex draperies.

Next on the right is the statue of the Jesuit saint, Francis Borgia, an elegant figure by Jan and Ferdinand Maximilian Brokoff, cast in 1710 and restored in 1937. The scrolled pedestal is equally refined. The next pair of statues is nineteenth-century, including a lusty St Christopher by Emanuel Max. Then on the right you'll come to a copy of Ferdinand Maximilian Brokoff's St Francis Xavier of 1711. Here too we encounter some distinctly exotic elements: an Indian chieftain, a Turk, a pigtailed Chinese, all alluding to the saint's missionary work. Further along on the left is Jäckel's St Anne with the Virgin and Child of 1707, characterized by the stooping pose of the saint that allows dramatically carved draperies to fly.

The following group includes a beautifully modelled Crucifixion, a replacement for a fifteenth-century crucifix that used to stand on this spot. This bronze work of 1629 was the first piece of religious statuary to adorn the bridge. Unfortunately it is now flanked by two figures by Emanuel Max, both of which are immensely dull. Max was also responsible for the uninspired Pietà opposite. The next group on the right, of saints Margaret, Elizabeth, and Barbara, is by Ferdinand Maximilian Brokoff. Created in 1707, it lacks some of the vitality of his other statuary on the bridge; there is no interaction between the three figures, each of which strikes an independent pose. Opposite is the more dramatic, if overcrowded, copy of Jäckel's Our Lady with saints Dominic and

OPPOSITE *From the exquisite filigree of its wrought-iron screen, the arcades of the university church of St Salvator march down towards its brilliantly lit choir.*

Thomas Aquinas, of 1708, the last of whom is appropriately portrayed clutching a book. The original of this group, as of many others subsequently replaced by modern copies, is in the Lapidarium of the National Museum (pp. 165–9). From here there is a good view to the right onto the sgraffito façade of the former water-works, now the Smetana Museum (p. 105), and the turreted waterworks tower.

The final pair on the bridge are also copies. On the left is Jäckel's elaborate Virgin with St Bernard of 1709, her pedestal plumped up with putti-heads and what look like profiteroles. Opposite is the tall figure of St Ivo made by Matthias Braun in 1711. Because Ivo, the scholarly bishop of Chartres in the early twelfth century, was the patron saint, incongruously, of both lawyers and the poor, Braun placed behind the figure allegories of Justice and of the impoverished.

You are now almost in front of the OLD TOWN BRIDGE TOWER, a solid, tur-reted structure rising above a broad gothic archway and completed in 1380. This vaulted passageway is painted with coats of arms, and, within wreaths, a king-fisher, the emblem of the wife of Wenceslas IV. The façade facing the Old Town is even more impressive. Plaques bear the coats of arms of the various territories that were part of the Holy Roman Empire at the time of Charles IV, who is depicted above, on the left. The other seated figure is Wenceslas IV, who wears the imperial crown. The arms separating them from the central figure of St Vitus are those of, on the left, the Holy Roman Empire, and on the right, the kingdom of Bohemia. All these figures are placed beneath elegant trefoiled canopies. These statues, and those of saints Adalbert and Sigismund (patron saints of Bohe-mia) on the tier above, are copies of products of Peter Parler's workshop, for it was Parler who designed the splendid tower itself. Before the battle with the Swedes in 1648 the bridge side of this tower was also richly ornamented, but the decorations were destroyed during the hostilities.

Descending the ramp from the tower to street level, you will see on the left the fussy neo-gothic, cast-iron monument of 1848 to Charles IV by the German sculptor J. Haehnel. It was erected to celebrate the five hundredth anniversary of the founding of Charles University, which may explain its rather austere academic correctness and lifelessness.

Also to the left of the ramp is the entrance to the church of ST FRANCIS, built by and for the Knights of the Cross, a central European military order founded during the Crusades. In the Middle Ages their principal task in Prague appears to have been guarding this bridgehead and collecting the tolls. The knights built the original church in the thirteenth century. The present façade dates from the 1680s and was designed by the French architect Jean Baptiste Mathey. The exterior is far from harmonious. The gaunt buff façade, rusticated in shallow relief and enlivened by statues in niches, seems stylistically at odds with the tall drum, with its columns in rust and beige, and the green copper dome. The best statuary is above the façade, where copies of dashing angels from Jäckel's work-shop strike poses.

The interior, restored in the 1960s, is much more successful, an airy space spanned by the oval dome. The somewhat chaotic frescoes of the Last Judgment on the dome were painted by Václav Reiner in 1723 and the main altarpiece depicting St Francis is by Jan Krystof Liška. The church contains one of those excessively decorated gilt baroque pulpits (by J.A. Quittainer, in this case) that I find irresistible, and the elongated white statuary around the church and above the altar adds to the liveliness of the decorative scheme. These statues are also by Jäckel, among others. Gluck and Mozart are among the many composers who played the organ here.

Straight ahead, on leaving the bridge, is the church of ST SALVATOR. Built in 1601, the church was enlarged, gaining a dome by Francesco Caratti in 1648 and towers by Kaňka in 1714. The façade, dominated by the three-bay portico designed by Carlo Lurago, is particularly elegant, and a decorative frieze spans the building above the tall pilasters. Along the top of the portico the balustrade that supports six statues and three urns is the work of Jan Bendl from 1659. There are more statues above the pedimented façade. The Jesuit insignia on the façade make it clear under whose auspices the church was founded.

Enter the church through the central marble doorway. The seventeenth-century interior, awash with Bendl's elegant cream stucco ornament, is absolutely lovely. The body of the church, with its broad nave and galleried aisles, is separated from the entrance narthex by a highly stylized and very beautiful seventeeth-century grille. The dome, filled with clear glass that pours down light, is situated over the crossing, but in place of transepts there are shallow bays with elegantly curved galleries. The stucco is particularly lavish in the squinches beneath the octagonal balustrades of the dome. The furnishings are few but what there is is of high quality. These include the lavishly carved pews, the exuberant baroque pulpit, and the powerful gilt reredos in the choir. Nowadays the church, associated with Charles University, is back in full operation, and the Sunday Masses, conducted with choirs and swinging censers, are invariably celebrated before a full house.

On leaving the church, turn left and follow the embankment. After a short distance turn right where the promenade juts out into the river. You will pass the tower, originally built in 1489 but rebuilt during the last century, as the date 1880 on the clockface confirms. Alongside is a very pleasant wine bar, the Three Graces, and at the very end the building of 1883 that until 1935 housed the old waterworks and is now the SMETANA MUSEUM, containing manuscripts and memorabilia associated with the composer. The noise of the weir drowns out the less welcome noise of the traffic and this can be a very pleasant spot to linger and watch the river sweep by. The modern sgraffito decorations on the house depict the battles with the Swedes that took place on the Charles Bridge.

Return to the embankment, and turn right. The house by the triangular park across the street, number 34 (208), conceals one of Prague's least known mansions. Walk through to the second courtyard, where you'll find Johann Joseph Wirch's PACHTA PALACE, a charming and unpretentious two-storey building from the 1770s with a *porte cochère* (carriage entrance), a staircase with statuary from Platzer's workshop, and wrought-iron lanterns. In the late eighteenth

ABOVE *This grand little organ of 1690, one of two placed within the Hall of the Mirrors in the Clementium, is still being played.*

OPPOSITE *The church of St Clement is worth visiting for two reasons: the fine architecture by Kilián Ignác Dientzenhofer and the carvings by Matthias Braun that are among the finest workmanship in Prague.*

century Count Jan Pachta was one of the patrons in Prague of Mozart and then Beethoven. Behind the little palace, in Anenské náměstí is the theatre Na Zábradlí, the base of the Fialka company. Ladislav Fialka was the best known exponent of the thriving Prague school of mime theatre, although on the one occasion when I sat through a performance I found it a lacklustre experience. Many other theatre-goers have disagreed, however.

Return to the embankment, backtrack, and just after you pass St Salvator turn into the doorway on the left. This leads into the four courtyards of the CLEMENTINUM, the former Jesuit college built from the sixteenth to eighteenth centuries on the site of a Dominican monastery. It also provided the order with its headquarters in Bohemia. It was Ferdinand I who summoned the order to Prague in 1556 as an expression of Counter-Reformation zeal, and the Jesuits gradually constructed the largest building complex in the city apart from the castle. Since 1777 the Clementinum has been part of the university, and nowadays it houses the immense state library of over five million printed books, as well as thousands of manuscripts. In the second courtyard you will find the entrance to the main reading room, which occupies the former college refectory. It's an immense room, designed by Carlo Lurago or Francesco Caratti in 1660; scrolled brackets support the stuccoed barrel vault of the ceiling, and at either end are large uninspired paintings of 1710. Heating was once provided by an immense ceramic stove of 1762, which is still in place close to the entrance. The doors have beautiful locks and metalwork, so intricate in their design that on one occasion when I was reading here, I and a few hundred university students found ourselves locked in for ten minutes.

Return to the entrance to the main reading room, where a staircase leads to a long corridor on the first floor, which in turn leads to the long narrow corridor of the west wing, facing the river. On either side of the barrel vault are panels of darkened paintings of admittedly medicore quality within stucco frames designed by D. Galli, richly if heavily decorated with leaves and cornucopias. Even though the paintings don't bear close examination, the overall effect is impressive. Far more splendid is Kaňka's magnificent library of 1727, one of the three great baroque libraries of Prague, but it is rarely open to the public. In addition to its books and manuscripts, the library houses a famous collection of globes.

Leave the building and continue to walk into the second courtyard and you will have a good view of the celebrated but rather ungainly Astronomical Tower, built in the 1720s by František Maximilian Kaňka. Bear left through the archway and you will soon come to the entrance of the former college chapel, also known as the Hall of Mirrors. This is another of Kaňka's designs and was also built in the 1720s. It contains two baroque gilt organs. The one in the loft, yet another organ on which Mozart used to perform, dates from 1743 and is only played once a year during the Christmas season; its mechanism is delicate and the pump action is by foot, which is labour-intensive and tiring. The other organ is older, from 1690, and its adaptation by means of the miracle of electricity means that it can be played more frequently. Beneath the organ loft is a fine wooden statue by Matthias Braun.

The hall derives its name from the panels of Venetian mirror glass inserted into the walls and ceiling. From certain standpoints the wall panels give the impression of receding into infinite space, a Jesuit conceit intended to demonstrate that reality and existence are not confined to what is visible. If you stand at the central point of the hall and stare upwards, you will find your face reflected in no fewer than three glass panels on the ceiling above. The ceiling frescoes, which are not of great interest, are by Josef Hayn, but another worthwhile feature of the hall is its splendid main door, which is ornamented with tongues of silver-plate. Today the hall is used for exhibitions and concerts.

On leaving the Clementinum turn right to the corner of Karlova. Facing you at number 2 is the baroque COLLOREDO-MANSFELD PALACE (about 1730) now housing the archives of the Academy of Sciences. The ground floor also contains an antiquarian bookshop specializing in German titles and old prints. The right side of Karlova is lined by the walls of St Salvator. On the left at number 4 (188) is the house At the French Crown, where the great German astronomer Johannes Kepler lived from 1607 to 1612. After the death in 1601 of Tycho Brahe, the Danish astronomer who had been summoned to Prague by Rudolf II, it was Kepler whom the emperor invited here to continue the work of his famous predecessor. The passage into the courtyard has a small display about Kepler, and in the courtyard itself is a modern three-storey loggia of some charm. Number 8 (166), the Pötting Palace built by Kaňka in 1720, has a fine baroque portal. At number 10 (185) is the cosy pub U Malvaze, serving the excellent Braník beer, if you can taste it through the pall of cigarette smoke. At 14 (183) look out for the statue of a mermaid on the corner. Number 12, with its slightly undulating façade, is another baroque palace, with shabby but airy courtyards within.

On the right, just behind St Salvator, is the entrance to both the Italian Chapel of that church, built from 1590 to 1600, and to the church of ST CLEMENT, designed by Kilián Ignác Dientzenhofer between 1711 and 1715. The two churches share the same porch, which was erected in 1715. The porch bays are filled with a very fine and elaborate ironwork grille, probably from the early eighteenth century. The interior of St Clement's is ravishing, although the church is usually open only in the late afternoon, when a Greek Orthodox service is held here. The ceiling frescoes over the barrel-vaulted church are not that exciting, but what is astonishing is the collection of sculptures over the side altars and the confessionals, as well as the more conventionally situated statues in niches along the side walls. The effect is cluttered but intensely dynamic, and this masterly sculptural complex by Matthias Braun is surely one of the great sights of baroque Prague, or for that matter, baroque Europe. The organ loft is almost as impressive, as here Kaňka, employing a lighter, more rococo style, displayed much the same kind of exuberance.

Opposite St Clement's, at 18 (181) Karlova, is the house known as the Golden Serpent, identifiable by the gilt plaque on the corner of Liliová. The house is now the café and restaurant U Zlatého Hada. Like so many of the restaurants and wine bars carved out of Prague's most charming houses, it has been tastelessly decorated in a vaguely modern style, with in this case tall booths of a distracting design. Facing the serpent, at number 3 (175) on the opposite side of the small square, is the renaissance House at the Golden Well. The stucco decorations, depicting the various saints helpful in warding off the plague, were added later by J.O. Mayer in 1701. The house, which today contains the wine bar U Zlaté Studny, is separated from St Clement by one of the entrances to the Clementinum, this one designed in 1715 by the ubiquitous Kaňka. The food at U Zlaté Studny is quite good, but service can be slow.

Continue down Karlova, passing on the left some charming baroque houses, recently restored and prettily painted, and on the right a handy waffle stall. Number 7 (168) is especially charming. Turn left on to Husova. Filling the entire right side of the block is the CLAM-GALLAS PALACE (1715–30), built for Count Gallas, who was the imperial ambassador to London. The façade is one of the finest in Prague, with superb and varied window frames and raised central bays with an attic storey and pediment. The entrance is not through the central bays but through two immense portals at either end of the building. Johann Bernard Fischer von Erlach set the standards for palatial architecture in the Habsburg capital of Vienna, but town palaces on this scale are less common in Prague's Old Town. On either side of each entrance, pairs of Herculean figures, bent under the weight, support the friezes and balconies over the doorway. The statuary is by Matthias Braun. Broad windows and curved railings rise up on each storey, and these portal bays soar to a height just above the balustrades at the top of the inner bays, thus forming a truncated tower at each end. It is a magnificent design, although hard to appreciate in narrow Husova.

Walk into the palace, which now houses the city archives, and climb the stone staircase, which has frescoed ceiling panels within stucco frames. From the steps you can see down into the very handsome courtyard. On the first floor the door frames, each with a different medallion above, are especially fine. The next section of the staircase is even grander, lit by tall windows; the banisters are topped with urns and lanterns. At the very top is a large painted ceiling done by Carlo Carlone in 1730, and even more lavish door frames than those below. Before returning to Husova, glance into the courtyard, where you can see Braun's Triton fountain.

On leaving the palace turn right and you will soon emerge into Marianské náměstí. This square used to be called Náměstí Primátora Dr V. Vacka, but since the 1989 revolution Mayor Vacka has evidently fallen from favour, and the square has reverted to its old name. Hug the Clementinum side of the square. Opposite the entrance to the Clementinum is the vaguely Jugendstil pile of the new town hall, designed by O. Polívka from 1909 to 1912. It is worth peeking into the foyer to have a glance at the coloured glass that provides the principal decoration of the entrance hall.

The rest of the square is filled by the rather brutal stone building of the city library, which was built in 1928. Continue to follow the Clementinum along Platnéřská. Cross to the other side of Křižovnická, from where there is a good

The heavy statues on either side of the portals of the Clam-Gallas Palace are reminiscent of the grandest palace doorways in the Habsburg capital of Vienna, which is unsurprising since the architect was the Viennese J.B. Fischer von Erlach.

view of the pilastered façade of the Clementinum (pp. 106–8) by Franceso Caratti. The grimness of the Platnéřská façade is here relieved not only by the pilasters but by the varied medallions and reliefs above them, as well as by the scrolled gables above the cornice.

Walk along Křižovnická away from the Clementinum. On the left you will pass grand institutional buildings in a bland nineteenth-century historicist style, and on the right the side streets are lined with florid tall apartment blocks dating from the late nineteenth and early twentieth centuries, buildings typical of much inner-city housing in Prague. A few buildings, such as the irregular extravaganza above the metro entrance on Kaprova, have a Jugendstil design. In this example, the finest feature is a set of very fine iron railings.

You'll soon reach, on the left, DŮM UMĚLCŮ, the Artists' House, with its gently curving façade. After it was completed in 1884, this structure, designed by Josef Zítek and Josef Schulz, served between the two World Wars as the Parliament building, but then became a concert hall, the home of the excellent Czech Philharmonic Orchestra. At time of writing, it was undergoing a very thorough restoration. Its design is clearly derived from such Viennese Ringstrasse buildings as the Staatsoper and the Burgtheater. For many years the hall was known as the Rudolfinum, a name derived from the unfortunate Count Prince Rudolf of Austria–Hungary, who committed suicide at Mayerling in the company of his teenage mistress. The square in which the hall is located has recently been renamed náměstí Jana Palacha, in honour of the student who immolated himself in protest against the Soviet invasion of Czechoslovakia. After his death, Palach became a non-person in official eyes, and even the location of his grave was kept secret. After the 1989 revolution, Palach's stature as the embodiment of desperate and heroic resistance to force was officially recognised.

On the other side of 17 Listopadu from the concert hall is the MUSEUM OF DECORATIVE ARTS. This is another pompous historicist building in vaguely renaissance-palazzo style, lavishly ornamented with reliefs in the spandrels between the arched windows. It was built at the very end of the last century by Josef Schulz, who also had a hand in the Dům umělců. Steep staircases with barrel vaults painted in hideously cheerful pastel designs lead up to the main exhibition halls. At the time of writing, the upper floors were closed to the public. The exhibits are wide ranging, and include renaissance furniture, much of it with fine *pietra dura* inlay work of coloured marble, ebony and ivory, mostly from the early seventeenth century and from Augsburg in Germany; pewter and ceramics; a small group of astronomical clocks and scientific instruments; sixteenth-century tooled bindings in calf and pigskin; an important collection of cheerfully painted glass pitchers and tankards and goblets as well as more refined engraved versions of the same vessels; Majolica dishes and sentimentally pretty Meissen figurines and other porcelain; renaissance and baroque chalices and monstrances, copes and mitres; the Czech equivalents of Viennese Empire and Biedermeier style furniture of the early nineteenth century; and a collection of nineteenth-century silk dresses clearly intended for the fuller figure.

From here it is only a short walk into Židovské Město, the Jewish Quarter. Although administratively incorporated within Staré Město, the Old Town, the Jewish area was a separate entity, delineated by a wall and gates until 1848. From their earliest recorded presence in the tenth century, the Jews of Prague led an uncertain existence. Because their skills as money-lenders were essential to the stability of the ruling house, they were much relied upon, and for that very reason were also resented and from time to time persecuted and expelled from the city. The life of the ghetto was focused around its commercial estabishments and around its synagogues, many of which still survive. The separation of the quarter from the rest of the Old Town ended during the rule of Joseph II, and the district became known as Josefov. The quarter was always overcrowded, there was no proper water supply and squalor existed side by side with scholarly and commercial enterprise. Josefov benefited from the bourgeois reconstruction of the inner city at the end of the nineteenth century, although the synagogues and the remarkable cemetery survived this redevelopment intact.

Continue past the museum, along the wall which screens the old Jewish cemetery, and turn right on Břehová, which has more of the characteristic Old Town apartment blocks in a debased Jugendstil style. Turn right again on U Starého Hřbitova, which soon brings you to the JEWISH MUSEUM. The museum is not a single unit, but a collection dispersed among several buildings, including former synagogues. Ironically, the Nazis made an important contribution to the collections, by gathering in items from all over Bohemia and Moravia in order to document the degeneracy of the people they sought to extinguish. The first building you come to is a neo-romanesque structure that houses a permanent collection of some of the 4000 surviving drawings made by children in the Terezín (Theresienstadt) camp. Terezín was not an extermination camp, but a ghetto created by the Nazis alongside the fortress that had long existed in this military town. There was a semblance of normality within the camp, to which Jews rounded up by the Nazis in Czechoslovakia and Germany and many other countries were dispatched, but nonetheless a quarter of the inmates died and many of those who survived the ghetto were to meet their gruesome end at the extermination camps to which they were transported from Terezín.

By 1944 the camp had been emptied of most of its 140,000 inhabitants, including the children who made these drawings, who had mostly been sent off to Auschwitz. Beneath many of these drawings is written the name of the child, his or her date of birth, and then the date of deportation to Poland and the gas chambers. Most of the drawings depict elements of the natural environment – animals and fields and houses – that children always like to draw, but a few show funerals, the grim buildings of Terezín, the gates of the ghetto, and a hanging. Some other children managed to produce a typewritten magazine on a regular basis, and photocopies of some of these editions are also on display. The young editors did not survive the war.

The other building on this corner is the former KLAUS SYNAGOGUE, built in 1694 and now a museum that documents Jewish communal life in Bohemia and

Moravia. Jews had made their mark on this part of Europe from the Middle Ages onwards, pursuing their own cultural interests – mostly relating to their religion – and contributing to the culture around them, especially in its more intellectual manifestations. On display are facsimiles of manuscripts and other holy texts, and early printed books in Hebrew, mostly from the printing house founded by Gershon Kohen in the early sixteenth century, the first of its kind in central Europe. Of particular interest are the works by the scholar and teacher, Jehuda Liwa ben Bezalel, better known as Rabbi Löw (1512–1609).

Löw may be best remembered today in association with the Golem, but other members of the Bohemian Jewish community were better known for their contributions to scientific inquiries, notably in the fields of astronomy, mathematics, and, in the nineteenth century, medicine. There are also displays of Jewish ceremonial objects, such as phylacteries, the ram's horn, and candelabra.

The interior of the Klaus synagogue has been thoroughly secularized, although the marble superstructure that contained the Ark and the Scrolls of the Law (the Torah) is still preserved. The former ladies' gallery is now used for temporary exhibitions. The old JEWISH CEMETERY – its gates are between these two museum buildings – has, however, survived intact. The oldest grave is that of Avigdor Karo of 1439, and the last burial took place here in 1787, when Joseph II prohibited any further burials within the city walls. It seems as though nothing has changed since. It's believed that 100,000 bodies were deposited over the centuries in these few acres, and about 12,000 gravestones are still here. Some of them are so closely packed that they resemble stacks of slates on a building site, but it is this incredible density of burial that gives the cemetery its extraordinary atmosphere. Moreover, many of the stones lean at crazy angles, creating the higgledy-piggledy tangle of the cemetery. Shortage of space meant that earth had to be piled on existing graves from time to time, so that fresh burials could take place, and this process explains the oddly undulating surface of the cemetery. Every stone is inscribed, and not just with a name but with what appears to be an entire essay celebrating the virtues of the deceased. The People of the Book remain bookish even after death. Nor is the cemetery a depressing place, for most of the stones are marble and of various colours, pink and white and grey and mauve, giving a hint of gaudiness to the place.

Wandering along the winding paths past the stones one can see the emblems of pine cones, pitchers and bunches of grapes that denoted either symbolic values such as fertility or to which of the twelve tribes the deceased had belonged; other symbols conjure up the occupation of the deceased or his heraldic device. By making your way to the wall that separates the cemetery from the Museum of Decorative Arts, you will find the tomb, suitably elaborate, of Rabbi Löw, marked by a small plaque inserted in the wall. When visiting a cemetery, Jews customarily place stones and pebbles on gravestones as a mark of respect, and Rabbi Löw's tomb is always dotted with stones, showing that he is far from forgotten.

The yellow building at the other end of the cemetery is the PINKAS SYNAGOGUE, originally built under the auspices of the Horowitz family, one of the

Gravestone upon gravestone, inscription upon inscription, memorial upon memorial – the old Jewish Cemetery crams in the dead with an intensity that is inadvertently picturesque.

The forms of gothic ecclesiastical architecture were occasionally borrowed by non-Christians, as here in the Maisl Synagogue.

leading clans of the Jewish quarter, and rebuilt in 1535 and again a century later. Although it serves as a memorial to the 77,297 Jewish victims of Nazism from Bohemia and Moravia, it has long been closed to the public, but after restoration it should be accessible once again. The process is being delayed by the unexpected discovery of such items as ritual baths which date from the eleventh century. The fine vaulting and elaborate bema (raised area from which the service is conducted) must make this the most beautiful synagogue in Prague after the Altneu synagogue. The MAISL SYNAGOGUE, a neo-gothic building just a block away from the Pinkas synagogue on Maislova, is also closed, 'for technical

reasons', although it used to contain, and still may, a magnificent collection of Jewish liturgical objects. The original synagogue on this site was founded in the sixteenth century by Mordechai Markus Maisl, the mayor of the Jewish quarter during the time of Rudolf II; he was responsible for many civic improvements. Maisl died in 1601 and is buried in the old cemetery.

Continue down the lane from the cemetery entrance and you will see ahead of you the fifteenth-century stepped gables of the Altneu synagogue. Before visiting this famous building, enter the door on the other side of the alley, which leads into the former HIGH SYNAGOGUE, now another part of the Jewish Museum. Although a textile collection does not sound especially alluring, this is a remarkable series of exhibits, probably unique. Some of the textiles on display are simple embroidered linens intended for domestic use, but the most impressive items in silk and velvet are connected with the synagogue. The scrolls, or Torah, are enveloped in velvet and placed within the Ark, which is adorned with curtains and draperies. Because of their religious associations, such items were usually prepared on the most lavish scale.

The oldest textiles here date back to the sixteenth century. Many of the finest, such as the draperies of 1606 from the Pinkas synagogue, are beautifully embroidered with gold and silver thread. Those from more rural parts of Moravia are more folksy in their decorative schemes and use less costly materials than those which the prosperous Jewish burghers of the capital could afford for their synagogues. Also on display is a fine collection of the silver finials, crowns, and shields with which the Torah scrolls were always embellished, as well as candelabra and other liturgical objects. The High Synagogue itself is not without interest, for the building, which dates from the mid sixteenth century, has a flamboyant vaulted ceiling; the elaborate Ark is a later addition.

The ALTNEU SYNAGOGUE is one of the marvels of the city, for it is the oldest synagogue still in regular use in Europe. In the much larger city of Vienna, for example, the Nazis, with the enthusiastic help of many of their Austrian hosts, destroyed every synagogue in the city bar one. Prague was more fortunate, although its Jewish inhabitants were not. The synagogue derives its curious name from the fact that when it was originally built, there was another, even older, house of worship in existence, and thus this became the New Synagogue. When, in subsequent centuries, more synagogues were built, this one became known as the Old New Synagoguge, which is logical enough.

The oldest part is the kind of vestibule into which a flight of steps leads from the street. This probably dates from the early thirteenth century. Later that century the vaulted gothic hall of the present-day synagogue was added on. The hall is divided by a three-bay arcade, and between the two piers of that arcade is placed the bema, surrounded by the congregation. The bema is protected by a tall wrought-iron grille from the fifteenth century, from which are suspended some of the chandeliers that illuminate the otherwise gloomy interior. Above the bema hangs the banner of the Jewish community, which was granted the right to fly its own flag by Charles IV in 1357, although this particular banner was given

OPPOSITE *The oldest synagogue still in regular use in Europe, the Altneu adapts gothic forms to the requirements of the Jewish liturgy.*

ABOVE *F.M. Brokoff made a speciality of statues of the beloved St John Nepomuk, here placed outside the Church of the Holy Ghost.*

OPPOSITE *Built on a more flamboyant scale than the medieval and renaissance synagogues of Josefov, the Spanish Synagogue reflects the prosperity of the Jewish community here in the nineteenth century.*

to the community at the end of the Thirty Years War as a tribute to its patriotism. Around the sides of the bema, and around the side of the walls, are narrow straight-backed pews and wooden lecterns. The slightly larger and taller pew to the right of the Ark was the seat of Rabbi Löw in the sixteenth century. The Ark itself is covered with ancient draperies, very similar to those which are on display in the museum opposite.

The interior, which was thoroughly restored in 1966, is naturally dark both because the building is below modern-day street level, and because the daylight can only enter a few narrow lancets and roundels. The slits on the left side of the building are squints placed there so that women, who had to be separated from the men during prayer, could observe the service without themselves being visible from the main chamber.

On leaving the synagogue you can see, adjoining the High Synagogue, the former JEWISH TOWN HALL, still the headquarters of Prague's Jewish community. The building, designed by Pankraz Roder, dates from 1568, although it was given a new façade by J. Slesinger in the 1760s. Its most curious feature is the clock with Hebrew characters that faces the Altneu Synagogue; its hands move in a counter-clockwise direction, reflecting the right-to-left movement of Hebrew script. The building also contains the only kosher restaurant in the city.

Follow the alley past the entrance to the Altneu Synagogue and climb the steps to Pařižská, and turn right; then turn left on Široká. On the left you will see the CHURCH OF THE HOLY GHOST, with its tall round-headed lancets. This is essentially a gothic structure from the fourteenth century, though it was much altered during the baroque period, most radically after a disastrous fire in 1689. An eloquent statue of St John Nepomuk by Ferdinand Maximilian Brokoff (1727) stands alongside the church.

Turn right down Dušní to the stylish renaissance church of ST SALVATOR, a foundation of the German Lutheran community built in 1614. The architect, J. Christoph, seems to have been unsure whether he was designing a church or a town house, but the overall effect is quite striking. The interior is light and attractive, despite the overgrown foliage on the capitals of the pilasters that separate the bays of the galleried aisles. The tall windows of the gothic-style choir are both elegant and efficient in providing light. St Salvator's, which was virtually reconstructed in 1970, has long been a Protestant church.

Return down Dušní. As you pass the Church of the Holy Ghost, you'll see on your right the façade of the so-called SPANISH SYNAGOGUE, an extravagant neo-Moorish design from the 1880s. This domed synagogue, built on the presumed site of the city's first synagogue, has been closed for many years. Continue along Dušní till you come, on the right, to the church of SAINTS SIMON AND JUDE, originally built in 1620, with considerable alterations in the following century. This is an attractive church, elegantly moulded, with a tall scrolled gable at one end, and pilasters and cartouches decorating the buff-coloured surfaces. The principal entrance is through a baroque portal on the south side, and the entire south wall is designed more like the front of a town mansion than the side of a church.

Not all the vaults of Prague are as complex and eccentric as those by Benedikt Ried in the castle, and this example from the cloister of St James's church is in the purest gothic style.

The interior is aisle-less, but there are galleries over the side bays as well as an organ gallery at the west end. The only ornament consists of some painted ceiling panels and stucco work in the side bays, and frescoes in the choir. At time of writing, the interior was a pile of rubble as the entire floor was being taken up. What appearance the eventually reconstructed interior will take on when all this subterranean work is completed, it is impossible to say.

Behind the church, along U Milosrdných, is a large hospital built in the eighteenth century with a gently undulating façade and thick grilles over the windows. The design of its bays is thoroughly asymmetrical. Continue along the lane towards the CONVENT OF THE BLESSED AGNES, a complex of buildings founded in 1234 for the Poor Clares and the Franciscans, whose monastery was close by. It was founded by Agnes, the sister of Wenceslas I, and she served as its first abbess. What we see today is largely a reconstruction of gothic buildings that began to be severely neglected in the sixteenth century; after the dissolution of the monasteries in 1782, the remaining buildings were used as storehouses.

As you enter the courtyard you will see medieval arches ahead of you, and on the right the soaring peak of one of the modern sections, a not wholly successful attempt to harmonize two very different idioms and sets of materials. The elegant medieval cloister is a reconstruction. Each bay has two lancets beneath a central quatrefoil, glazed with inappropriate blurred glass. The vaults spring from corbels on the wall and from three slender columns on the cloister side.

From the cloister you enter the reconstructed choirs of two churches that lie side by side: ST FRANCIS dates from the 1240s, and ST SALVATOR from 30 years later. Here the tomb of Wenceslas I was unearthed, as were the remains of other members of the Přemyslid dynasty. Today the choirs reveal little more than the outlines of the slender ribbed vaults and the tracery in the tall narrow windows. Apart from a few tomb slabs, the churches are unfurnished. St Salvator is the larger of the two, St Francis the smaller. The bays preceding the choir of St Salvator are also vaulted and have beautifully carved corbels. At the back of St Francis's is a concert hall, the Josef Mánes Hall; it preserves some of the church walls but is completed by the modern design visible from the courtyard.

The convent is more than a shell, for it houses an extensive collection of nineteenth-century Bohemian paintings, which may be seen in the galleries upstairs. You can see gloomy Claudesque landscapes by Karel Postl (1769–1818), inept historical paintings by Antonin Machek (1775–1844) – although his portraits are competent and straightforward – and supremely awful religious paintings by František Tkadlik (1786–1840). Some landscapes by August Piepenhagen (1791–1868) do show considerable skill and charm. The versatile Josef Navrátil (1789–1865) is at his best with lively genre scenes. The work of Josef Mánes (1820–71), one of the best known of these nineteenth-century painters, is displayed in abundance, and there are some good portraits; his nudes and landscapes, however, are less convincing, and his religious canvases exhibit sickly Victorian sentimentality. The numerous portraits by Karel Purkyné (1834–68) are marred by the fact that all his subjects have identical eyes like marbles.

Forest scenes were the particular speciality of Julius Mařák (1832–99), but the landscapes of Antonin Chittussi (1847–91) are quite attractive. There are some atmospheric if formulaic nocturnal streetscapes by Jakub Schikaneder (1855–1924), and in the last room, some good portraits, and frightful nudes, by Vojtech Hynais (1854–1925).

On leaving the convent, walk along Anežská towards another church, ST GASTULUS. Founded in the late twelfth century, it was rebuilt in the fourteenth, as its fenestration still indicates, although the church was given a baroque appearance in the late seventeenth century. The finest feature of the interior is the gothic double north aisle. At the west end of these aisles stand polychrome figures presenting a series of single-image summaries of the Passion story. Although claimed to be the output of Brokoff's workshop, they are excessively emotional, even sentimental. The main part of the church is relatively austere, with few baroque intrusions in the nave, other than the handsome black and gold pulpit.

If, on entering the little square where the church is located, you take the nameless alley on the left, it will bring you out near the river, with a good view of the choirs of St Francis and St Salvator. Return to the square, and bear left onto Haštalská, with its plain old houses, then immediately turn right down Rybná. Turn left on Dlouhá until you come to number 37 (729), the House at the Golden Tree. Enter the courtyard to look at the remarkable two-storey renaissance loggia, which was built by the former mayor of the Old Town who lived here. The spandrels of the upper storey are prettily decorated but unfortunately the whole loggia is in very shabby condition.

Return down Dlouhá, passing some lovely elaborate baroque façades. Number 29 (733) is especially fine, with delicate cartouches in the window hoods, and above the portal of number 30 (711) is a statue of the Virgin and Child in a small niche. Number 32 (712) is even grander, though less refined in its ornamentation.

Take a sharp left into Masná. Follow the street to the right and continue straight to the church of ST JAMES. Just before the church, a gate leads into the cloister, two sides of which are gothic and elegantly vaulted. The western side has two bays, vaulted from piers without capitals, an unusual feature. St James's was originally built as a Minorite church in 1232, but was repeatedly rebuilt; the cloister is a survival of the fourteenth-century church. The latest rebuilding took place in the 1690s. The main façade is enlivened by Ottavio Mosto's riotous baroque stucco ornament of 1695 over the three doorways. So relentless is the swirl of clouds and putti that the figures of saints within the niches at the core of each carving become obscured.

The interior of St James's is extraordinary. It's very long and tall, with frescoed barrel vaults over the nave, and lofty galleried arcades separating nave from aisles. Against each pier, and in almost every side chapel, stand dark gilt baroque altarpieces, which only serve to pull the eye down from the marvellous vertical thrust of the architecture, with its marble pilasters reaching from ground level to way above the gallery balustrades. The choir is even more amazing, since here there are two tiers of galleries, giving a theatrical feeling to the whole space, as

though one were in an opera house rather than a church. (Indeed, in late 1990, when Placido Domingo came to Prague, he gave a televised recital in this church. Prague residents complained that the tickets were so expensive that only western tourists could afford to buy them.) As in the nave, an urn and putto balance on each balustrade of the galleries. The painting on the high altar of the beheading of St James is by Václav Reiner, and many of the other altars contain paintings by Peter Brandl. Turn back to look at the superb gilt organ in the west gallery.

In the north aisle stands a baroque masterpiece, the tomb of Count Jan Václav Vratislav of Mitrovice, a former chancellor of Bohemia. It was designed between 1714 and 1716 by the great Viennese architect Johann Bernard Fischer von Erlach and executed by Ferdinand Maximilian Brokoff. The effigy portrays the dying Vratislav, a crucifix clutched in his hand; heavily encased in armour, he is supported by a female figure in the act of planting a laurel wreath on his bewigged head. Above, an angel hurls himself at the pyramidal inscription, contributing to the text in mid-flight. As befits a theatrical church, St James's is one of the better places in the city to hear sung Masses. On successive Sundays I was able to hear Gregorian chants and a Mass by Guillaume de Machaut, musically somewhat insecure but welcome nonetheless in such a setting.

Just beyond the church on the right is the entrance to the UNGELT courtyard. In the Middle Ages visiting merchants along this important trade route would stay here, and until 1774 the customs house was also located within the complex. For years the Ungelt has been undergoing restoration, and seems no nearer completion than when I visited it four years earlier. But if you can sneak through the gate and brave the mud, it's worth taking a glance at the buildings that surround this large courtyard. The most interesting is the Granovský house, with is splendid loggia, in the far corner. The tax collector Jakub Granovský had this mansion built on the site of the former customs house in the 1560s.

Continue along the lane from St James's until you reach the pleasant wine bar U Pavouka (the Spider) and turn right. As you walk you'll have a good view of the spires and turrets of the Týn church, and its tall choir (pp. 124–6). Turn right, following the walls of the Ungelt, and on the right you will come to the main entrance to the courtyard, which has been kept closed during the restoration work. Of the sgraffito decoration on the walls above the entrance, which also served as the entrance to the Granovský house, only a few traces remain. Straight ahead are other renaissance houses, such as number 7, the Golden Ring of 1609, which has quite an attractive courtyard.

Bear left, following the curving Týnská Ulička. At number 10 (611) is a baroque house with a painting of three feathers above the portal. There is a pretty courtyard within, painted a garish canary yellow. Turn left, and in a few paces you will find yourself in the Old Town Square.

OPPOSITE *Baroque ecclesiastical architecture doesn't come much more theatrical than this multi-tiered interior of the church of St James, a perfect setting for the many concerts held here.*

5
The Old Town
Square

....

THE TÝN CHURCH *to* THE OBECNÍ DŮM

Prague, a relatively small city, is blessed with many large squares, an unusual feature in a medieval town plan. The Staroměstské náměstí, the Old Town Square, is one of them. The oldest visible remains in the square are gothic, although foundations of some of the houses around the square are from the romanesque period. Nor are the predominant baroque façades to be trusted, for many of them conceal far older houses. To inspect the square thoroughly you should go there during the day, but it is worth returning at night when the huge expanse is brilliantly floodlit, the lights picking out the lively and colourful architecture. In December the whole square becomes a Christmas fair.

In many respects this is the true core of the city, since it has often been consciously chosen as the place to stage historically important events, usually, it has to be said, executions. Some of the Hussite leaders were put to death here, as were the Protestant leaders of the Bohemian Estates whose movement was decisively defeated at White Mountain; they were executed *en masse* here in 1621. Large demonstrations were often held here, and it was to large crowds in this square that Klement Gottwald, standing on the balcony of the Golz-Kinský Palace, proclaimed the establishment of the Communist state in February 1948. More recently, in particular during the Velvet Revolution of 1989, the focus for popular action has shifted towards Wenceslas Square.

The focal point of the square is the HUS MONUMENT in its centre. This is commemorative sculpture on the grandest scale, erected in 1915 to celebrate the five hundredth anniversary of the execution of Jan Hus. Not content with a mere statue, the sculptor Ladislav Šaloun provided an entire scene, peopled by over-sized, grim-faced figures with elongated bodies. Much of the monument is embraced by evergreen shrubbery, which goes some way towards relieving the impassioned severity of the memorial.

With your back to Hus, you'll see on your left the lovely GOLZ-KINSKÝ PALACE, which has recently been restored. It was built on the site of two gothic

OPPOSITE *Side by side in the Old Town Square stand palaces and mansions from the gothic, renaissance and baroque periods, establishing a surprising harmony that confounds all conventional expectations.*

The grandiloquent Hus monument in the Old Town Square is cut down to size by the more discreet elegance of the towers of St Nicholas's church.

houses by Lurago in 1755 to 1765 to plans by Kilián Ignác Dientzenhofer. In 1786 the palace was bought by Count Kinský, and it remained in his family until the end of World War II. The interior was remodelled in 1835 by Jindřich Koch and Josef Kranner in the Empire style fashionable at the time. Since 1949 it has housed the graphics collection of the National Gallery and constantly varying selections from that collection are displayed in the second-floor galleries. The delicacy of its charming rococo decoration above and below the windows and in the pediments of the two entrance bays is somewhat undermined by the heavy statuary by Ignác Platzer on the balustrade between the pediments. No matter. It remains a delightful building, and is among the finest examples of rococo architecture in Prague.

To the right of the palace is the gothic house known as At the Stone Bell, a name reflected in the presence on the corner of the building of a large bell. Before its reconstruction in the 1980s this house had an entirely baroque façade. The restorers stripped that away to reveal, all in lovely buff stone, two tiers of gothic windows and tracery dating back to about 1340. The windows are evidently renewed, as are the cornice and steeply pitched roof, but it is good to have this reminder that behind many a baroque façade in Prague stands a gothic house. The modern interior houses an art gallery.

Next to the house, on the other side of Týnská, is the former TÝN SCHOOL, another gothic structure, probably from the mid thirteenth century. The curious rounded gables, reminiscent of the Lombard style and of fifteenth-century Venetian churches such as the Lombardos' Santa Maria dei Miracoli, were added in the second half of the sixteenth century. A doorway within the gothic arcades of this house leads through a medieval passage to the west door of the TÝN CHURCH. A romanesque chapel stood on the site in the twelfth century, and it was replaced at the end of that century.

The church we see today dates from 1365 onwards. Work on the two highly distinctive towers, with their numerous sharp turrets, began in 1402; the north tower was completed in 1466, and the south tower in 1511. The north tower had to be replaced in 1835 after another fire. It took as long as it did to complete the church because of the Hussite wars and other disturbances. After a fire in 1679 the gothic vault over the nave was replaced by vaulting in a more baroque style, but this did not seriously jeopardize the stylistic harmony of the church's architecture. More disruptive was the presence of passionate preachers, such as the precursors of Jan Hus, and subsequently the Utraquists, including the bishop Lucian Augustin, who is buried in the Týn. As moderate Hussites, their central belief was that the communion wine should be given to laymen as well as priests. Despite persecutions at various times between the early fifteenth and the mid sixteenth century, they were left alone by Maximilian II, and, after some initial difficulties, were included in the tolerant brief of the Letter of Majesty issued by Rudolf II in 1609.

Despite its chequered history, the Týn church retains its tall medieval arcades and narrow aisle windows, giving it a thoroughly gothic atmosphere.

It may seem curious that so important a church is thoroughly encircled by other buildings, but in medieval times this was by no means unusual. The harmony of the interior is not aided by the numerous baroque altars lining both the piers of the nave and the side bays. Along the north aisle you can see the rather heavy-handed late gothic stone baldacchino built by Matthias Rejsek in 1493 over the tomb of Bishop Augustin. The underside of the canopy is intricately carved, with bold rib vaulting.

Against the pier on the other side of the nave is a fine gothic stone pulpit, although the paintings and other embellishments are much more recent. On the west side of this pier is a splendid late gothic wooden winged tabernacle with beautiful reliefs depicting the Annunciation, the Nativity, and other biblical scenes. The principal panel portrays the Baptism of Christ and is of exceptional quality, and at the very top is a small but vivid Crucifixion by the I.P. Master. A little further up the south aisle, along the wall, is a large seated Madonna and Child, an expressively carved early fifteenth-century work. At the end of the south aisle is the oldest font in the city, from 1414; made from pewter, it resembles an up-ended bell and has a matching font cover.

Close to the carving of the Madonna and Child are two splendid monumental tomb slabs of 1575 and 1603 depicting figures in armour. Other

THE OLD TOWN SQUARE

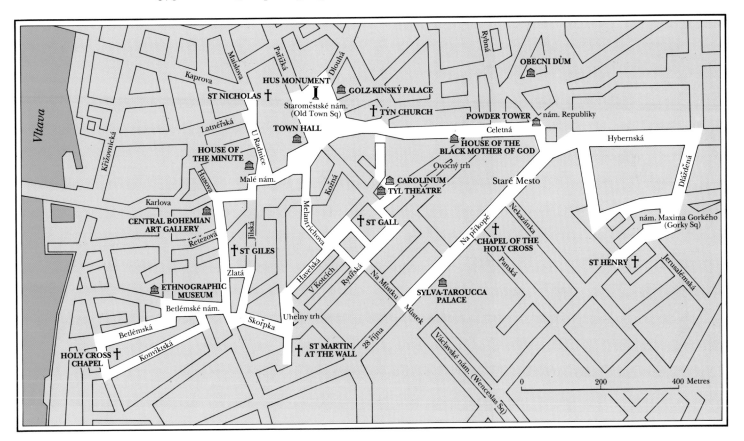

monuments are clustered around the pier just east of the pulpit, one of them in memory of the great Danish astronomer Tycho Brahe (1546–1601), whose burial place is marked by a simple slab just a few feet away. Brahe had been invited to Prague by Rudolf II in 1597; he was already a distinguished scientist and designer of astronomical instruments before his arrival here, and who knows what further discoveries he might have made had he not been struck down by the plague in 1601. As it was, he went to his grave still convinced that the universe revolved around the Earth rather than the Sun.

The high altar is a ponderous baroque construction of 1649 and the painting is by Karel Škréta. Of greater interest is the early fifteenth-century crucifix in the apse of the north aisle, flanked by the solemn figures of Mary and St John. Look back towards the west gallery, which contains the superb black and gold organ. Although the side porch, which boasts a copy of a superb medieval tympanum by Peter Parler's workshop, has been inaccessible for years, thanks to building works, the original carvings are on display at the Bohemian collection of the National Gallery in St George's Convent (pp. 50–54).

On emerging from the church and returning to the Old Town Square, turn left through the arcades of the Týn school and those of the medieval building adjoining it known as the White Unicorn; the façade we see today is eighteenth-century but the house itself is far older. Just around the corner, at 3 Celetna is a fairly unremarkable house, although it is of gothic origin, where Kafka lived from 1896 to 1907. To the right, along the south side of the square facing the Hus statue, is a range of buildings that have been very thoroughly restored in recent years. In some cases the restoration has been so thorough that the unveiled versions are scarcely recognizable. I do have occasional doubts about the results, which sometimes resemble a stage set, but overall the restoration has been vivid and successful. No attempt has been made to drive the more modern houses into a baroque mould. The Storch house of 1896, number 16 (552), for instance, has a luridly modern façade, with an unsubtle painting by Mikoláš Aleš of St Wenceslas on a horse alongside the fantastical oriel.

Number 17 (551) has a chunky sixteenth-century portal with a bay window above. To the right of the bay is the contemporary carving of a ram. Number 18 (550), At the Stone Table, is a salmon-pink baroque house with delicate stuccowork above and below the windows. Like many of the houses on this side of the square, it has a tall central gable. Number 20 (548), at the Golden Unicorn, is of similar design but a touch more stolid; the composer Smetana ran a music conservatory here. Further along the south side, the baroque façades rise above another range of gothic arcades. Numbers 25–26 (478–9), the fifteenth-century Štěpánovský house, have an old stone archway that leads to the restaurant U Bindrů and its adjoining snack bar. Arches crossing Melantrichova link these houses with a baroque mansion, 27 (462), At the Ox, with a statue of St Joseph in a corner niche. Number 29 (460) is the restaurant U Prince, and an elaborate statue of St Florian, possibly by Ignác Platzer, occupies the corner. The house also has a large handsome bay window.

An extravagant lion roars from the corner of the House of the Minute, with its stately seventeenth-century sgraffito decoration.

Among the stylistic cacophony of the Town Hall, these renaissance windows strike a grand but elegant note.

Opposite stands the HOUSE OF THE MINUTE, with its early seventeenth-century sgraffito ornament, mostly depicting allegorical and biblical scenes. Some of the best designs, a series of heads, appear beneath the eaves. The eighteenth-century carving of a lion on the corner above the arcades dates from the time when the building housed a pharmacy known as At the White Lion.

To the right of this house stretch a number of old houses that were knocked together on the inside to form a TOWN HALL after permission was granted to the citizens of the Old Town in 1338 to establish their own municipal headquarters. The first house is U kohouta, At the Cock, and next to it is a large house with glassed-in gothic arcades and a façade dated 1879 in a grandiloquent neo-renaissance style. To the right is a lovely façade of the 1520s, with lavish renaissance windows, this time the genuine article, decorated with fluted pilasters,

turrets, inscriptions, and a round-headed tympanum. Next door is the main entrance to the town hall, now only used on ceremonial occasions, with its magnificent ogee-arched late gothic doorway carved by Matthias Rejsek in about 1475, and the equally splendid carved renaissance windows.

The famous ASTRONOMICAL CLOCK fills the lower part of the Town Hall tower. This remarkable object, the oldest working clock of its kind in Europe, was constructed by Mikuláš of Kadaň in about 1410. The clock was frequently renewed and altered, most recently after the partial destruction of the town hall by German troops in May 1945. The clock is framed within exuberant gothic carvings: men peek above the lintels, while beneath the platform to the left of the clock is a jungle of carved vegetation. The polychrome statues above and below the clock face are delightful. When the clock strikes the hours or quarters, the four figures on either side of it – portraying Human Vanity, Miserliness, Death in the form of a skeleton, and a Turk – begin to nod and move. The skeleton tugs ominously at a bell rope and raises an hour glass to remind us all that our time on earth is limited. At the same time the blue panels above the clock open to reveal a procession of the twelve apostles – these figures are replacements from 1948 – filing slowly past. The chimes and parade conclude with a raucous blast, the crowing of the gilt rooster that surveys the proceedings from the top of the clock.

Beneath the astronomical clock is an equally incomprensible calendar, a copy of 1864 by Josef Mánes of the original. For the convenience of those of us who simply want to know what time it is, two conventional clocks are placed on top of the tower and next to the town hall entrance. E.I. Robson, the wayfarer of the 1920s, found himself completely baffled by the famous clock:

> This clock is popularly supposed to do various odd things: you stand in a crowd, and when nothing happens, you slink off and pretend you were looking for a tram.... I found out afterwards that it worked by 'astronomical time'. But how is one to know that? And what is it, all said and done? You cannot ask Czecho-Slovakian policemen for the 'astronomical time'.

The 69-metre-high tower of 1364 is ornamented with a number of canopied statues – nineteenth-century work by Max, although the corner statue of the Madonna and Child is a copy of a medieval original – which perch on tall columns with corbel heads below. The tall oriel of the chapel with its fine gothic tracery juts from this end of the town hall, and the façade is also decorated with painted coats of arms. The pink building adjoining it to the right is a ruinous tower with immense gothic and renaissance windows. This part of the town hall was destroyed by the Germans the day before the city was liberated on 9 May 1945, and it has never been restored. Just in front of the town hall here is the memorial to the Protestant nobles executed here after the battle at White Mountain; embedded in white stone in the pavement of the square are 27 white crosses and the date 21 June 1621.

It is possible to visit the interior of the town hall. The building is now used primarily for ceremonial purposes and weddings, while administrative work

OPPOSITE *Just before the hour strikes, the plaza in front of the Town Hall Tower will fill with people waiting to watch the antics of the figures around the astronomical clock.*

connected with the running of the city is conducted in the new town hall in Marianské náměstí (pp. 109–10). The areas behind the gothic arcades, and part of the floor above, are used for special art exhibitions. The events of May 1945 did enormous damage to these buildings, and many portions were either destroyed totally or have had to be reconstructed. Nevertheless elements of the old town hall do survive, such as the painted beams on the ceilings in some rooms on the first and second floors. One room, which dates from the fifteenth century, preserves some fragmentary sgraffito decorations. The main hall is located behind the neo-renaissance façade and contains two enormous historical paintings by Václav Brožík. One of them depicts the election of George of Poděbrady as king of Bohemia in 1458, which took place here. The council chamber next door has fine painted beams and a gilt ceramic stove. The pair of beautiful marquetry doors dated 1619 were brought here from the Lesser Town Hall (p. 79) in the last century.

You can also visit the chapel, built by Peter Parler in 1381. The walls are decorated with heraldic frescoes, some of which may date to the foundation of the chapel, though they have frequently been restored. The glass in the oriel and other windows was of course destroyed in 1945, and it has been replaced with completely inappropriate blue, pink and mauve modern glass. Canopied statue niches survive on either side of the oriel. It is also possible to climb the tower, from which there are splendid views of the city.

Beneath the present ground floor is a network of rooms and passages that dates back to romanesque times. In the early Middle Ages, what now appears to be a basement was in fact the ground floor. The ground level of the Old Town was raised to prevent the frequent flooding that used to take place. Consequently many of the houses around the square have romanesque basements, although few are as complete as those of the town hall. In recent years these basements have been closed to the public, but there are plans to reopen them eventually. The former prison is located at the base of the tower, and still preserves its original thick doors; in other parts of the basement are an ancient well, a deep trough that was either a cistern or a dungeon, or both, and a number of large interlinked chambers.

Behind the town hall a small park has been laid out, and the row of houses alongside it is called U Radnice. These modest old houses painted in pastel shades face the Týn church. At the end of this little square within the square is the church of ST NICHOLAS. There are references to a church on this site in 1273, and until the Týn church was completed, St Nicholas served as the parish church of the Old Town. It was rebuilt in 1650, and again in 1732–5 by Kilián Ignác Dientzenhofer, and that is the church that stands here today.

This is a complex building with a very broad façade. The two side towers are separated from the equally tall central bays by narrow and much lower bays, allowing the paired half-columns on either side of the dramatic doorway to soar upwards. The façade is decorated with excellent statues and busts by Antonín Braun, the nephew of Matthias. The south door itself is impressive, with

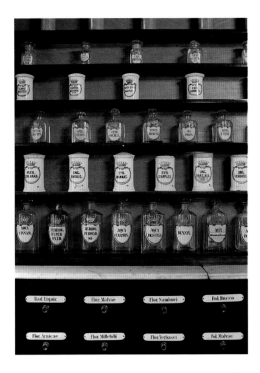

ABOVE *Within the charming old pharmacy on Malé náměsti, little seems to have changed since the times of the Habsburgs.*

OPPOSITE *Viewed from the Town Hall Tower, the roofs of the Old Town and Malá Strana seem almost indistinguishable as the Vltava becomes a dip in the middle distance.*

ornamental metalwork applied to the surface. On entering the church by the doorway to the left, it becomes clear that the length of the façade reflects the fact that this is the south side of the church, not its west front. The church is essentially cruciform, topped by a squarish dome with dim frescoes by Peter Assam. There is lavish stucco ornament by B. Spinetti throughout the church and fine iron railings on the galleries that run the length of the building on both sides. The only jarring note is the colossal and hideous late nineteenth-century chandelier suspended from the dome.

On leaving the church, take a look at the adjoining house on the right, which is the birthplace of Franz Kafka. From the other side of St Nicholas you can see the houses on the north side of the square. They are mostly nineteenth- or early twentieth-century, but to the right is the former Pauline monastery of 1689, which retains the statues of the saints carved by Jäckel in 1696.

Return to the House of the Minute and pass through its arcades to the Malé náměstí, or Little Square, which in medieval times served as a fruit market. A number of printing houses were also located here. In the centre is the renaissance fountain with its exceptionally lovely protective grille of 1560. There are some attractive houses in the square, many of them with romanesque cellars, attesting to the antiquity of the original structures. Number 2 (143), At the White Lion, has a gothic doorway, but the windows are decorated with rococo cartouches. The house has recently been painted a rather startling pink and grey. Next door at number 3 is the Rott house, named after the enlightened ironmonger who commissioned from the popular painter Mikoláš Aleš the paintings that enliven the entire façade.

Number 9 (5) preserves some sgraffito decoration in similar style to that of the House of the Minute. The large mansion at number 11 (459) is the Richter house, fashioned from a number of previously existing medieval houses; it has a fine portal by Josef Kranner dating from 1798. Next door, number 12 (458), At the Golden Lily, is a narrow two-bay house, originally gothic but rebuilt in the late seventeenth century and decorated with a blue and gold plaque of the fleur-de-lis. It houses an art gallery. Next door, number 13 (457), At the Crown, is one of the most beautiful pharmacies in Prague, reminiscent of those frequently found in Vienna. It retains its wooden cabinets and other furnishings in Empire style, and its labelled drawers and jars. The ceiling is panelled and even the clock, perched on by gilt eagles, is in full-blown Empire style. The house still displays Habsburg regalia on the façade.

This whole part of the city, which is crowded at the best of times, becomes jammed solid in the weeks before Christmas, when some of the narrow lanes become almost impassable. The congestion is even worse on St Nicholas's Day in December, when youths dress up as bishops and devils with tails and horns, and younger children don the wings of angels and play musical instruments as they wander the streets. Small children being wheeled along in their push-chairs become distraught at the sight of devils prancing about them, but they are soon pacified with sweets and smiles.

OPPOSITE *The white surfaces of the interior of the Dominican church of St Giles provide a backdrop for these ebullient baroque furnishings.*

Leave the square on Karlova, which soon makes a sharp right turn. Number 21 (149) is a baroque house with very broad windows and a façade that is like a sheet of folded paper that just will not lie flat. In the centre of the first floor is a baroque statue in a niche. Today a casino operates within. Next door is a baroque house with a more recent but very handsome wooden shop front. From here turn left into Husova. The house on the other side of the street is now the CENTRAL BOHEMIAN ART GALLERY, and if you look up you will see its quirky irregular renaissance gables. Next door is the pub At the Golden Tiger, with an appropriate relief over the entrance. The whole lane is lined with handsome baroque façades. Number 14 has plentiful and varied stucco work over the windows. Most of the houses on the right are identified by polychrome carvings over the door or in niches.

Shortly before you come to the church of St Giles, turn down the narrow alley Řetězová. At number 3, you'll find a pleasant mid nineteenth-century mansion which conceals a far more interesting medieval past. George of Poděbrady lived here, in the 1440s, but even then it was an old building, as the basement, with its vaults and fireplaces, is entirely romanesque, and was, before the raising of the level of the Old Town, the ground floor of a twelfth-century town house.

Return to Husova and continue to the church of ST GILES, with its tall blunt buttressed towers, which have been clumsily restored. The church dates from the fourteenth century, but was thoroughly worked over by baroque artists in the 1730s, by which time it had been handed to the Dominicans by the ardently Catholic Ferdinand II. A round-arched portico shelters the severe portal. The interior is in a thorough baroque style, and even the confessionals and pews are luxuriantly carved. Václav Reiner's frescoes of 1733–4 over the nave and aisles celebrating the achievements of the Dominicans, are, with their powerful architectural backgrounds, highly effective. (Reiner is also buried in this church.) Naturally, both the pulpit, of 1735, and high altar are awash with gilt statues, urns, medallions, and all the other devices so beloved of high baroque designers. Yet the interior has a stylistic coherence that is most successful. Little stands out from the riot of ornament, but neither does anything detract from its costly baroque swagger.

Continue down Husova. Number 5, which is part of the technical university, has a baroque portal. Return a few yards to the corner of Zlatá to look at the south side of St Giles, which has a few damaged traces of its original gothic ornament. By the choir, turn right down Jilská. On the next corner is a shabby renaissance house, number 4 (353), which in the eighteenth century was the home of the lord mayor of the city, whose arms are carved above the doorway. There are some sgraffito decorations in the courtyard, which also leads to the restaurant occupying the ground floor of the mansion. Scaffolding has been up for years. I originally supposed this was to allow some restoration and repairs to take place, but now I suspect that it is to prevent the building from falling down.

At the end of Jilská, turn right, then left into Betlémské náměstí, a pleasant, irregular square. The chapel here was built in the 1390s and has considerable historical importance, since it was built specifically as a church where Mass could be held in Czech. The Catholic authorities were unhappy about this but gave permission for a chapel to be erected, but this particular chapel was larger than many of the principal churches of the city. Jan Hus preached here from 1402 to 1413, as did other leading reformist preachers. The chapel, inevitably, fell into Jesuit hands in the seventeeth century, and was demolished in the 1780s. It was rebuilt in the 1950s, with the addition of two modern gables. The interior is now a large hall, brutally supported on concrete colums, with some frescoes modelled on medieval codices and transcriptions from the writings of Jan Hus and others.

In the square there are some attractive houses, such as number 10 (258), with its baroque statuary and elegant window hoods; the ground floor is now a wine bar. Number 1 (269), at the end of the square, is U Halánků. In the nineteenth century it belonged to Vojta Náprstek, a philanthropic businessman who founded the museum which, considerably enlarged, is still attached to the house at the far end of an attractive galleried courtyard. After four years of reconstruction, this ETHNOGRAPHIC MUSEUM has recently reopened. On the ground floor you will find jewellery and accessories from all over the world; the first floor is devoted to American Indian artefacts, from north and south; the second floor is closed, but the third floor concentrates on Australasia. Unlike many Prague museums, this one is well laid out and the general standard of exhibits is high.

Continue down Betlémská, and turn left at the next corner. You will soon come to the tiny HOLY CROSS CHAPEL, an early twelfth-century romanesque rotunda. When it was constructed it stood alongside the major riverside route to Vyšehrad. It is not usually open to the public. Take Konviktská back to Betlémské náměsti and continue to Husova. Continue straight into Skořepka. At the end, turn right, and you'll see ahead of you the church of ST MARTIN AT THE WALL, its name derived from the medieval walls and a town gate of the Old Town that were once adjacent to it. It is an essentially gothic structure, but for 100 years after its closure in 1784 it was used as a storehouse and flats, and had to be almost entirely rebuilt in the early years of this century. Despite some lively window tracery, the exterior is somewhat grimy and charmless. The sixteenth-century tower is quite striking, if only because it is capped, rather inappropriately, with renaissance gables. There's a memorial to the Brokoff family on the church wall, as they were buried in the former church cemetery.

Retrace your steps and just before you reach the square, take a look at the house on the right. As a plaque and medallion testify, Mozart lived here in 1787 as the guest of the Dušek family, who were also his hosts at the then suburban Villa Bertramka. Continue straight into the square, Uhelny trh, the former coal market. Beneath the arcades is the spacious restaurant U Dvou Koček, which serves excellent Pilsen beer, and, unusually in a Prague beer hall, fresh vegetables with some of the main courses. The cooking, however, is hardly the best in town. The last house over the arcades, number 8 (413), is evidently of renaissance origin, as are some of the curiously gabled houses across the street in Rytířská, which means the Street of the Knights.

Bear left up the side of the square. The first street you pass on the right, V Kotcich, is now used as a clothes market. Continue to Havelská and turn right. There has been a market in this street since 1232, but in the years before the revolution you were lucky to find a few old carrots on sale. Now the stalls are overflowing with fruit, vegetables and flowers, as well as seasonal items such as walnuts and gingerbread.

There are some lovely houses along this street, mostly renaissance and mostly over atmospheric gothic arcades, a survival from the fourteenth century. Number 3 (511), At the Golden Scales, has an elaborate if faded fresco of the Archangel Michael above the seventeenth-century façade, and a grand scrolled gable. The house was once the headquarters of the Czech Repeal, a radical nationalist group active in the city in the 1840s. Next door, number 5 (510) has beautifully carved renaissance window frames on the first floor, while number 7 has baroque stucco decoration on the façade. The last house on the block, number 20 (514), has wooden doors dated to 1643.

Continue to the church of ST GALL, the scene of many a fiery sermon by reformist preachers in the fourteenth and fifteenth centuries, including Jan Hus. This church has an attractive curvaceous baroque façade embellished with statues. This façade is a later addition, possibly by Giovanni Santini and Paul Ignaz Bayer in the 1720s, and is placed in front of the church's two tall towers with their bulbous steeples. The present structure dates from the fourteenth century, but was of course subject to the usual baroque modifications in the late seventeenth century, under the auspices of the Carmelites, into whose hands the church had fallen during the Counter-Reformation. The interior has considerable charm. It is baroque, of course, but the numerous altarpieces, dark green and gold, some with spiral columns, are on a modest scale and do not overwhelm the simple architectural design. The pulpit, however, is more lavish, with beautiful gilt ornament. In the west bay of the north aisle, which retains its gothic rib vaults, is a charming, unaffected polychrome Madonna beneath a canopy. She faces a blood-bespattered and mournful Christ seated beneath a similar canopy. In the north apse is a rustic carved Crucifixion and Entombment of 1726, believed to be by Ferdinand Maximilian Brokoff.

On leaving the church, turn left into the passage alongside the large palazzo of 1892–4 in front of you, a building that can be entered round the corner on Rytířská. Before the Communists were ousted, this was the Gottwald Museum, named after the first leader of the country during its Stalinist years. The museum documented the revolutionary struggle of the Czech people, while being careful to omit such unfortunate lapses as the democratic rule of Tomáš Masaryk in the 1930s. I once spent a rather tedious hour exploring the museum, gazing forlornly at photographs of Stalin, Gottwald and Gustáv Husák shaking hands with visiting foreign politicians. Naturally, I was the only person there.

Since the revolution, the museum has lost its appeal. Indeed, there is no longer any trace of the museum, and the full-length statues of Lenin and the rest of them are probably languishing in a distant warehouse. The palazzo has now

This rococo sunburst is only a detail above a doorway on Celetná, but it makes a radiant contribution to the charm of the façade.

been returned to its original use as part of the state savings bank, but it's still worth climbing the grand staircase to have a look at the lavishly decorated halls.

You will emerge onto Rytířská, a street with many splendid baroque mansions, marred by coarse shopfronts below. Straight ahead is the green, cream and gold TYL THEATRE, originally built for the Nostitz family by Anton Haffenecker in 1781–3. This theatre won lasting fame when on 29 October, 1787, Mozart's *Don Giovanni* was given its first performance here. The composer Carl Maria von Weber was the director of the Tyl, then known as the Estates Theatre, from 1813 to 1816. It is a handsome neoclassical building undergoing perpetual restoration, but there does seem to be a fighting chance that before too long the theatre will once again be giving performances.

Turn left in front of the theatre. The building with the gothic arches below and the very tall windows above is the CAROLINUM, now the core of Charles University. As the name suggests, the university was founded by Charles IV in 1348, and the Carolinum was established eight years later. Charles's vision of the Carolinum as an international centre of learning was seriously tarnished during the Hussite revolution, when German students and teachers were discriminated against, and many of them left Prague, thus impoverishing the university. After the defeat at White Mountain, the Carolinum became a Jesuit institution. Not surprisingly, it became a focal point for students and other dissidents during the revolutionary rumblings of 1848. Later in the century, the profound cultural divisions of the country were reflected in the division of the university into separate Czech and German institutions, a schism that was only healed after independence in 1918.

The oldest buildings here are medieval, as the university set up shop in what had been private houses. Just down the lane alongside the Magna Aula, the Great Hall with the tall windows, you will find the splendid fourteenth-century oriel of the former chapel, with its quatrefoil balustrade and its vigorous carved and crocketed brackets beneath. Stay on the main road, passing the fine renaissance double windows, and enter the complex through Kaňka's baroque portal of 1718.

The staircase on the left leads up to the first floor, where a baroque doorway gives access to the Magna Aula, insensitively modernized in the late 1940s. The hall is used for ceremonial purposes, and I once watched as university dignitaries in long robes and birettas handed out degrees to grey-suited candidates ranged on either side of the platform. Some of the dignitaries' robes were not black, but lilac, orange, red or green, which lacked some academic dignity and faintly suggested costumes for a school play. In the body of the hall, the graduates' relatives looked on attentively, bouquets on their laps, while the organ played softly in the background.

On returning down the stairs, cross into the cloakroom area where you can see the surviving fourteenth-century gothic arcades of the Carolinum. Follow the corridor, passing the courtyards, and head towards the modern part of the complex. Once you emerge into a courtyard, follow signs to the Celetná exit which will bring you out on the street of that name. Celetná, which is named after

The heroic figure of a miner, seeming to emulate Samson, helps to support the former Mint building on Celetná.

the bakers who plied their trade here in the Middle Ages, is full of charming baroque and rococo houses, many of which were renovated in 1987.

Turn left, passing the imposing baroque portal at number 13 (597), formerly the Caretto-Millesimo Palace. Some romanesque masonry survives here, as well as gothic gables and tracery, but the palace as a whole was rebuilt in 1756 by Anselmo Lurago. It is now part of the philosophical faculty of the university. Number 12 (558), the Hrzán Palace, another romanesque structure heavily altered by Giovanni Battista Alliprandi in 1702, has a rather pompous portal, but number 10 (557) has some exceptionally charming rococo stucco on its salmon-pink façade. Over the sleek portal of number 8 (556) is a startling rococo sunburst cartouche. Return down Celetná. Just beyond the back entrance to the Carolinum, you'll come to U Supa (At the Vulture), a well-known beer hall. In warm weather you can drink in the courtyard; at other times the hospitable dining room indoors serves simple meals. In the fourteenth century a brewery was located in this gothic structure, but the complex was rebuilt after a fire in 1945. The pub serves the excellent dark Braník beer.

Opposite U Supa, the severe portal of number 17 (595), dated 1700, leads into an attractive courtyard with two baroque statues. This is the Menhart house, and is of gothic origin, despite its obvious baroque appearance. On the eighteenth-century façade of number 23 (592) is a joyful Madonna and Child of 1720 from Matthias Braun's workshop.

On the corner with Ovocný trh, you'll find a modern building at number 34, the HOUSE OF THE BLACK MOTHER OF GOD. Erected in 1912, this is in the style known as architectural cubism, presumably because it sought to break up surfaces, just as cubism in painting dislocated direct images. Josef Gočár's building, whatever the ideology behind it, is a remarkably individual contribution to the city. It blends certain Jugendstil principles – large windows, spiky railings, broad eaves – with a clarity of line and expansiveness oddly reminiscent of the Chicago architect Louis Sullivan; and there are elements specific to Gočár's own cubist style, such as the recessed bay windows, the stumpy Egyptian-style pillars around the entrance, and the thick-set pillars between the third-floor windows. Gočár was careful to use the same proportions for his house as were employed for its baroque neighbours, so the building isn't obtrusive. It has certainly worn far better than many post-war buildings that are no more than twenty years old.

Just beyond, on the right, at number 36 (587) is the grandiose façade of the former MINT, which ceased to operate in 1783. Johann Joseph Wirch designed the palace in 1755, and it was remodelled in 1784 as military offices. Ignác Platzer contributed the balcony over the gateway and its four heroic figures of miners. The portrayal of miners was by no means novel in Bohemian art. Matthias Braun contributed a carving of a miner to the Vladislav oratory in St Vitus's Cathedral (p. 45), and in the church of St Barbara in Kutná Hora, to the east of Prague, some remarkable gothic frescoes of miners have been preserved.

The end of Celetná is dominated by the POWDER TOWER. This large and magnificent structure, part of the city fortifications, was designed by Matthias

OPPOSITE *The late gothic Powder Tower and the debauched art nouveau of the Obecní Dům hardly blend well together but the juxtaposition is undoubtedly arresting.*

Rejsek towards the end of the fifteenth century. It was convincingly rebuilt in the 1880s. With its sheer bulk and its steeply pitched roof, it's an unmistakable contribution to the Prague skyline. Like the similarly named tower in Hradčany (p. 49), it was used to store gunpowder. The ornamentation on both sides is as exuberant as any late gothic Manueline cloister in Portugal. Arches and ogees sweep across the surface, collapsing onto pedestals or undergoing sudden transformations into canopies, crockets and gargoyles. The niches are all filled with statues, admittedly uninspired nineteenth-century work for the most part, and for good measure attached to the walls are coats of arms and plaques depicting bagpipers. Jutting from the balustrade at the top are polygonal turrets, each with a spire and finial.

As you pass through the tower, you'll see on the left the immense OBECNÍ DŮM, the Municipal House, a complex of restaurants, cafés and public halls. It was built on the site of the royal court that existed here in the fifteenth century as the seat of kings such as Wenceslas IV, George of Poděbrady, and Vladislav II Jagellon. The whole complex glories in a kind of Parisian art nouveau design. The exterior bears more than a passing resemblance to a large railway station, but the railings alongside it are highly inventive. The architects A. Balšánek and O. Polívka designed this building from 1906 to 1911. They certainly made quite a statement with the decidedly eccentric metal and glass porch over the main entrance. An even more important statement was made in October 1918, when the new Czech republic was proclaimed here.

The coffee house on the ground floor has a decor which is closer to Viennese Jugendstil than Parisian art nouveau, and I find it thoroughly enjoyable. Moreover, the well-spaced tables and the height of the galleried hall at least allows some of the cigarette smoke to rise. The bronze chandeliers (apart from their awful white lamps) and the other brass fittings over the entrance are stylish and original. The restaurant on the right of the entrance is a rather less well defined version of the same scheme.

Upstairs is the colossal Smetana concert hall spanned by glass domes. It's immensely vulgar but there's an unfettered exuberance to the design that makes it oddly invigorating. Of Ladislav Šaloun's grandiloquent sculptures and other decorations inside the hall, the less said the better. On leaving the Obecní dům, turn left to the next corner, from where you'll see to the left the Paříž Hotel, where the wood-panelled coffee house serves some of the better pastries of Prague. This is one of the best places in town in which to sample game during the winter months.

Opposite the porch of the Municipal House is the hideous exhibition hall U Hybernů, originally the church of the Irish Franciscans. It was built in the 1650s but closed down by Joseph II in the 1780s. It was subsequently given an Empire-style face-lift by Jiří Fischer in 1811. If its proportions were more modest, it might not seem so crass.

The street alongside the hall is Hybernská. On the left at number 3 is the splendid Sweerts-Sporck Palace, reconstructed in 1783 by Anton Haffenecker, who preserved the baroque portals at either end. With Stalinist cruelty, the first of them has been converted into a greengrocer's. Statuary from Ignác Platzer's workshop decorates both the portals and the attic. At number 5 (1034) is another mansion with statues on the attic and with an unusual rounded pediment filled with playful stucco imps. Number 7 (1033) is the thoroughly unimaginative Kinský Palace, originally built in about 1660 by Carlo Lurago but given a neoclassical face-lift in 1798. Until recently the palace housed the Lenin Museum, which has suffered the same fate as the Gottwald Museum (pp. 136–7). Lenin himself was here in 1912, chairing the year's All-Russian conference of the Social-Democratic Party which saw the establishment of the Russian Bolsheviks as a separate party.

Turn right down Dlážděná, walk across Gorky Square (náměstí Maxima Gorkého), and on the right you will soon see the church of ST HENRY. Although much altered in the nineteenth century, it retains its fourteenth-century gothic outlines. Some old tomb slabs from the cemetery that once surrounded the church have been arranged around the west entrance. The interior, despite baroque alterations, still has its gothic vaulting, although with stucco decoration between the ribs. The choir is richly decorated, with panelling and gilt statuary by Jan Bendl. The pulpit too is full-blown baroque. The altarpieces are by Škréta and Reiner and other leading artists of eighteenth-century Prague.

The belfry is detached and now stands on the other side of Jindřišska. It was built in the 1470s and has the same kind of spiky turrets as the towers of the Týn church (pp. 124–6). Cross back into Gorky Square. At the far side, one of the covered shopping arcades that are quite common in this commercial part of Prague leads through to Na příkopě. The name means 'at the moat', which is an exact description of what stood here until the late eighteenth century, when it was filled in. The moat formed the boundary between the Old and New Towns.

Turn left down Na příkopě. Immediately on the left is the broad baroque façade of the former Prichovsky Palace, now the Slovanský Dům. Its present appearance dates from 1797. Ironically, this palace was in effect the headquarters of the substantial German-speaking population of Bohemia, but its present name means the Slav house. The palace was suitably downgraded into a complex of snack bars. Next door is the useful Prague Information Service, which provides information about walking and sightseeing tours and interpreters. The next building on this side of the street is occupied by the Čedok travel service, from where you can book rail and air tickets.

The Information Service is located in the Živnostenská bank building of 1896, a grand neo-renaissance palazzo with a lavishly carved façade and pretty floral decorations beneath the eaves. The entrance hall with its complex of staircases is thoroughly theatrical, and the glass-roofed banking hall upstairs is, despite the folksy statuary, shapely and resplendent. It's all unashamedly historicist, but none the worse for that. The brass signs over the counters and the mosaic floor are particularly memorable.

At the end of this block of Na příkopě is an awful neoclassical design, the galumphing CHAPEL OF THE HOLY CROSS by Jiří Fischer, built between 1816 and

1824 for the Piarists, an education-oriented religious order which made its first appearance in the city in 1752. The interior is of little interest. At number 10 (852) is the sumptuous SYLVA-TAROUCCA PALACE (or Nostitz Palace), a precursor of 1743–51 to the Golz-Kinský Palace in Old Town Square (pp. 123–4). The architect was Kilián Ignác Dientzenhofer, and Anselmo Lurago was responsible for the interior design. The façade is decorated with rococo swags, some of which hang down from the window hoods, giving a luxurious three-dimensional effect. The statues on the pediment are by Ignác Platzer the Elder. The palace is much deeper than it looks and two airy courtyards are ranged behind the façade.

Just inside the gate, a door on the right leads to the main staircase. On the landing are rococo railings and stucco ornaments by Carlo Bossi, but they lack the lightness of touch one looks for in rococo craftsmanship. This part of the palace is filled with meeting halls where cultural and other activities, notably jazz concerts, take place.

Further up Na příkopě on the right, above the Pelikán restaurant, is a well-preserved Jugendstil house of 1905. In a few yards you are at Můstek at the head of Václavské náměstí. Můstek means 'little bridge', a reference to medieval times when a bridge was required to cross the moat that existed here. A couple of spans from this bridge are visible below ground in the Můstek metro station. Turn right on Na Můstku. The house on the left, number 15 (378) is a late baroque structure, with curious stucco ornament in the pediment.

The street leads into Melantrichova, which curves towards the Old Town Square. On the right, at the corner of Kožná you will see the hefty renaissance doorway of 1559 at number 1 (475), At the Two Golden Bears. The spandrels and lintels are elaborately carved and on either side are the reliefs of the said bears. A plaque commemorates the house as the birthplace of the influential left-wing journalist Egon Erwin Kisch (1885–1948), whose most celebrated feat was to expose Colonel Redl, the Austrian officer whose homosexuality was exploited by Tsarist Russia's spymasters. Redl's suicide and the ensuing scandal proved to be yet another nail in the coffin of the Habsburg Empire.

A dark passage leads into the house's austere but beautiful courtyard with a renaissance loggia. In a few paces you will be back in Old Town Square.

OPPOSITE *An unexpected renaissance delight just yards away from the Old Town Square: the elegantly carved doorway to At the Two Golden Bears.*

6
Nové Město

....

WENCESLAS SQUARE *to* CHARLES SQUARE

In its medieval heyday Nové Město, the New Town, must have had a powerful character of its own, and not only because it was intended by Charles IV to be a coherent piece of urban planning. Habitation was focused around major squares, and building regulations controlled the kinds of dwellings that could be erected in different parts of the town. The regulations also stipulated the width of the streets, the height of the houses and the materials from which they were to be constructed. The New Town soon became the haunt of traders and craftsmen; it was never one of the most prosperous parts of medieval Prague. So it is not surprising that it became a hotbed of support for the Hussite revolution. Like the other districts of Prague, it lost its independent status in 1784. In the course of the following century the New Town became the commercial centre of Prague, and much of its character was lost as individual dwellings, dissolved monasteries and other institutions were torn down to make way for shops and businesses, streets and embankments. There are still attractive corners of the district to be found, and a wealth of churches founded by Charles IV, but they are more scattered than those in Malá Strana or Staré Město.

Begin at Václavské náměstí, Wenceslas Square, which you will have seen flung before you like a great urban carpet at Můstek, but position yourself at the other end of the square, near the National Museum. The metro stop Muzeum will bring you out at exactly the right spot. Of course Wenceslas Square, which is 700 metres long and 60 metres wide, is no more a square than is the Champs Elysées: it is a boulevard. Yet now that traffic other than taxis and essential service vehicles is kept out of the square, it is gaining some of the attributes associated with squares, not the least of which is being able to walk across and through it without risk to life and limb.

This is where it all happens. Some of the most fashionable hotels, cafés, cinemas, the best shops and the worst restaurants now overlook this former horse market, and like the castle and the Old Town Square, it is one part of

OPPOSITE *The gilded hump of the roof of the National Theatre, with chariots at each corner, dominates the embankment of the New Town.*

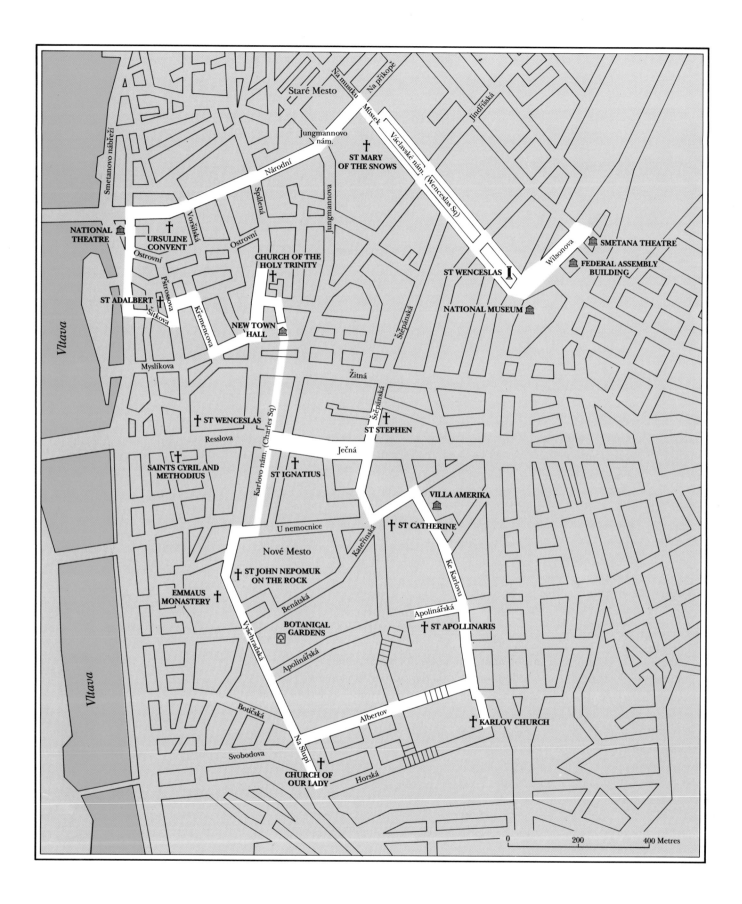

Staré Mesto

Na můstku

Na příkopě

Jindřišská

Jungmannovo nám.

St MARY OF THE SNOWS

Můstek

Václavské nám. (Wenceslas Sq)

Smetanovo nábřeží

Národní

Spálená

Jungmannova

NATIONAL THEATRE

URSULINE CONVENT

Voršilská

Ostrovní

SMETANA THEATRE

Wilsonova

St WENCESLAS

FEDERAL ASSEMBLY BUILDING

Ostrovní

Pštrossova

CHURCH OF THE HOLY TRINITY

Šítková

St ADALBERT

Křemencova

NEW TOWN HALL

Štěpánská

NATIONAL MUSEUM

Myslíkova

Žitná

Vltava

Resslova

St WENCESLAS

Karlovo nám. (Charles Sq)

Štěpánská

St STEPHEN

Ječná

SAINTS CYRIL AND METHODIUS

St IGNATIUS

VILLA AMERIKA

U nemocnice

Kateřinská

St CATHERINE

Nové Mesto

Ke Karlovu

St JOHN NEPOMUK ON THE ROCK

EMMAUS MONASTERY

Benátská

Apolinářská

St APOLLINARIS

BOTANICAL GARDENS

Vyšehradská

Apolinářská

Botičská

Albertov

Na Slupi

KARLOV CHURCH

Vltava

Svobodova

CHURCH OF OUR LADY

Horská

0   200   400 Metres

Prague that every tourist knows and can find easily. This means that it is also frequented by some of the less savoury characters in town, the pickpockets and black market touts who grow fat off the tourist trade. The amnesty granted to many prisoners after the revolution and the greater ease of travel within eastern Europe have brought highly skilled petty thieves into the city, and nowhere in Prague should women be more careful of their handbags and men more wedded to their wallets. Yet one should not be dissuaded from promenading here, for it remains a genuine core of the city, as the events of November 1989 proved. The major political changes of the century were urged on by mass rallies here, and the square played its part as a focal point for the Velvet Revolution too.

A focal point is provided by the presence of a national symbolic statue at the top of the square. Josef Myslbek's equestrian statue of St Wenceslas surrounded by the patron saints of Bohemia of 1912 is, however, a relatively recent arrival. It replaced Jan Bendl's seventeenth-century equestrian statue of the duke of Bohemia and subsequent saint, now displayed in the Lapidarium of the National Museum (pp. 165–9) and in a copy at Vyšehrad (pp. 169–70). It was close to the statue that Jan Palach immolated himself in January 1969 in protest against the Soviet invasion of 1968. After his death the authorities did everything they could to prevent his grave from becoming a shrine, but they failed. Now the spot near the statue has itself become a shrine, to Palach and to others who fought against oppression. A year and a half after the revolution fresh bouquets were still being placed on the spot each day, and day and night candles burn in front of the photographs of those whose yearnings for freedom have at last, after 41 grim years, become realized.

Overlooking the statue from the top of the square is the NATIONAL MUSEUM, which was founded as an institution in 1818 and built in its present form in 1885–90. Although the museum is identified with this very grand piece of nineteenth-century historicism, built by Josef Schulz, who also designed the National Theatre (pp. 151–2), the National Museum is in fact a network of different museums all under centralized control. The Museum of Musical Instruments (pp. 87–9), the Lapidarium, and the Historical Museum in the Lobkovic Palace (pp. 56–7), for example, are all administered by the National Museum.

Despite its institutional importance, the contents of the museum are a disappointment. It appears to be little more than a depository for some substantial collections, no doubt of importance as a place of reference and education, but hardly inspiring. Architecturally, it is clear that, as in the case of the National Theatre which was built a few years earlier, no expense was spared. The main staircase rises beneath a roof glazed with milky glass. At the front of the building on the first floor is the so-called Pantheon, a square galleried hall beneath a glazed cupola, filled with bronze busts and statues of worthy Czechs, and with historical paintings above the gallery, some of which, inevitably, are by Václav Brožík.

To the right is the huge collection of prehistoric artefacts, filling many rooms with bones and flints and pots, many of them evidence of early Czech and Slav

ABOVE *The bulk of the National Museum and Myslbek's commanding equestrian statue of St Wenceslas lord it over the upper end of Wenceslas Square.*

OPPOSITE NOVÉ MĚSTO

cultures. Adjoining these rooms, incongruously, is an exhibit featuring the development of Czech national consciousness in the last two centuries. The remaining rooms are filled with cases of minerals and meteorites, all identically displayed. The second floor is devoted to the zoological collections: stuffed birds, animals, fish, shellfish, insects, reptiles, and furry creatures of all kinds. The remaining rooms contain exhibits of fossils. Coral and other marine life is displayed in a room at the back of the staircase on the ground floor.

On leaving the museum you should turn right and take the underpass to the FEDERAL ASSEMBLY BUILDING on Wilsonova. In a country not renowned for daring modern architecture, this building has much to be said for it. It is in fact two buildings, one from the 1930s, the other by K. Práger, dating from 1967–73. The new parliament building, placed on stilts, soars over and rests on top of the old. It sounds strange, but it works. A sensible and stylish use of stone and glass – clearly no expense was spared for this national institution – also contributes to the success of the design.

An old joke from before the revolution asks why the parliament building was put where it is, to which the answer is that it is half-way between a museum and a theatre. Indeed, next door is the SMETANA THEATRE (1888), a dull neoclassical job with a shallow Corinthian portico and a *porte cochère*. With the National Theatre established as a Czech house, the Smetana Theatre provided an auditorium for German-language performances. It is still used as an opera and ballet house, but visitors expecting performances of the standard of international opera houses are likely to be disappointed. Before 1989, any truly talented Czech singer would find the constraints of working within the national system so confining that he or she would inevitably leave Czechoslovakia for the international circuit. Those that stayed were rarely first-rate, and the producers and conductors were often hacks. Standards were dire in the mid-1980s, and can only improve, although judging by a performance of a Martinů opera I saw here late in 1990 movement in that direction has yet to begin.

The theatre has, however, an exceptionally attractive interior. The foyer is decorated with slightly anaemic gilt rococo-style work, but the auditorium is much more confident. It adopts the same basic style of decoration and handles it with greater exuberance, showing more lightness of touch and vivacity than the other major nineteenth-century theatrical interior at the National Theatre. The few spaces on the ceiling not frothing with stucco are filled with vapid frescoes of mythological subjects.

Further up Wilsonova you can see the tall outline of the eclectic main railway station, a fairly dramatic and spacious building erected between 1901 and 1909 and combining art nouveau with other styles. But return to Václavské náměstí and begin to stroll down the right side. Most of the architecture is uninspired, but there are exceptions, usually hotels. The EUROPA COFFEE HOUSE (1905) has one of the most handsome modern interiors in Prague, wood-panelled and with art nouveau echoes. This is easily the most enjoyable spot on the square for coffee and a snack.

OPPOSITE *The lobby and staircases of the National Museum are on a palatial scale not matched by the rather lugubrious halls of exhibits.*

Shortly before Můstek, you'll find a shopping arcade at number 28. This leads to the Franciscan Garden. This little park used to be a pleasant corner, but at time of writing it had been closed off for reconstruction. It's a good place to know about if you want to find a quiet spot to sit and rest in the middle of town. Continue up to Můstek, and just before the end of the block you'll see on the left at number 12 (777) the Peterka House of 1900 by Jan Kotěra. This is a pure Jugendstil building, even employing the sunflower motif and idiosyncratic railings so beloved of Kotěra's teacher, the Viennese architect Otto Wagner. Inside, the staircase and mosaic flooring swirl with Jugendstil grace and eccentricity.

At Můstek take a sharp left into Jungmannovo náměstí. You'll come to a gateway that leads into the forecourt of the church of ST MARY OF THE SNOWS. A humdrum renaissance doorway brings you into an extremely lofty church. Very clumsy reconstruction at various times has left the lower part of the building an unsightly mess, but then the ribs soar to a height of 33 metres, framing tall, narrow gothic windows. Charles IV founded St Mary's in 1347 and a small church was constructed, followed in the 1370s by the new church, for which Charles had the most ambitious plans; but only this aisle-less choir, the highest in Prague, was completed when construction was halted in 1397. The Hussite wars, and a shortage of money, meant that his church, intended to rival the cathedral itself, was left in its present truncated form. Baroque furnishers have done the building no favours by blocking the east bays with a monstrous seventeeth-century altarpiece the full height of the church. The side chapels are equally barbaric. One of the few furnishings of any interest is the pewter font of 1459, similar to that in the Týn church (pp. 124–6), placed just to the left of the west entrance. St Mary of the Snows is a church to inspire awe rather than affection. It did play an important historic part in the life of the city, as the radical Hussite preacher Jan Želivský preached here from 1419 to 1422, and the church remained a centre of Hussite activity for some time after his death.

Just north of St Mary's in a broad alley leading off the square you will find a gothic gate and above it the badly mutilated remnants of a former fourteenth-century tympanum (the original is in St George's Convent, pp. 50–54). This cul-de-sac also contains the beer hall U Pinkasů, which serves the Pilsen brew.

Continue into the main part of Jungmannovo náměstí, focused around the seated statue of the Czech philologist and nationalist Josef Jungmann (1773–1847). To the right at number 1 (761) is a fine art nouveau doorway of 1905. Across the street looms the Adria Palace, a perfectly hideous building from the 1920s, now the home of the famous Magic Lantern Theatre. This company offers a poetic combination of theatre, mime, and dance, employing sophisticated technical effects and lighting to achieve its ends of perfect illusion. Cross the street and continue straight down Národní, a thoroughfare created, like Na příkopě, when the moat that divided the Old and New Towns was filled in during the 1780s. It soon became a major shopping street of the city, with a large Swedish-built department store, Máj, about halfway down. Before you get to Máj, you will see on the right at number 37 (416) the heavy neoclassical

An art nouveau gem in the heart of Wenceslas Square: the coffee house of the Europa Hotel, where the interior design is usually more pleasing than the coffee.

apartment block called the Platýz, with a large courtyard in the same style; the first tenement building in Prague, it was designed by H. Hausknecht in the early nineteenth century. Inside, is a hall where Franz Liszt often gave concerts.

Beyond Máj, through a rather dark arcade on the left side of the street, you will come across a small bronze plaque with the date 17.11.89; there are usually flowers, sometimes candles, left here, in the precise spot where the police dragged demonstrators in November 1989 and beat them up. A short distance beyond, there is a lane on the left called Voršilská, and at number 12 (140) is the Valter Palace, a small neo-rococo mansion of 1891 – an unusually successful pastiche – that is now the seat of the papal nuncio. Return to Národní. On the left you will see the broad pink and white flank of the URSULINE CONVENT, a conventional and compartmentalized design of 1704 by Marc Antonio Canevale, yet considerably more attractive than most of the buildings along this street. The centre-piece of the statuary to the left of the portal is of St John Nepomuk, executed by Ignác Platzer the Elder in 1747 – he and Brokoff must have produced so many of these that it is amazing that they had time to do anything else. Inside, there are crowded ceiling frescoes of 1707 by J.J. Steinfels within stucco frames, a grand but pompous high altar, and side altars framed by a lurid spaghetti of gilt rococo ornament. Crisp baroque statues of saints, which are probably by František Preiss, flank the side altars.

Next to the church, in the former convent buildings, is the Klášterni wine tavern, a comfortable and moderately expensive restaurant, but handy for the National Theatre just down the street. Opposite the church are two splendid art nouveau buildings by O. Polívka. At number 9 (1010) is the resplendent Topič building of 1908, and at number 7 (1011) the former building of the Prague Insurance Company of 1907, with some lovely reliefs on the façade by Ladislav Šaloun.

The NATIONAL THEATRE consists of two separate auditoriums, a modern glass-wrapped new theatre designed by K. Práger in 1983 and the hefty neo-renaissance building at the end of the street close to the bridge. The new theatre tends to be used mostly for plays, whereas the older theatre is also equipped to stage opera and ballet, and often does. The foundations of the National Theatre were laid in 1868, and the design, by Josef Zítek, was completed and ready for audiences in 1881. The triumph of the opening was short-lived. A few months later the theatre was destroyed by fire, but it was swiftly rebuilt under the supervision of Josef Schulz, so that it was ready for its reopening by 1883. The theatre is, as it was always intended to be, a triumphant expression of Czech nationalism in the face of a politically dominant Germanic culture. That it is architecturally elephantine concerns nobody, and the design is redeemed by a shapely roof modelled, surely, on that of the Belvedere (pp. 33–4). The gilt railings on the very top, especially when floodlit at night, have become one of the city's landmarks. No opportunity for pompous display has been overlooked, and there are even bronze chariots being raced up on the roof.

Given the bulk of the building, one would imagine that the interior is also vast, but it is not. In fact the auditorium is relatively intimate, despite its considerable height. The tiers and boxes are a riot of gold, yet this decoration is surprisingly restrained. A more exuberant note is sounded up on the ceiling, from which thinly clad young women appear to be plummeting contentedly out of the sky onto the audience. Compared to the major cultural institutions of, say Vienna, the public spaces are meagre, with few of the immense salons and bars one would expect in a building of this size. The principal salon, while of modest size, is certainly lavishly decorated, with frescoes by Mikoláš Aleš in a sentimental historicist style, and busts of theatrical worthies by Myslbek and others.

It is dangerous to generalize, but in my experience the standard of opera performances at the National Theatre is superior to that at the Smetana Theatre (p. 149). As a rule of thumb I would tend to avoid productions of, say, Mozart or Verdi, and choose instead to see works by the major Czech composers, such as Dvořák, Smetana, Janáček, or Martinů. The chances are that, by international opera standards, a production of, say, *Rigoletto* won't be all that exciting, whereas the opportunity to see an unfamiliar Smetana or Janáček opera performed by artists thoroughly at home with the idiom is nearly always worthwhile, whatever the deficiencies of individual performances.

One always hears that it is hard to get tickets for performances at the National Theatre. I hardly ever had difficulty, and often picked up opera seats just a few hours before the performance. On the first day of booking, however, the large foyer is packed with multiple queues as hundreds of people line up to secure seats for the most sought-after productions.

Czech audiences puzzle me. I once sat through a perfectly adequate performance here of Janáček's intense opera *Katya Kabanova*. The reception was, to put it mildly, tepid. An admittedly half empty house clapped as though there were only twenty people awake in the whole place. I could see the cast, during their curtain calls, looking at each other in bewilderment, as though to say: What have we done wrong? They were fine, but the collection of tourists, Russian delegates, guests of diplomatic missions, and a handful of Czechs probably wished they were somewhere else, such as a night club. On the other hand, if the citizens of Prague can't be bothered to attend and support their own opera houses, it is their own fault if at times those institutions feel like mausoleums.

Opposite the National Theatre is the Slavia coffee house, one of the largest in the city. It is about as close as Prague gets to the great Viennese coffee houses, but it still has a long way to go. There is an interesting mixture of people here: weary shoppers, theatre-goers, tourists, friends meeting for a drink after work (or, just as likely, during work), and a small but highly visible punk element. The café occupies the ground floor of the Lažan Palace, where Smetana lived in the 1860s. Turn left at the embankment and before long you will see the tower of the New Town Waterworks (the Sitek Tower) in the distance, which, like the Old Town Waterworks, was built in 1489 but has been much renewed since. On the right is Slovanský ostrov, the Slavonic island. In the mid nineteenth century there was a famous restaurant and ballroom here, and composers including Berlioz, Liszt, and Wagner gave performances here. The present building dates from 1884.

OPPOSITE *Between the acts at the National Theatre, the audience can stroll through spacious and elegant salons and repose on velvet sofas, relics of a time when opera-going was a social as much as a musical recreation.*

In the 1840s J.G. Kohl in his book *Austria* described the island as

perhaps one of the most beautiful places of public resort in all Germany [sic]. . . .
In the centre of the island are some elegant buildings, which stand open all day
long for the entertainment of strangers. In the rear of those buildings, he who
feels himself disposed for sedentary enjoyment, will find abundance of benches
and tables laid out under the canopy of huge spreading trees, and a tribune
erected for the accommodation an orchestra will seldom be found unoccupied.

Turn left on Šítkova and you will soon come to ST ADALBERT'S CHURCH.
The exterior is irregular but essentially the design of 1778 of Johann Joseph
Wirch, with an onion dome capping the detached belfry, which was built in
1700. The choir is neo-gothic. The interior is most peculiar: the round-arched
nave arcades rest on stumpy little piers, in complete contrast to the tall gothic
windows to east and south. Between the ribs of the vaults are vestigial and barely
discernible early sixteenth-century frescoes. What is worth seeing is the very
lovely fifteenth-century statue of the Madonna and Child (known as Our Lady of
Zderaz), both figures gracefully elongated, at the east end of the north aisle.

Cross the little square behind the church to Pštrossova, turn left, then right
and right again into Křemencova. Half-way down the block you will find,
beneath a huge clock, the entrance to U Fleků. This former brewery is one of the
best-known beer halls in Prague, and it has a good deal going for it. The rooms
are cosy, and in clement weather it's possible to sit at the long tables in the rustic
beer garden. Moreover, the dark beer is delicious.

It is also large enough to accommodate coach parties and other groups of
tourists, and throughout the year it tends to be packed with them. U Fleků also
mounts a cabaret for visitors, a performance I have neither seen nor intend to.
Germans and Austrians in large groups with a few beers inside each of them can
certainly command attention, and I find the undoubted picturesque qualities of
U Fleků insufficient to counter its daily conversion into a Bavarian beer cellar.
There is one great point in its favour, however, which is that one of the rooms is
reserved for non-smokers.

On emerging from U Fleků, turn right – if you can still tell left from right –
then left along Myslíkova. Turn left up Spálená, where the broad-gabled façade
of Ottaviano Broggio's CHURCH OF THE HOLY TRINITY of 1712–13 has recently
been given a face-lift in colours of white and rust. It apparently contains an altarpiece by the late eighteenth-century Austrian artist Anton Maulbertsch, whose
work is usually worth seeing, but at the time of writing the church was closed for
restoration. Next door, on the right, is another cubist building, the Diamant
House, designed in 1912 by M. Blecha. Like 34 Celetná, this building is characterized by thick, heavily moulded portals, and equally heavy angular ornament
on the upper storey. The building certainly has its admirers, but unlike the
Celetná house, it strikes me as awkward and lacking in stylishness.

Return down Spálená to Karlovo náměstí, Charles Square. During the spate
of town planning prompted by Charles IV's decision to establish the New Town

in 1348, this space, 530 metres in length, was chosen for the cattle market. The park in the centre of the square was laid out in the mid nineteenth century. Most of the buildings around the square are of no great interest, since there is a high concentration of bland commercial blocks and fussy nineteenth-century apartment houses, but on the left, in the corner, is the NEW TOWN HALL, yet another major Prague building that has been undergoing constant restoration. Judging by the wreckage in the courtyard last time I saw it, it will not be reopened for some years to come.

Its most conspicuous feature, other than the powerful and much rebuilt tower, originally built in 1425 and restored to an approximation of that appearance, is the group of three traceried renaissance gables on the side of the building facing the square. This section of the town hall dates from 1520 but was rebuilt early in the twentieth century. Many other parts of the town hall are older, including the gothic main hall, which it has long been inaccessible. In front of the building is a fountain with a statue of St Joseph by Matthias Jäckel put up in 1698. The greatest claim to fame of the town hall is that the first defenestration of Prague took place here in 1419, when Catholic officials, accused by Jan Želivský and others of persecuting Hussites, were thrown out of the window. A splendid gesture, but it had the unfortunate consequence of igniting the Hussite wars. Like the other town halls of Prague, it lost its administrative role in 1784, and in the nineteenth century served as a court house and jail.

With the town hall behind you, walk down the left side of the square to the church of ST IGNATIUS, which has a façade more powerful than refined, especially the porch, with its row of statues by Tomasso Soldati on the balustrade. The porch of 1699 was constructed slightly later than the body of the church, which dates from 1665–77. The gable is stuccoed, and the obelisks on either side prevent the façade from appearing too broad. It is not certain who the architect was. Some sources favour Carlo Lurago, but it may have been Giovanni Domenico Orsi; the porch is by Paul Ignác Bayer, with statues by Soldati.

The interior is very impressive. The sheer thickness of the piers is such that the nave is only three bays long, and because of the breadth of the nave the aisles are little more than passages between side chapels. The decoration is mostly in stucco, also by Soldati, with some uninspired ceiling frescoes confined to the chapels. The overall effect is somewhat coarse and it certainly doesn't make the spirits soar. This was a Jesuit foundation, and, judging from my experience of Jesuit churches in this part of Europe, the order was more interested in intimidation than in charm. This is easily demonstrated by taking a look at the former Jesuit college, built in the 1660s and since 1770 a hospital, that adjoins the church and fills one half of one side of this enormous square. It is marginally more ingratiating than the Jesuit college alongside St Nicholas's in Malostranské náměstí.

On leaving the church, turn right up Ječná, then left onto Štepánská, where you can see the church of ST STEPHEN, with its fifteenth-century Týn-style steeple. The church, another of Charles IV's foundations, dates from the late fourteenth century, and retains its gothic apperance. On the north side of the church you will see tomb slabs and, behind a wrought-iron grille, a skull-laden funeral monument. Just behind this side of the church is the second of Prague's romanesque rotundas, dedicated to St Longinus. Before the New Town was established, this tiny church served the village of Rybníček that once stood outside the city here.

The interior of St Stephen's is gothic, with simple rib vaulting, and above the nave arcades are rather faded gothic frescoes that seem to be finely drawn. Gothic too are the pulpit and the pewter font of 1462 in the north aisle. The font, still with its matching cover, bears a family resemblance to the fifteenth-century font in the Týn church; inscriptions and rather crude medallions ornament the surface. Also in the north aisle is an image of the Madonna and Child of 1472, with tiny painted medallions around the frame. Some of the altarpieces by Karel Škréta that used to hang in St Stephen's are no longer here. Matthias Braun, who died in 1738, is buried in the church.

Return along Štepánská and cross Ječná. As Lipová curves to the left, you'll see the high wall of St Catherine's gardens. Overlooking this small park is a narrow, many-tiered gothic church tower, with an often noted resemblance to a minaret. The body of the church was redesigned by Kaňka (1737–41) but has long been used as a storehouse, and thus is closed to the public. This is regrettable as the church apparently contains fine frescoes by Václav Reiner. The park, planted on a gentle slope next to a psychiatric hospital, is a welcome bit of greenery in a part of Prague which, Charles Square apart, lacks it.

On leaving the park, turn left up Kateřinská, then turn right up Ke Karlovu. This part of Prague has strange resonances for me. One of the huge institutional buildings in this neighbourhood was the workplace of a dissident who wrote, and had been published in France, under the name Fidelius. Some years ago I managed to spend an afternoon with him in his workplace, a boiler room in the depths of one of these buildings. Like so many dissidents before the Velvet Revolution, Fidelius could only find employment as a stoker. Since, I was informed, the police would have been keenly interested to learn the true identity of Fidelius, I had to be vague in my descriptions when I wrote about this interview. This meant that I was unable to reveal that this particular boiler room was probably the only one in Prague to contain a piano.

On the left you will soon see the VILLA AMERIKA, a boxy house with very fussy stucco decorations. The summer house of Count Michna, it was possibly designed by Kilián Ignác Dientzenhofer and built from 1712–20 but has surely been considerably altered since. The statuary in the garden comes from the workshop of Antonín Braun, the nephew of the great Matthias. The villa houses the DVOŘÁK MUSEUM, with scores and memorabilia of the great composer, but the museum is in the course of being revamped, and the exhibits will, when the villa is eventually reopened, be completely rearranged. Antonín Dvořák (1841–1904) deservedly remains the most internationally popular of all Czech composers. Like Smetana, he made ample use of the glorious folk melodies of Bohemia, but was far from parochial in the use he made of them. The often

OPPOSITE *Inventive stucco decoration dominates the interior of the church of St Ignatius, which soars above the expanses of Charles Square.*

poignant lyricism of his finest works, which includes the cello concerto, the late symphonies, and the abundant chamber music and serenades, is irresistible.

Just beyond the villa, in a lane to the left, is the pub U Kalicha, the Chalice, immensely popular with tour groups as the favourite drinking hole of the good soldier Schweyk. Behind the touristic exploitation of the character is a very resonant symbol. The modest resilience and cunning of this fictional hero have so fully encapsulated certain aspects of that dubious concept, the national character, that it is sometimes difficult to recall that Schweyk is no more than the invention of a gifted and eccentric novelist, Jaroslav Hašek. It was not a depiction of the Czech character that was likely to find favour with Bohemians of a more aristocratic or snobbish disposition, but Schweyk represented other facets of Czech resourcefulness that seemed, and perhaps still seem, appropriate in an era when the Czechs, swamped first by the Germanic Habsburgs and subsequently engulfed within the wriggling boundaries of competing nationalisms, were striving to define and exert their own specific culture and personality.

Continue down Ke Karlovu, a street lined with schools and hospitals, and turn right on Apolinářská, which brings you to the tall, finely proportioned gothic church of ST APOLLINARIS, yet another of Charles IV's foundations. On the interior walls of this aisle-less church are the remains of fourteenth-century frescoes of saints, but these are very faded.

Return to Ke Karlovu, and turn right. You will see ahead of you the shallow, vaguely byzantine red domes of the KARLOV CHURCH. The pretty building that used to be part of the monastery on the right side of the forecourt housed, until 1989, the most repulsive of all Prague's museums, the police museum. Or as the official guidebook used to put it:

> 'An Exposition of the Museum of the National Security Corps and the Army of the Ministry of the Interior, documenting the historical development and activity of these armed bodies in the protection of the Czechoslovak state, is now installed in the former monastery.'

It came as no surprise when the ghastly place was closed soon after the 1989 revolution. The church itself is fascinating, however. It was built to an octagonal plan at the wish of Charles IV, who clearly had in mind the Palatine church of Charlemagne in Aachen. Construction began in 1358 but proved protracted; the church was only truly completed after the court architect Bonifaz Wohlmut, whose work is so important up at the castle (p. 49), constructed in 1575 the splendid vaulting, which has the extraordinary span of 23 metres.

The church has the usual baroque furnishings, but which Prague church does not? What is special here are the theatrical goings-on above the entrance porch. Polychrome figures enact the Visitation, while on either side onlookers lean out of windows to see what is hapening. Kaňka conceived all this in the 1720s and the figures were carved by J.G. Schlansovský. On the opposite side of the church is the CHAPEL OF THE HOLY STEPS, with the setting of a renaissance

mansion, but it is peopled more sparsely; on the other hand, flights of steps beneath the windows actually invite you in and lead you up to the chapel.

The organ loft is crowded with polychrome figures and putti with horns jigging about on top of the pipes. The crypt provides more illusions in the Chapel of the Nativity, which was built as a grotto in 1709. The stone of the wall is painted in low relief so as to suggest gardens and views glimpsed through neoclassical ruins. The exuberance of the Karlov church is irresistible, and only its relative isolation can explain why so few visitors come here. From the terrace behind the church there is a good view of the bridge that used to be named after Klement Gottwald and of the modern Palace of Culture across the Botič valley.

Return a few paces up Ke Karlovu, and turn left on Albertov. At the end of the street turn left and you will see the rebuilt gothic CHURCH OF OUR LADY, another of Charles IV's foundations. A curious feature is that the mid fifteenth-century vaulting of the nave springs from a single central pier. As the nave is only two bays long, this is a less astonishing feat than it may sound. The street on which the church stands is Na Slupi, which means On the Pillar, a clear reference to this feature. All the furnishings are neo-gothic.

Continue up Na Slupi to the BOTANICAL GARDENS (1897), which are on the right. The gardens are not especially large, but they contain well-stocked

This early eighteenth-century residence, the Villa Amerika, once a country house, has been swallowed by the burgeoning city and now houses the Dvořak Museum.

greenhouses. Na Slupi now becomes Vyšehradská. As this road curves upwards you reach another Dientzenhofer church, that of ST JOHN NEPOMUK ON THE ROCK, built between 1730 and 1739. Its south flank is remarkably undulating, not unusual in a church from this master of the baroque, but the west front is more unusual, with the two towers set at an angle, thus pinching in the façade and seeming to offer protection to the central bay. The steep staircase which gives access to this façade from the street was a later addition by A. Schmidt in the 1770s. Because the church is on a crag high above the street level, it makes a highly dramatic impression.

Opposite, you can see the gothic choir of the EMMAUS MONASTERY. On entering the gates, take the path on the left, which brings you to the cloisters concealed behind a perfectly ordinary eighteenth-century block. These gothic cloisters are frescoed with mostly fourteenth-century paintings, depicting scenes from the Old and New Testaments, but unfortunately they are badly damaged. But a lovely Annunciation remains intact, and the Flight into Egypt reasonably so. The Emmaus monastery was founded in 1347 for the Slavonic Benedictines, essentially as a political strategem to secure the loyalty of those who dwelt in the easternmost parts of Charles IV's domains. Completed in 1372, the monastery became an international centre of Slavonic piety, and illuminated religious texts and other works of art were produced at its workshops.

After the defeat at White Mountain the occupants were replaced in 1635 by Spanish Benedictines, who made many alterations, as the exterior of the cloister confirms. Many vicissitudes followed – the monastery became a hospital, and then an art gallery to house paintings from religious houses that had been dissolved – until in 1880 the German Benedictines arrived and re-gothicized the place. In 1919 they were thrown out in turn. Monks returned here after World War II, during which the buildings had suffered considerable damage, but they were too few in number to put matters right, and in 1950 the monastery became a branch of the Czech Academy of Science. The authorities at least repaired the damage, and tried to do so in an imaginative way, as you can see from the tall sail-like towers built over the church by F.M. Černý in 1967. Just behind the church is the chapel of saints Cosmas and Damian (1657), a baroque reworking of a romanesque church on this site.

On leaving the grounds, turn left and you will soon be in Charles Square. On the right corner is the Faust House, a renaissance mansion, much altered, where the alchemist Edward Kelley is believed to have practised his arts during the time of Rudolf II. Unfortunately Kelley fared no better than his fellow alchemists at turning base metals into gold, and for his efforts was thrown into prison, where he later died of poison. The Faust House derives its name from the fanciful connection made by fabulists between alchemical research and the Faust legend. The mansion now presents a debased baroque façade. Continue up the left side of the square and turn left on Resslova.

Adjoining a large neoclassical palace, now part of the Czech Technical University, is Kilián Ignác Dientzenhofer's church of SAINTS CYRIL AND METHODIUS

OPPOSITE *One of the truly delightful church interiors of Prague: the organ loft of the Karlov church with its parade of music-loving polychrome figures.*

of 1736, now used as Greek Orthodox church. A plaque at ground level commemorates the spot where the killers of the bestial Reinhard Heydrich, whom Hitler had sent to Prague to oversee the 'Final Solution of the Jewish problem', took refuge in June 1942. After some weeks their hiding place was revealed and the assassins tried unsuccessfully to defend themselves against the Nazis; realizing that they were cornered, they eventually took their own lives. Bullet marks are still visible above the window. It is not unusual to find fresh flowers placed here. Steps lead up to the forecourt, which is entered through an elaborate gatepost. Dietzenhofer's façade of 1730–6 is fairly narrow, and above the pediment seems somewhat undernourished by his standards. Although the furnishings, such as the iconostasis, are thoroughly in the Orthodox tradition (unlike St Clement's, p. 108), the stuccoed ceiling by M.I. Palliardi, with panels of lively frescoes by J.A. Schöpf, remains intact.

On the other side of Resslova is the late fourteenth-century church of ST WENCESLAS, a tall building with a steeply pitched roof. Above the west front are oddly positioned pairs of romanesque windows, remnants of the original structure of 1180. The aisle-less interior preserves its gothic lines, especially in the choir. The nave, which is frescoed, has a broad late gothic vault dated to 1587 and reminiscent of, if not nearly as impressive as, that of the Karlov church (p. 158). In the choir and on the east wall of the south aisle are fragmentary gothic frescoes from about 1400. The underside of the organ loft is panelled and each panel is painted, not well, but cheerfully.

ABOVE *Despite a long and chequered history, the cloisters of the Emmaus Monastery have preserved some of the finest medieval frescoes in Prague.*

OPPOSITE *In his church of St John Nepomuk on the Rock, Kilián Ignác Dientzenhofer skilfully angled the towers so as to accommodate them within a narrow and precipitous site.*

7

Outside the city

································

THE LAPIDARIUM *to* THE MUNICIPAL MUSEUM

Medieval Prague evolved as a series of municipalities that were gradually linked together without losing their independence. Each town had its own character, its own administration, and its own walls, and this structure gave the city an unusual density and cohesion. Only late in its history did Prague evolve a network of suburbs, and their relative newness means that suburban Prague is not notably rich in monuments or churches or houses of major interest. The development of the city, until well into the nineteenth century, took place within its formal boundaries. The Bohemian countryside is rich in castles and ancient towns and villages, but the immediate environs of Prague itself are somewhat impoverished architecturally, although some villas were built on the outskirts of the city. There are, however, a number of places well worth visiting, and, thanks to the excellent public transport system of the city, they are all easily accessible.

From the C line terminus of Nádraži Holešovice, take tram 5, 12 or 17 one stop to the immense exhibition buildings and planetarium which fill the east end of the STROMOVKA PARK. The huge hall facing the entrance gates that resembles a French railway station was built to house the Jubilee Exhibition in 1891. The pavilion on the right is the LAPIDARIUM of the National Museum, which contains sculptures, almost all of them original, from the eleventh to the nineteenth centuries. The collection was first assembled and displayed in 1905, but was often closed for reorganization, and more recently the Lapidarium was closed for decades because of the poor condition of the building. Reconstruction began in 1988 and is due for completion in May 1992.

Visitors will see a series of halls with exhibits arranged in chronological order. The first hall contains romanesque and early gothic carvings, all from Bohemia, and most of them from Prague itself. There are many tomb slabs from the Benedictine abbey of St John the Baptist at Ostrov, and a copy of the tympanum from the north door of the Týn church (pp. 124–6). Although the original

OPPOSITE *Château Troja and its gardens, built for the Sternberg family in the 1680s and surely the grandest of the country mansions still standing on the fringes of the city.*

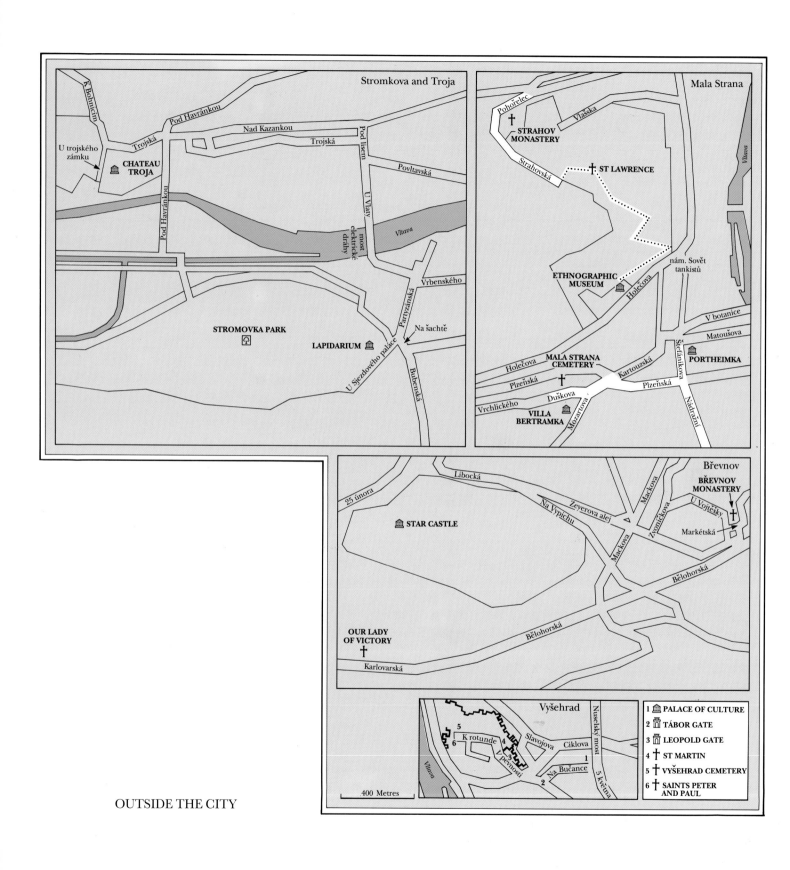

Stromkova and Troja

K Bohnicim
Pod Havránkou
Nad Kazankou
Trojská
Pod lisem
Trojská
Povltavská
U trojského zámku
CHATEAU TROJA
U Vlaty
Pod Havránkou
most elektrické dráhy
Vltava
Vrbenského
Partyzánská
Na šachtě
STROMOVKA PARK
LAPIDARIUM
U Sjezdového paláce
Bubenská

Mala Strana

Pohořelec
Vlasská
STRAHOV MONASTERY
Strahovská
ST LAWRENCE
Vltava
ETHNOGRAPHIC MUSEUM
nám. Sovět tankistů
Holečova
V botanice
Matoušova
MALA STRANA CEMETERY
Kartouzská
Štefánikova
PORTHEIMKA
Holečova
Plzeňská
Duškova
Mozartova
Nádražní
Plzeňská
Vrchlického
VILLA BERTRAMKA

Břevnov

Libocká
Mackova
BŘEVNOV MONASTERY
25 února
Zeyerova alej
Na Vypichu
Zvoníčkova
U Vojtěšky
STAR CASTLE
Mackova
Markétská
Bělohorská
OUR LADY OF VICTORY
Bělohorská
Karlovarská

Vyšehrad

5
K rotunde
6
Slavojova
Ciklova
Nuselský most
4
3
V pevnosti
1
Vltava
Na Bučance
2
5 května

400 Metres

1	**PALACE OF CULTURE**
2	**TÁBOR GATE**
3	**LEOPOLD GATE**
4	**ST MARTIN**
5	**VYŠEHRAD CEMETERY**
6	**SAINTS PETER AND PAUL**

OUTSIDE THE CITY

can be seen in the museum at St George's Convent (pp. 50–4), the justification for keeping this copy at the Lapidarium is that it was made early in this century and records details that are no longer visible on the more eroded original.

In the second medieval hall are high and late gothic sculptures, including originals from Parler's workshop, notably the marvellous sandstone carvings of the 1380s from the Old Town Tower (p. 104) on the Charles Bridge. Also from the bridge is the original Roland Column from the Malá Strana end; it makes one appreciate all the more keenly how feeble the nineteenth-century replacement is.

The major exhibit in the renaissance hall is the Krocín fountain of 1591–6. The identity of the sculptor is unknown but the fountain stood in Old Town Square until 1864, when it was dismantled. Despite its great beauty, it apparently only worked properly for about 50 years and was widely regarded as a nuisance rather than as an ornament to the square. It was badly damaged in the course of its removal. What is left of it suggests how magnificent the fountain as a whole must have been. The surviving portions are embellished with carvings of Neptune and creatures of the deep and shallow, great fish and small frogs, as well as other allegorical figures.

The central hall contains a number of the statues that originally stood on the Charles Bridge: Jan Brokoff's Baptism of Christ, Matthias Braun's St Ivo, Ferdinand Maximilian Brokoff's St Francis Xavier, and Brokoff's St Ignatius Loyola, of which there is no copy on the bridge, so the only place to see this superb sculpture is at the Lapidarium. Intended, not surprisingly, to show how the influence of the founding father of the Jesuit Order has spread throughout the world, the figure of the saint stands on a globe, surrounded by figures representing Africa, Asia, Europe, and America. Jäckel's original of the Madonna and Child with saints Thomas Aquinas and Dominic is also here, and so is another group of which no copy exists, Ottavio Mosto's St Wenceslas and Angels.

In the 1650s the early baroque sculptor Jan Bendl was commissioned to produce a column to commemorate Prague's survival of the terrible Thirty Years War. He did so, and for two and a half centuries this column stood in Old Town Square. On 3 November 1918, a large crowd, mistakenly believing that the column had been erected to celebrate Habsburg rule, tore it down. What is left of what must have been an impressive composition is here too. So is Bendl's last work, the celebrated equestrian statue of St Wenceslas, which stood in various places in Wenceslas Square. A copy has been erected on Vyšehrad, but this is the original, and a delightfully characterful sculpture it is. There are other statues by Jäckel and some unknown baroque masters, and Brokoff's original statue of the Virgin Mary from the pillar in Hradčanské náměstí (p. 64).

The long hall contains mostly late baroque work, including the original of the fountain by F.X. Lederer, of which a copy now stands in Uhelny trh, and four allegorical figures by Ignác Platzer which came from the Golz-Kinský Palace (pp. 123–4). In the last hall are the Habsburg monuments, victims of the declaration of the republic in 1918, just as in 1989 and 1990 the statues of Lenin and

ABOVE *The Lapidarium contains a huge anthology of original statuary from the medieval period to the present century, including this splendid statue by F.M. Brokoff.*

Gottwald were swiftly removed from squares and public buildings. Perhaps in 20 years they will appear in the Lapidarium, yet somehow I doubt it.

Return to Nádraži Holešovice and take the 112 bus to the zoo. You will pass through one of the city's most attractive villa districts. Opposite the entrance to the zoo is CHÂTEAU TROJA, a fine house built between 1679 and 1685 for the Sternberg family and set in magnificent walled grounds. The architect was Jean Baptiste Mathey, which, since he was a Frenchman, may explain why the park is laid out in the French style, with parterres both on the terrace of the villa and in the main part of the gardens. The modern lamps shaped like light-bulbs are intrusive and mar the stylish cohesion of the park. The villa itself is boxy, with four-square pavilions and towers at either end and little decoration apart from pilasters between bays. At Château Troja there is little of the fluidity of Prague baroque at its most vigorous, with the one remarkable exception of the superb double staircase. This is a slightly later addition to the house and is crowded with statuary by J.J. and P. Heermann of 1686–1703 and the workshop of Jan Bro-koff. The wall of the terrace is busily lined with a bewildering variety of late seven-teenth-century urns. It would all seem *de trop* except that against the grand but plain façade of the villa itself, it seems a welcome frenzy of embellishment. Inside the house there are frescoes of the 1690s by the Dutch artist Abraham Godin extolling the Habsburgs.

Take the bus back to Nádraži Holešovice and take the metro directly to Vyšehrad. You will emerge onto the terrace of the PALACE OF CULTURE, (Palác kultury), an impressive and well-planned modern building designed by a consor-tium of Czech architects in the 1970s. It is an all-purpose, or rather multi-purpose, building, with five concert halls, conference rooms, exhibitions halls, restaurants and cafés, and a night club. Walk across this terrace, keeping the fine view of the New Town to the right across the Botič valley. This is an excellent place to see the only surviving fortifications of those built around the New Town in 1350. A ramp on the right slopes down to Na Bučance and you soon see the fortress walls of VYŠEHRAD ahead of you.

It was here that princess Libuše made her legendary prediction about the future greatness of Prague (p. 10), and Vyšehrad unquestionably became a great fortress, founded in the tenth century and second only to Hradčany in import-ance. This hilltop overlooking two rivers formed a kind of plateau, which made it relatively easy to build on and to defend. By the reign of Vratislav II at the end of the eleventh century, it had become the royal residence as well as the seat of the bishop. Of the palaces that must have stood here nothing, alas, remains, since they were all destroyed during the Hussite wars. Vyšehrad's period of glory was brief, for after three generations the Bohemian ruling family moved back to Hradčany in 1140. Charles IV, who ignored no opportunity to expand and glor-ify his city, took an interest in Vyšehrad as in everything else and strengthened the fortifications, linking them with the city walls. He also instituted a Czech cor-onation route, which began here and passed across the rest of city and then over the river to the castle at Hradčany.

OPPOSITE *The finest feature of the Château Troja is the tremendous double staircase, packed with dynamic late seventeenth-century statuary.*

The Hussites occupied Vyšehrad for a time in the fifteenth century, and made alterations and constructed new buildings, but the next major period of construction took place in the seventeenth century to designs by various Italian architects. By the late nineteenth century, however, such buildings no longer served any military purpose, and the fortress was gradually dismantled, leaving only the gates and walls and, as the sole survivals of medieval Vyšehrad, the rotunda of St Martin and some foundations of a romanesque church. Archaeological excavations have been under way for decades now, and given the antiquity of the site, it is probable that many interesting discoveries remain to be made that will shed light on the long history of Vyšehrad.

The first gate you come to is the Tábor gate, which was the main entrance to the fortress when it was used as a citadel. The gate is a clumpy little structure of 1655 and has almost certainly been rebuilt . The road widens as you near the second set of walls and the Leopold gate, a more imposing rusticated baroque structure by Carlo Lurago of about the same period, with coats of arms and lions by G.B. Allio on the superstructure.

On the right you will see another of Prague's three romanesque rotundas. This, dedicated to ST MARTIN, is the earliest, from the late eleventh century. It is all that remains of Vyšehrad during its heyday under Vratislav II. Take the left turn, past the little park and into the cemetery. Laid out in the 1860, the VYŠEHRAD CEMETERY has become a kind of pantheon for the Czech good and great. Opposite the entrance is the grave of the poet Jan Neruda (1834–91). Smetana is buried here too, as is Antonín Dvořák, in the arcades to the right. Other cultural heroes whose graves are here include Emmy Destinn, Karel Čapek, Alfons Mucha, Mikoláš Aleš, and Josef Myslbek.

The cemetery church of SAINTS PETER AND PAUL, quite a landmark with its two spires, has been closed for many years; it is essentially nineteenth-century and the towers date from 1902, although a church has stood here for nine hundred years. Indeed, the crypt served as the burial place for four Přemyslid kings. On the south side of the church is another park, with some rather intimidating sculptures by Myslbek.

The lane facing the west front of the church overlooks the Vltava far below, giving one a view of the city rarely encountered. Just beyond, in a shady little park, is the copy of Bendl's statue of St Wenceslas. Retrace your footsteps, as Vyšehrad is not particularly well served by public transport other than the metro by which you arrived.

Take the metro back to Muzeum, then the A line to Hradčanská. Take either tram 1 or 18 to the terminus, Petříny. Bear left along U Hveždy after the tram stop, then turn right at the end of the road, and you will soon see the entrance to the fine park, originally a game reserve established by Ferdinand I in 1530, in which the STAR CASTLE is set. To the right a splendid avenue, one of a number created when the park was redesigned in 1797, leads directly to the castle across the top of White Mountain. With its six radiating points, like the prows of a ship, the castle has a most unlikely and most compelling shape. It was built in the 1550s

OPPOSITE *Set within a quiet corner of Vyšehrad, the cemetery contains the graves of most of Czechoslovakia's greatest musicians and artists, including Smetana, Dvořák, and Karel Čapek.*

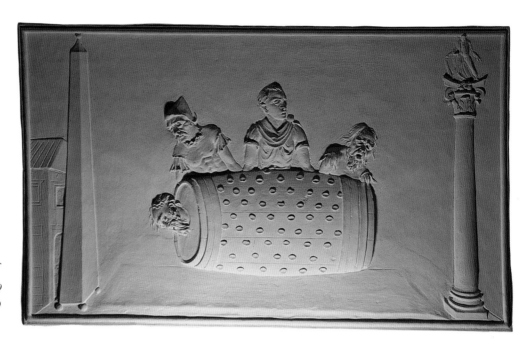

RIGHT *The highly original exterior of the Star Castle is in complete contrast to the exquisitely detailed Italianate stucco work that adorns the halls inside.*

by Italian architects, notably J.M. Aostali, as a hunting lodge for Ferdinand of Tyrol, the son of Ferdinand I. Ferdinand fancied himself as an architect, and it seems probable that he had a hand in the highly original design. It was used by various occupying armies in the seventeenth and eighteenth centuries, and under Joseph II it became a powder store and remained so until 1874, but it was thoroughly renovated after World War II.

Inside, the central hall, from which passages lead off to the six points, is suprisingly low, but this makes it easier to admire the superb renaissance stuccowork on the ceiling. The decoration, completed in 1563, depicts scenes from Greek and Roman mythology, varied with more standard items from the plasterer's repertoire: swags of fruit, medallions, and grotesques. The decoration was the work of G. Campione and A. Avostalis del Pambio.

The ground floor is used to display a permanent exhibition devoted to the work of Alois Jirásek (1851–1930), a popular writer at the turn of the century, and the display manages to incorporate plenty of information on Czech cultural history. On the first floor is a similar exhibition about the work of the painter Mikoláš Aleš (1852–1913), who was responsible for the painting of St Wenceslas on the Storch house in Old Town Square (p. 126), as well as other façades and the frescoes within the National Theatre (pp. 151–2). For foreign visitors the most rewarding exhibits are those in the basement, which include fascinating and informative displays about the founding of the castle and about the decisive battle that took place here in 1620.

Return to the park gate and walk down Na Vipichu to Vipich. From Bělohorská take tram 8 or 22 to the terminus at Bílá Hora (White Mountain). Just beyond the tram terminus is the church of Our Lady of Victory, surrounded by a

OPPOSITE *The lavish decoration of the portals of Our Lady of Victory on White Mountain whets an appetite to pass through them that can only infrequently be satisfied.*

wall which is arcaded on the inside, rather like the cloisters of the Loreto complex (pp. 65–6). It was built in the early eighteenth century as a pilgrimage church by an unknown architect. To me, it has a Russian air to it, with its numerous cupolas and turrets. Since it contains frescoes by Václav Reiner, it seems a pity that the church is rarely open.

Return with the 8 or 22 tram for three stops, which brings you to the BŘEV-NOV MONASTERY. Surrounded by high walls and watched over by an onion-domed tower, the monastery is clearly visible on the left. This is a complex of immense historical importance, since it was founded in 993 and was the very first monastery established in Bohemia. It was rebuilt in the fourteenth century and again in the eighteenth century, and it is that version which survives today. It was a Benedictine foundation, established by Boleslav II in the late tenth century. You enter through a powerfully designed gateway by Kilián Ignác Dienztenhofer of 1740 and straight ahead is his father Christoph's church of ST MARGARET, built between 1708 and 1714, a fairly austere sculptural baroque design coloured in rich buff tones. The main entrance is on the south side of the church, where Dientzenhofer has created gables with lunettes to add grandeur.

St Margaret's is a large aisle-less church with the flat-topped capitals between side chapels reminiscent of St Thomas's in Malá Strana (p. 91) by the same architects. The organ gallery at the west end is elegantly curved and the organ itself is covered with carvings of putti, many of whom are portrayed as instrumentalists. For a baroque church there is a surprising lack of stucco ornament, or even of baroque furnishings, other than the high altar. Side altars are painted onto the walls, framing the actual paintings of the altarpieces. The choir stalls have elegant marquetry and are topped with statues, some of which are by Jäckel. A few of the altarpieces are by Peter Brandl, and the mediocre ceiling frescoes of 1719 to 1721 are by J. J. Steinfels. In a crypt beneath the choir are the remains of the original church of the early eleventh century. To the east of the church stand the early eighteenth-century abbey buildings, also mostly the work of Christoph Dientzenhofer.

Return to the 22 tram and get off at the Strahov Monastery. Instead of entering the gates of the monastery, take Strahovská, the road to the right of the gateway, which gradually climbs the Petřín hill. For most of the way it follows the so-called HUNGER WALL, built in 1360–2 at the command of Charles IV, apparently as a kind of public works project. For many years the wall was under restoration, and a joke used to circulate in Prague that it was taking longer to restore the wall than it took Charles IV's crew to build it in the first place.

When you reach the television tower, enter the park. On the right is ST LAWRENCE'S church, an eighteenth-century rebuilding by Ignác Palliardi of a romanesque chapel that served one of the hamlets incorporated within Malá Strana by Charles IV. Keep the Hunger Wall on the right as you gradually descend, passing the cable car line and then the observatory. There are superb views on the left onto the whole city. After the road zig-zags, take the fork that leads under the bastion of the Hunger Wall, and keep heading downwards.

With any luck you should end up close to náměstí Sovětských tankistů, the square named after the fact that a Russian tank, symbolizing those that liberated the city in 1945, stood on a high pedestal here until 1991, when it was removed to the military museum at Žižkov. Don't enter the square, but bear right along the path inside the park parallel to Holeckova. This leads to the ETHNOGRAPHIC MUSEUM in the neoclassical building formerly known as the Villa Kinský, built between 1827 and 1831, and now in rather shabby condition. The museum specializes in exhibits relating to Czech and Slovak folklore, but has been closed for years and nobody seems to know when it is likely to repoen.

Return to the square, and take tram 9 to Bertramka and walk back past the MALÁ STRANA CEMETERY, which is dominated by the huge memorial of 1830–31 to Bishop Leopold Thun-Hohenstein, by V. Prachner. From Duškova turn right into Mozartova and climb the short hill. The VILLA BERTRAMKA is an unpretentious house set on a steep wooded slope close to a former vineyard. It is a reconstruction of the eighteenth-century house, mostly destroyed by fire in the 1870s, that became Mozart's retreat during his visits to Prague.

At that time this was still very much a suburb of Prague, and must have been an idyllic spot, so one can see why Mozart was drawn to it during his stays in the city in 1787, 1789, and in 1791, shortly before his death, when he came to Prague for the premiere of *La Clemenza di Tito*. The other draw was Josefina Dušek, for whom he wrote here in 1787 the ravishing and extremely taxing concert aria *Bella mia fiamma*. She was the wife of the villa's owner, František Xaver Dušek, and a celebrated singer who specialised in concert and oratorio performances.

As the MOZART MUSEUM established here during the last century makes clear, many of Mozart's finest works were either composed in Prague or composed for Prague audiences. *Don Giovanni*, first performed at the Tyl (p. 137), is the best-known but not the only example; according to Alfred Einstein, Mozart's biographer, it was completed at Bertramka. (The museum, incidentally, preserves an original poster from that memorable premiere.) The sublime clarinet concerto was another glorious work composed here. The museum, which is considerably more interesting than the better-known Mozart houses in Vienna, contains a harpsichord played by the composer, as well as a lock of his hair, scraps of autograph manuscript, and other memorabilia.

On leaving the villa, walk to the bottom of Mozartova, turn right and follow the tram tracks along Plzeňská. Turn left up Štefánikova, and just past the church of St Wenceslas you will see the summer house Kilián Ignác Dientzenhofer built for himself in 1729 (it is also known as PORTHEIMKA, after a family that later lived in the house). As a family house it was of course built on a more modest scale than his great churches, but it shows the same fluidity of line and the same sculptural quality. The entrance bay projects forward and has a balcony; indeed, the façade has a prettiness one doesn't usually expect from this architect. The house was originally much larger, but part of it was knocked down when the church was built. The small park in front of the house is a vestige of the park that once stretched down to the river bank. The interior is now used as an art gallery called 'D'.

Return along Štefánikova to Anděl metro station and take the B line to Florenc, where, incidentally, the main bus station is located. The large late nineteenth-century cream-coloured building near the overpass is the city's MUNICIPAL MUSEUM, built in 1898. It is not, I have to say, one of Prague's great museums, and I include it in the hope that one of these days it will be revamped and that a more convincing tribute to the city's evolution will be installed. One of the problems in Prague is that too many museums overlap in subject matter (there are historical surveys along similar lines in the National Museum and the Lobkovic Palace (pp. 56–7)), so the available material is stretched rather thinly between them.

The first room deals with the early medieval period, and relies heavily, as do the other rooms, on photographs and diagrams. The few actual exhibits consist of coins and jewellery and some thirteenth-century frescoes. In the next room are more interesting exhibits from medieval Prague: frescoes, metal flails and other alarming weapons, seals, and carvings of high quality, including the statue of the Madonna that came from the corner niche of the Old Town Hall (pp. 127–31), and a thick-set Pietà from the Týn church (pp. 124–6).

The third room deals with Prague between 1437 and 1620. There are more polychrome Madonnas, early printed books, a bronze horse by Adriaen de Vries and a fine three-legged sixteenth-century font, not unlike the one in the Týn church. Here too you will see weapons: pikes and swords and muskets. The main hall upstairs is dominated by an immense model of the city as it appeared in the early nineteenth century, as well as paintings from a slightly later period, all demonstrating that the city has hardly changed at all since that time. The history of Prague from the sixteenth century to the present day is, unfortunately, not covered, or if there are rooms containing such exhibits, they do not appear to be open. The principal effect of visiting the museum is to send you rushing back into the streets and alleys of the city, which are invariably more interesting and dynamic than the relics sporadically deposited in this museum.

This book has inevitably focused on old Prague, on Prague as an almost unrivalled repository of the medieval and the baroque, a city that has inadvertently acquired the finest roofscapes in Europe, and a city with its oldest districts left virtually untouched by war and modern urban redevelopment. Yet Prague is also on the brink of major changes as a city. Unless the programme outlined by the new government goes seriously off course, western capital will lead to new construction and to restoration programmes that will eclipse anything achieved so far. The huge and drab housing projects undertaken by the Communists were all on the fringes of the city. The new schemes, however, are intended to rejuvenate districts that adjoin the most historic parts of the city. No one can predict the outcome with any exactitude, but what is certain is that Prague will be transformed. The city, long in danger of becoming ossified as a kind of baroque theme park, should recover its commercial and artistic vitality without jeopardizing the achievements of the past. If all this can be achieved, the Prague of the future will be one of the most exciting cities of Europe.

OPPOSITE *The Villa Bertramka was Mozart's suburban retreat when he came to Prague, and within its quiet rooms and steep gardens he composed some of his very finest music, inspired in part by his hostess, the singer Josefina Dušek.*

Appendices

....

CHRONOLOGY OF EVENTS • RULERS
ARTISTS AND PATRONS • OPENING TIMES

CHRONOLOGY

723 Traditional date for the founding of the city by the legendary Princess Libuše.

late ninth century The Přemyslids, the first Czech ruling house, create settlement on the site of Prague; according to legend, the dynasty was founded by a ploughman, Přemysl, who married Princess Libuše.

928 St Wenceslas, duke of Bohemia and patron saint of Czechoslovakia, murdered by his brother Boleslav.

950 Boleslav acknowledges overlordship of Emperor Otto I, Bohemia becomes part of Holy Roman Empire.

973 Bishopric founded in Prague.

1124 First mention of a synagogue in Prague.

1158 Vladislav II granted title of King of Bohemia. Reigns as Vladislav I.

1170 First stone bridge constructed across River Vltava.

1257 Malá Strana (Lesser Town) founded by Ottakar II.

1306 Murder of Wenceslas III ends Přemyslid dynasty.

1310 John of Luxemburg elected king; Luxemburg dynasty rules until 1437.

1344 Prague becomes archbishopric; St Vitus's Cathedral begun.

1346–78 Reign of Charles IV, the golden age of Bohemia.

1348 Charles founds university.

c.1352 Peter Parler becomes architect of cathedral.

1357 Charles Bridge begun.

1415 Execution of Jan Hus.

1419 First Defenestration of Prague; Hussite rebellion begins.

1437–1526 Bohemia ruled – with interruptions – by royal houses of Hungary and Poland.

1493–1502 Vladislav Hall in Prague Castle built by Benedikt Ried.

1526 Accession of the Habsburg ruler Archduke Ferdinand (later Emperor Ferdinand I): the Habsburgs rule Bohemia until 1918.

1538–63 Belvedere built at Prague Castle.

1575–1611 Rudolf II is King of Bohemia; his court is a brilliant intellectual and cultural centre.

1618 Defenestration of Prague begins Thirty Years War.

1648 Peace of Westphalia ends Thirty Years War.

1669–97 Černín Palace built.

1704 St Nicholas's Church (Lesser Town) begun, the most famous baroque building in Prague.

1749 Maria Theresia begins administrative reforms, including making German the official language.

1787 Mozart conducts premiere of *Don Giovanni*.

1848 The Year of Revolutions; Czech nationalism stirs, but Austrian domination continues. Franz Joseph becomes Emperor and rules until 1916.

1868	National Theatre begun.	**1938**	Germany annexes Sudetenland (a largely German-speaking border region of Czechoslovakia).	**1968**	Soviet Union invades Czechoslovakia to end growing liberalization of the regime under Alexander Dubček.
1874–9	Smetana composes *Ma Vlast* (My Country).				
1885	National Museum begun.				
1918	At end of World War I Bohemia, Moravia and Slovakia combine to form Czechoslovakia, with Prague as its capital.	**1939**	Germany invades Czechoslovakia.	**1989**	The 'Velvet Revolution' – Communist regime collapses. Václav Havel becomes president.
		1945	Czechoslovakia liberated.		
		1948	Communists gain control.		

RULERS

Dukes					
Bořivoj	*c.*870	Konrád Ota	1182	Matthias	1611
Spytihněv I	*c.*894	Bedřich	1182	Frederick of the Palatinate	1619
Vratislav I	*c.*905	Konrád Ota	1189	Ferdinand II	1620
Wenceslas (Václav)	*c.*921	Václav II	1191	Ferdinand III	1637
Boleslav I (the Cruel)	*c.*935	Otakar I	1192	Ferdinand IV	1646
Boleslav II (the Pious)	*c.*967	Břetislav Jindřich	1193	Leopold I	1657
Boleslav III	999	Vladislav III Jindřich	1197	Joseph I	1705
Vladivoj of Poland	1002	Otakar I	1212	Charles VI	1711
Břetislav I	1034	Wenceslas I	1230	Maria Theresia	1740
Spytihněv II	1055	Otakar II	1253	Joseph II	1780
Vratislav II	1061	Wenceslas II	1278	Leopold II	1790
Břetislav II	1092	Wenceslas III	1305	Francis I	1792
Bořivoj II	1100	Jindřich of Carinthia	1306	Ferdinand V	1835
Svatopluk	1107	Rudolf Habsburg	1306	Franz Joseph I	1848
Vladislav I	1109	John of Luxemburg	1310	Charles I	1916
Bořivoj II	1117	Charles IV	1346	*Presidents*	
Vladislav I	1120	Wenceslas IV	1378	Tomáš Masaryk	1918
Soběslav I	1125	Sigismund	1420	Edvard Beneš	1935
Vladislav II (*1158 becomes king as Vladislav I*)	1140	Albert Habsburg	1438	Emil Hácha	1938
		Ladislav the Posthumous	1440	Edvard Beneš	1945
Bedřich	1172	George of Poděbrady	1458	Klement Gottwald	1948
Soběslav II	1173	Vladislav II Jagellon	1471	Antonín Zápotecký	1953
Bedřich	1179	Ludvik Jagellon	1516	Antonín Novotný	1957
		Ferdinand I	1526	Ludvík Svoboda	1968
		Maximilian II	1564	Gustáv Husák	1975
		Rudolf II	1576	Václav Havel	1989

ARTISTS AND PATRONS

Aleš, Mikulás (1852–1913), the most prolific Czech decorative painter of his period: Rott House; Star Castle; Storch House; and National Theatre.

Alliprandi, Giovanni Battista (1665–c.1720), Italian architect; Hartig Palace; Kaiserstein Palace, Sternberg Palace; and Trinity Column.

Bendl, J.J. (1620–80), Czech sculptor: Lapidarium; St George's Convent.

Brandl, Peter (1668–1735), Czech painter: Castle Picture Gallery; Loreto Pilgrimage Church; St James's Church; St George's Convent.

Braun, Matthias (1684–1738), with Brokoff, the leading Czech Baroque sculptor: Charles Bridge; portal of Clam-Gallas Palace; Lapidarium; Museum of Musical Instruments; St Clement's Church; St Vitus's Cathedral; and much public statuary.

Brokoff, Ferdinand Maximilian (1688–1731), with Braun, the leading Czech Baroque sculptor: Charles Bridge; Lapidarium, Morzin Palace; St George's Convent; and much public statuary.

Caratti, Francesco (d.1677), Italian architect who became the leading architect in Prague after settling there in 1652: Černín Palace; Clementinum; Nostitz Palace, Church of St Salvator.

Charles IV (1316–78), King of Bohemia 1346–78 and Holy Roman Emperor 1355–78: the greatest figure of medieval Prague, known as the 'Father of the Country', an enlightened ruler and major patron of the arts and sciences.

Dietzenhofer, Christoph (1655–1722), German-born architect who settled in Prague, the father of Kilián Ignác: St Margaret's Church; St Nicholas Church, Malá Strana.

Dietzenhofer, Kilián Ignác (1689–1751), Czech architect, the outstanding member of a family of architects and the most prolific designer of buildings in baroque Prague: Church of our Lady, Golz-Kinsky Palace; Loreto Pilgrimage Church; St Clement's Church; St Cyril and St Methodius's Church; St John Nepomuk, Hradčany; St John Nepomuk on the Rock; St Nicholas, Malá Strana; St Nicholas, Staré Město; St Thomas' Church; Villa Amerika; and many additions and alterations to other buildings.

Fischer von Erlach, Johann Bernard (1656–1723), the greatest Austrian baroque architect: Clam-Gallas Palace; design of Vratislav (Mitrovitz) monument in St James's Church.

Fischer von Erlach, Josef Emanuel (b.1693), Austrian architect and designer, son of the great J.B. Fischer von Erlach: design of tomb of St John Nepomuk and of monument to Count Schlick, both in St Vitus's Cathedral.

Gocar, Josef (1880–1945), Czech 'Cubist' architect: House of the Black Mother of God.

Jäckel, Mathiaz Wenzel (1655–1738), Czech sculptor: Charles Bridge, Lapidarium, Pauline Monastery.

Kaňka, František Maximilian (1674–1766), Czech architect: Černín Palace (interior): Černín Palace (in Sněmovní); Clementinum; Hartig Palace, Karlov Church; Oettingen Palace; St Catherine's Church; St Clement's Church; St Salvator's Church: Vrtba Gardens.

Kracker, Johann Lukas (1717–79), Austrian painter: dome of St Nicholas Malá Strana.

Kupecky, Jan (1667–1740), Czech painter, an outstanding portraitist: St George's Convent.

Lurago, Anselmo (c.1702–65), Italian architect: Caretto-Millesimo Palace; Golz-Kinsky Pallace; gateway of Strahov Monastery.

Lurago, Carlo (c.1618–84), Italian architect: Leopold Gate; Lobkovic Palace, St Mary under the Chain; Schönborn Palace.

Mánes, Josef (1820–71), Czech painter, regarded as the founder of a national school of painting: Saint Agnes's Convent; Old Town Hall Tower.

Master of the Litoměřice Altar (early sixteenth century), Czech painter: St George's Convent; Wenceslas Chapel in St Vitus's Cathedral.

Master of the Třeboň Altarpiece (late fourteenth century), Czech painter: St George's Convent.

Master of the Vyšší Brod Altarpiece (active c.1350), Czech painter: St George's Convent.

Master Theodoric (active 1348–70), Czech painter: St George's Convent.

Mathey, Jean Baptiste (c.1630–95), French architect (originally a painter) who settled in Prague in 1675: Chateau Troja; Our Lady of the Theatines; Riding School at Castle; St Francis's Church; St Joseph's Church.

Matthias of Arras (d.1352), French architect who began St Vitus's Cathedral in 1344.

Maulbertsch, Franz Anton (1724–96), Austrian painter, the leading fresco decorator of his day in Central Europe: Holy Trinity; Strahov Library.

Mosto, Ottavio (1659–1701), Italian sculptor: Kaiserstein Palace; Lapidarium, St James's Church; Toscana Palace.

Mucha, Alfons (1860–1939), Czech painter, graphic artist and designer, a leading exponent of art nouveau and an ardent patriot (even though he made his name in Paris): stained glass in St Vitus's Cathedral.

Mylsbek, Josef Václav (1848–1922), Czech sculptor, the creator of most of the major public statues erected in Prague at the turn of the century: Cemetery Church of SS Peter and Paul; National Theatre; St Vitus's Cathedral; Statue of St Wenceslas, Wenceslas Square.

Oswald of Prague (active c.1370), Czech painter: Wenceslas Chapel in St Vitus's Cathedral.

Pacassi, Nikolas (1716–90), Austrian architect: tower of St Vitus's Cathedral.

Palliardi, Ignác (d.1751), Czech architect: Kolowrat Palace and Gardens; Ledebour Palace, Lobkovic Palace, St Lawrence's Church; Strahov Library.

Parler, Peter (d.1399), German architect, sculptor and engineer who took over as architect of St Vitus's Cathedral after Matthias of Arras died in 1352 and became the dominant artistic figure at the court of Charles IV: Charles Bridge; Lapidarium; continuation of St Vitus's Cathedral, including Wenceslas Chapel; Old Town Hall Chapel.

Philippi, G.M., Italian architect: former Lesser Town Hall, Mathias Gate; Our Lady of Victories; former Church of St Roch.

Platzer, Ignác (1717–87), Czech sculptor: Archbishop's Palace; Lapidarium; St Nicholas's, Malá Strana.

Reiner, Václav (1689–1743), the leading Czech fresco painter of the baroque period: Church of the Nativity; St Catherine's Church; St Francis's Church; St George's Basilica; St George's Convent; St Giles's Church; St Henry's Church; St James' Church; St John Nepomuk; St Thomas's Church.

Ried, Benedikt (c.1454–1534), German-born architect, the outstanding figure in late gothic architecture in Central Europe: Vladislav Hall.

Rudolf II (1552–1612), King of Bohemia 1575–1611 and Holy Roman Emperor 1576–1612: he was mentally unstable and politically incompetent (he was forced to abdicate the throne of Bohemia to his brother Mathias), but he was one of the greatest patrons of his age, bringing distinguished artists to Prague from all over Europe.

Šaloun, Ladislav (1870–1946), Czech sculptor: Hus Monument, Old Town Square.

Santini (Santini-Aichel), Giovanni (1667–1723), Czech architect of Italian extraction, an off-beat genius: Ledebour Palace Gardens; Morzin Palace; Schönborn Palace; Palace on Thunovska; Valkounsky House.

Schultz, Josef (1840–1917), Czech architect: House of Artists (with Zítek); Museum of Decorative Arts; National Museum; National Theatre (with Zítek).

Skréta, Karel (1610–74), Czech painter: St Henry's Church; St Mary under the Chain; St Nicholas's, Malá Strana; St George's Convent; Týn Church.

Stella, Paolo della (d.1552), Italian architect: Belvedere.

Vries, Adriaen de (1546–1626), Netherlandish sculptor, appointed court sculptor to Rudolf II in 1601: Castle Picture Gallery; Municipal Museum; St George's Convent; Sala Terrena.

Wirch, Johann Joseph (1732–83), Czech architect: façade of Archbishop's Palace: St Adalbert's Church.

Wohlmut, Bonifaz (d.1579), German-Czech architect, court architect to the Emperor Ferdinand I: Belvedere (completion); Karlov Church; St Vitus's Cathedral (including organ gallery and tower).

Würth, Joseph (fl.1733–57), Austrian goldsmith: tomb of St John Nepomuk in St Vitus's Cathedral.

Zítek, Joseph (1832–1909), Czech architect: House of Artists (with Schulz); National Theatre.

OPENING TIMES

Most public buildings and churches are open daily, but the latter are liable to be closed to visitors, without notice, during services, and all public buildings are likely to be closed on public holidays. All hours of opening, including some of those given in the following list, are periodically liable to alteration (winter hours, too, often differ from summer), and it is always advisable to check before planning a visit.

Archbishop's Palace, Hradčany náměstí: Maundy Thursday 9.00–5.00.

Belvedere, Hradčany: Tuesday– Sunday 10.00–6.00.

Château Troja, Troja: April– September, Tuesday–Sunday 9.00–5.00.

Ethnographic Museum, Petřinské sady, Smíchov: Tuesday–Sunday 10.00–6.00.

Hradčany Castle: April–September, Tuesday–Sunday 9.00–5.00; October–March, Tuesday–Sunday 9.00–4.00.

Jewish Museum (Jewish Town Hall, Maislova; High Synagogue, Cervená; Altneu Synagogue, Cervená; Klaus Synagogue, U starého hřbitova; Maisl Synagogue, Maislova; Spanish Synagogue, Dušni): April–October, Sunday–Friday 9.00–5.00; November–March, Sunday–Friday 9.00–4.30 (Altneu Synagogue 9.00–4.00 Friday).

Mozart Museum, Villa Bertramka, Mozartova: April–September, Tuesday–Friday 2.00–5.00, Saturday and Sunday 10.00–12.00, 2.00–5.00; October–March, Tuesday–Friday 1.00–4.00, Saturday and Sunday 10.00–12.00, 1.00–4.00.

Musical Instruments Museum, Grand Prior's Palace, Velkopřevorské náměstí: Tuesday–Sunday 10.00–12.00, 1.00–5.00.

Municipal Museum, Sady Jana Švermy, Karlin: Tuesday–Sunday 9.00–12.00, 1.00–5.00.

National Gallery:
Bohemian Collection, St George's Convent, Hradčany: April– November, Tuesday–Sunday 10.00–6.00.
European Art Collection, Sternberg Palace, Hradčany náměstí: Tuesday– Sunday 10.00–6.00.
Graphics Collection, Golz-Kinsky Palace, Staroměstské náměstí: Tuesday–Sunday 10.00–6.00.

National Museum, Václavské náměstí: Monday and Friday 9.00– 4.00, Saturday, Sunday, Wednesday and Thursday 9.00–5.00.

Old Town Town Hall, Staroměstské náměstí: March–mid October 8.00–6.00; mid October–February 8.00–5.00.

Powder Tower, náměstí Republiký: Saturday, Sunday and public holidays, April and October 10.00– 5.00, May–September 10.00–6.00, closed November–March.

St Agnes's Convent, Anežská ulice: Tuesday–Sunday 10.00–6.00.

St George's Basilica, Hradčany: April–September, Tuesday–Sunday 9.00–5.00; October–March, Tuesday–Sunday 9.00–4.00.

St Vitus's Cathedral, Hradčany: April–September, Tuesday–Sunday 9.00–5.00; October–March, Tuesday–Sunday 9.00–4.00.

Schwarzenberg Palace (Museum of Military History), Hradčany náměstí: May–October, Tuesday–Sunday 9.00–3.30.

Strahov Monastery, Strahovské nádvoří or Pohořelec: Tuesday– Sunday 9.00–5.00.

Stroma Park (including Lapidarium of National Museum): closed Monday.

Valdštejn gardens, Valdštejnské náměstí: May–September, 9.00–7.00.

Villa Amerika (including Dvořak Museum), Ke Karlovu: Tuesday– Sunday 10.00–5.00.

Vrtba Palace, Karmelitská ulice: May–September 8.00–7.00.

Glossary of Terms

....

Aisle A side part of a church, running parallel to the main space (NAVE or chancel) and usually divided from it by a row of pillars or columns.

Art Nouveau A style in art (mainly the decorative arts) that flourished from about 1890 until World War I, its chief characteristic is the use of flowing, plant-like forms.

Baldacchino A canopy over an altar (or occasionally over some other hallowed object).

Balustrade A row of balusters (small decorative posts) supporting a rail and forming a parapet of a balcony, terrace, etc.

Baroque A style of art and architecture flourishing in the seventeenth and early eighteenth centuries; it is characterized by fervent emotion, a strong sense of movement, and often by rich decorative display.

Barrel Vault A simple type of semi-circular VAULT, like the roof of a tunnel (an alternative name is tunnel vault).

Bay A major, repeated vertical division of a building (exterior or interior); a church NAVE, for example, is said to have four bays when there is a series of four arches and four windows on each side.

Berretta or Biretta A square cap worn by some Roman Catholic clergymen (red for a cardinal, purple for a bishop, black for a priest).

Belvedere A building or part of a building situated to command a beautiful view; it may be a gallery, a garden summerhouse, tower, etc.

Bema A raised or enclosed area in certain churches on which the altar stands or from which services are conducted.

Biedermeier A style of art (particularly furniture and interior design) flourishing in Central Europe from about 1815 to 1850, it is characterized by cosiness and unpretentiousness.

Cartouche An ornamental panel in architecture or sculpture, usually consisting of a central area with an inscription or coat of arms enclosed by scrolling decoration resembling cut parchment.

Choir The part of a church where services are sung; the term is often loosely applied to the whole eastern part of a typical cruciform church, in distinction from the NAVE.

Cloister A covered walkway around the walls of buildings opening onto a quadrangle; cloisters are particularly associated with monasteries.

Cope A long cloaklike garment worn by clergymen on ceremonial occasions.

Corbel A bracket (often carved) projecting from a wall to support a roof or similar feature.

Corinthian A type of column used in classical architecture, having an elaborate capital (crowning feature) carved with acanthus leaves.

Cornice In architecture, a horizontal decorative projection, particularly along the roofline of a building.

Crocket An ornamental leaf-like projection found on spires, canopies, etc. in GOTHIC architecture.

Cubism A movement in painting (and to a lesser extent other arts) developed from about 1907. In painting, forms were being broken into a multiplicity of facets, rather than being represented from a single fixed viewpoint; in architecture, the term is rather imprecise but is most commonly applied to the work of certain Czech architects who used applied cubist detail.

Defenestration The act of throwing someone out of a window (*fenestra* in Latin); there have been several instances in the history of the city, but 'The Defenestration of Prague' invariably refers to the occasion on 23 May 1618 when a

group of Protestant Czech nobles threw representatives of
the Emperor Mathias out of a window at Hradčany Castle in
protest at Catholic repression. This event touched off the
Thirty Years War.

Drum A circular wall supporting a dome.

Fresco A technique of wall (and ceiling) painting in which the
colours are applied directly to wet plaster to produce an
extremely permanent result, bonded to the structure.

Gable The triangular upper area of wall at the end of a
pitched roof; the term is also applied to any similarly-shaped
canopy.

Gothic The dominant style of European architecture from
the later twelfth century until the fifteenth century (or in
many places the sixteenth century); its most obvious feature
is the pointed arch.

Historicist A term most commonly used in architecture –
that can be applied to any style that deliberately imitates or
revives the forms of past art. It is applied particularly to
nineteenth-century buildings; the revival of numerous styles,
including GOTHIC, was then particularly popular.

Hussites Followers of Jan Hus (1369?–1415,) the Czech
religious reformer and national hero, burned at the stake in
1415.

Iconostasis A screen in an Eastern Orthodox church on
which icons were placed; it divided the main body of the
church from the part reserved for the clergy.

Ionic A type of column used in classical architecture
distinguished by the pair of volutes (scroll-like forms) of the
capital (crowning feature).

Jugendstil The German name for ART NOUVEAU.

Lancet A narrow pointed window, with little or no
ornamentation – a characteristic feature of early GOTHIC
architecture.

Loggia A gallery open on one or more sides.

Lunette A semi-circular window, more generally, the term is
applied to any flat, semi-circular panel in architecture.

Majolica A type of richly coloured and decorated pottery
popular in RENAISSANCE Italy.

Mannerism A movement in art that originated in Italy in
about 1520 and spread throughout Europe in the sixteenth
century; it was characterized by exaggerated elegance and
flourished particularly at sophisticated courts, such as that of
Rudolf II in Prague.

Mitre A tall pointed hat worn by bishops on ceremonial
occasions.

Monstrance In the Roman Catholic church, a receptacle in
which the consecrated Host (the bread or wafer signifying
Christ's body) is held up to the congregation for veneration;
monasteries are often elaborate examples of the goldsmith's
and jeweller's arts.

Narthex A portico or vestibule at the main entrance to a
church.

Nave The western 'arm' of a typical cruciform church,
leading from the entrance to the crossing, where the four
arms meet; more specifically, the term can be applied to the
central part of the arm when it is flanked by AISLES.

Neoclassicism A movement in European art and
architecture in the late eighteenth and early nineteenth
centuries in which the forms and spirit of Greek and Roman
art were revived.

Neo-Gothic The revival of the GOTHIC style of architecture
in the eighteenth and nineteenth centuries; Gothic Revival is
an alternative term.

Ogee A curved line with both a concave and a convex part
(like the letter S); in architecture, the term is applied mainly
to window arches with a double curve.

Oriel A bay window that projects from an upper storey.

Parterre A flower garden, usually adjoining a house, in which
the beds and paths are arranged in a formal pattern.

Pediment A wide, low-pitched GABLE over the facade of a
classical building or any similar feature used decoratively in
architecture, especially over windows or doors.

Phylactery A small leather box containing parchment
inscribed with quotations from the Hebrew scriptures; some
Orthodox Jewish men wear them.

Piarist Order A Catholic educational order founded at
Rome in 1597.

Pier An architectural term for any masonry support that is
more substantial than a column or pillar.

Pieta A representation in painting or sculpture of the Virgin
Mary supporting the dead Christ in her lap.

Pietra Dura A type of mosaic in which semi-precious stones
are arranged to create pictures, imitating as far as possible
the effects of painting, the term is Italian for 'hard stone'.

Pilaster In classical architecture, a flat 'column' attached to
and projecting slightly from a wall; it is used decoratively
rather than as a structural support.

Pointillism A painting technique in which dots of pure
unmixed colour are placed on the canvas in such a way that
they seem to blend in the eye of a viewer standing a suitable
distance from the picture; this produces a more vibrant effect
than if the colours were physically mixed together. The
technique was invented by the great French painter Georges
Seurat (1859–91).

Polychrome A term meaning 'many-coloured', applied particularly to statues that have been painted in more or less naturalistic colours.

Porte-cochere A porch at the entrance to a public building or mansion to shelter people getting in or out of carriages or other vehicles.

Quatrefoil An ornamental feature with four curved lobes (shaped rather like a four-leaved clover); it is found particularly in TRACERY in GOTHIC windows.

Renaissance An intellectual and artistic movement based on the revival ('Renaissance' means 'rebirth') of the values of ancient Greece and Rome; it began in Italy in the fourteenth century and spread throughout Europe.

Rib One of the arches that form the skeletal framework of a VAULT, or any similar projecting band used decoratively.

Rococo A style of art and architecture prevailing in the early and mid eighteenth century (until almost the end of the century in Central Europe); it was characterized by elegance, delicacy and playfulness.

Romanesque A style of architecture and art prevailing in most of Europe in the eleventh and twelfth centuries; the most obvious feature of romanesque architecture is the use of the round arch.

Rotunda A circular building, particularly one with a dome.

Rustication Masonry that has been given a bold texture or keep grooves between the joints to convey a feeling of massive strength; it is most commonly used on the lower parts of exterior walls, but is sometimes applied to whole buildings or to individual features.

Sala terrena A ground floor room that opens directly onto a garden.

Sezession The name adopted by several groups of painters who broke away (seceded) from official art academies in the 1890s – in Munich (1892), Vienna (1897) and Berlin (1899). Secession artists were associated with progressive styles, particularly ART NOUVEAU and in Austria art nouveau is in fact known as Sezessionstil.

Sgraffito Decoration produced by scratching through a thin coating surface (as for example a glaze in pottery) to reveal a different colour beneath.

Squinch One of four segments of masonry or vaulting built obliquely at the upper inside corner of a square tower or similar structure, forming the transition to a circular or octagonal dome or other superstructure.

Squint A small opening in a pier or interior wall of a church to allow worshippers whose view would otherwise be restricted to see the altar; it is also called a hagioscope.

Stucco A kind of light, easily moulded plaster used for sculpture and architectural decoration (both external and internal).

Swag A carved ornamental feature consisting of flowers, fruit and foliage (often tied with ribbons) arranged like hanging folds of draperies.

Tabernacle A canopied niche or recess in a wall, often containing a statue or used as a repository for holy objects.

Tracery Decorative stonework in windows, usually the upper part of windows – a feature particularly characteristic of GOTHIC architecture; the term is also applied to similar decorative forms used elsewhere, for example on furniture.

Trompe-l'oeil A painting (or part of a painting) that is intended to deceive the viewer into thinking that it is a real object rather than a two-dimensional portrayal of it; the term is French for 'deceives the eye'.

Tympanum The triangular or segmental area between the flat top of a door and the PEDIMENT above it.

Vault An arched roof or ceiling, particularly one built of stone or brick.

Further Reading

....

Brook, Stephen, *The Double Eagle*, Hamish Hamilton, 1988

Garton-Ash, Timothy, *The Uses of Adversity*, Granta Editions, 1989
We the People: The Revolutions of 1989, Granta Editions, 1990

Green, Gerald, *The Artists of Terezín*, Hawthorn Books, New York, 1978

Grusa, Jiri, *Franz Kafka of Prague*, Schocken, New York, 1983

Hašek, Jaroslav, *The Good Soldier Švejk*, Penguin, 1974

Havel, Václav, *Living in Truth*, Faber, 1986

Kafka, Franz, *The Diaries of Franz Kafka*, Penguin, 1964

Klíma, Ivan, *Love and Garbage*, Chatto & Windus, 1990

Kundera, Milan, *The Unbearable Lightness of Being*, Faber, 1984

Roth, Philip, *The Prague Orgy*, Jonathan Cape, 1985

Stern, J. P., ed., *The World of Franz Kafka*, Weidenfeld & Nicolson, 1980

Zeman, Z. A. B., *Prague Spring*, Penguin, 1969

Index

....

References to illustrations appear in italics, after the text references.

Adalbert, St 44, 99, 104
Aichbauer, J.G. 66
alchemy 50, 93, 161
Aleš, Mikoláš 84, 126, 133, 152, 170, 172
Alliprandi, Giovanni Battista 60, 78, 79, 82, 94, 138
Anna Jagellon 33, 43
Aostali, J.M. 172
Assam, Peter 133
Astronomical Clock 129, *129*

Balšánek, A. 140
Bassano family 38, 61
Bayer, Paul Ignác 136, 155
Becherovka 69
Bechteller, Caspar 43–4, 45
beer halls:
    At the Golden Tiger 134
    St Thomas's 91
    U Fleků 154
    U Kalicha 158
    U Kocoura 77
    U Malvase 108
    U Pinkasů 150
    U Supa 138
Beethoven, Ludwig van 87
Belvedere, *see* palaces
Bendl, Jan 38, 54, 105, 141, 147, 167, 170
Biederle, J.M. 66
Blecha, M. 154

Bohemia 40, 45, 49, 54, 66, 104, 111, 112, 113, 121, 141, 147, 156, 158, 165, 174
Bohemian Estates 36, 40, 49, 57, 79, 123
Böhm, J.K. 98
Boleslav the Cruel 45, 47
Boleslav II the Pious 50, 174
Bořivoj II 44
Botič valley 159, 169
Brahe, Tycho 108, 126
Brandl, Peter 38, 54, 66, 84, 91, 121, 174, *53*
Braník brewery 91, 108, 138
Braque, Georges 63
Braun, Antonín 131, 156
Braun, Matthias 45, 54, 77, 87, 99–102, 104, 106, 108, 109, 138, 156, 167, *106*
Břetislav I 35, 44
Břetislav II 44
bridges:
    Charles 35, 43–4, 53, 90, 95, 97–105, 167; *96, 98, 100*
    Judith 86, 97, 98
Broggio, Ottaviano 154
Borkoff, Ferdinand Maximilian 54, 64, 75, 77, 86, 91, 98, 99, 102, 116, 119, 121, 135, 136, 151, 167, *116, 167*
Brokoff, Jan 73, 102, 167, 169
Bronzino 61

Brožík, Václav 131, 147
Bruegel, Pieter, the Elder 62
Brueghel, Jan, the Elder 62
Bruni, Karl 54
Bys, Jan Rudolf 54

Canaletto 61
Canevale, M.A. 151
Čapek, Karel 170
Caratti, Francesco 65, 66, 86, 105, 106, 109
Carlone, Carlo 109
Carolinum 137
Casanova, Giacomo 77
Castle 33–58, *37, 39*
    Ball Games Court 34, *34*
    Black Tower 34, 56
    Bohemian Chancellery 47
    Chapel of the Holy Cross 37
    Dalibor Tower 34
    Golden Lane 54, *55*
    Hall of the Diet 49
    Lobkovic Palace 56–7, *56*
    Matthias Gate 36, 38, 79, 84
    Powder Tower 49–50
    Provost's House 38, 40
    Riding School 34
    Royal Gardens 34
    Royal Palace 47–9
    St George's Basilica 36, 49–50, 54, 59, *51*

St George's Convent 50–4, 59
Spanish Hall 38
Vladislav Hall 47, 49, *48, 49*
White Tower 34
see also galleries and St Vitus's Cathedral under churches
Catholicism, Roman 57, 60, 134, 135
Čedok 141
Černy, F.M. 161
Čertovka, River 89, 90
Český Krumlov 53
Cézanne, Paul 62
Charles IV, Emperor 36, 38, 40, 45, 47, 49, 56, 69, 75, 98, 104, 115, 137, 145, 150, 154, 155, 158, 159, 161, 169, 174
Charles University 56, 104, 105, 137, 138
Christoff, J. 116
churches, etc:
    Bethlehem Chapel 56, 134–5
    Břevnov Monastery 174
    Capuchin 66
    Convent of the Blessed Agnes 118–9
    Emmaus Monastery 161, *163*
    Holy Cross Chapel 135
    Holy Cross Chapel (Na příkopě) 141–3

Holy Ghost 116, *116*
Holy Trinity 154
Karlov 158–9, 163, *160*
Loreto 65–6, 174, *67*
Order of the Cross 53
Our Lady 159
Our Lady at the Theatines 77
Our Lady of Victories 84–6
Our Lady of Victory 172–4, *173*
SS Cosmas and Damian 161
SS Cyril and Methodius 161–3
SS Peter and Paul 170
SS Simon and Jude 116–7
St Adalbert 154
St Apollinaris 158
St Clement 108, 109, 163, *107*
St Francis 104–5
St Francis (St Agnes's Convent) 118, 119
St Gall 136
St Gastulus 119
St Giles 134, *132*
St Henry 141
St Ignatius 155, *157*
St James 119–21, *118, 120*
St John (Malá Strana) 90
St John Nepomuk (Hradčany) 69
St John Nepomuk on the Rock 161, *162*
St Joseph 90–1
St Lawrence 174
St Longinus 156
St Martin (Vyšehrad) 170
St Martin at the Wall 135
St Mary of the Snows 50, 150
St Mary under the Chain 86–7, *85*
St Nicholas (Malá Strana) 73, 78, 80–2, 90, 155, *58, 81*
St Nicholas (Staré Město) 131–3, *124*
St Salvator 105, 106, 108, *103*
St Salvator (Dušní) 116

St Salvator (St Agnes's Convent) 118, 119
St Stephen 155–6
St Thomas 91, 174
St Vitus's Cathedral 36, 37, 38–47, 50, 59, 64, 65, 73, *39, 41, 42, 43, 45*: Bohemian Crown Jewels 47; Golden Gate 40; Great Tower 40, 43; Holy Cross Chapel 45; Martinitz Chapel 45; Schlick Monument 45; St Adalbert's Chapel 44; Sigismund Bell 40; tomb of St John Nepomuk 44, 45; Vladislav Oratory 45, 138; Wenceslas Chapel 45, 54; *46*
St Wenceslas 163
Strahov Monastery 34, 54, 59, 69–73, 174, *58, 71, 72*
Tyn 35, 44, 53, 73, 121, 124–6, 131, 141, 150, 156, 165, 177, *58*
Ursuline Convent 151
see also Castle
Clementinum 106, 109, 110, *106*
coffee houses:
　Europa 149, *150*
　Malostranská 79
　Slavia 152
Collin, Alexander 43
Costa, Lorenzo 60
Counter-Reformation 57, 60, 66, 106, 136
Cranach, Lucas, the Elder 37–8, 60
Cranach, Lucas, the Younger 61
Cyril, St 44

defenestration of 1419 155
defenestration of 1618 45, 64
Degas, Edgar 62, 63
Destinn, Emmy 79, 170
Dientzenhofer, Christoff 80, 174, *81*
Dientzenhofer, Kilián Ignác 65, 69, 80, 91, 108, 124, 131, 143, 156, 161, 174, 175–7, *81, 106, 162*
Dobrovský, Josef 90

Dům Umělců 110
Dürer, Albrecht 54, 61
Dušek family 135, 175
Dvořák, Antonín 152, 156, 170

Elisabeth of Pomerania 40

Federal Assembly Building 149
Ferdinand I, Emperor 33, 36, 43, 56, 60, 106, 170, 172
Ferdinand II 57, 93, 134
Ferdinand of Tyrol 172
Fialka, Ladislav 106
Fischer, Jiří 140, 141–3
Fischer von Erlach, Johann Bernard 44, 66, 109, 121, *109*
Fischer von Erlach, Josef Emanuel 44, 45
Frederick V of the Palatinate 44
Frederick the Great, Emperor of Prussia 40

galleries:
　Castle Picture Gallery 37–8
　Central Bohemian Art Gallery 134
　National 60–3, 91, *62*
　St George's Convent (Bohemian art) 38, 50–4, 126, 150, 167, *52, 53*
gardens:
　Botanical 159–61
　Franciscan 150
　Kolowrat 94
　Ledebour 94
　St Catherine's 156
　Valdštejn 94–5, *74, 92*
　Vojanovy 95
　Vrtba 84
　see also Castle
George and Martin of Cluj 38, 52
George of Poděbrady 45, 97, 131, 134, 140
Gočár, Josef 138
Gottwald, Klement 123, 136, 159, 169

Goya, Francisco 62
Granovský, Jakub 121
Greco, el 62

Habsburg rule 33, 36, 38, 49, 56, 64, 70, 75, 91, 133, 143, 158, 167, 169
Haehnel, J. 104
Haffenecker, Anton 80, 86, 137, 140
Haffenecker, T. 87
Hals, Frans 62
Hašek, Jaroslav 158
Havel, Václav 40, 64
Hayn, Josef 108
Heermann, Jan Jiří 54, 169
Hilbert, Kamil 41
Hochhaus, T. 69
Hollar, Václav 54
Holy Roman Empire 104
Hotel Paříž 140
houses:
　At the Crown 133
　At the Golden Lily 133
　At the Golden Scales 136
　At the Golden Swan 93
　At the Golden Tree 119
　At the Golden Well 109
　At the Stone Bell 124
　At the Stone Table 126
　At the Two Golden Bears 143, *142*
　At the White Lion 133
　Château Troja 169, *164, 168*
　Diamant 154
　Faust 161
　House of the Black Mother of God 138
　House of the Minute 127, 133, *126*
　Menhart 138
　Peterka 150
　Platýz 151
　Portheimka 175–7
　Rott 133
　Štěpánovský 126
　Storch 126, 172
　Topič 151
　Valkounsky 77
　Villa Amerika 156–8, *159*
　Villa Bertramka 135, 175, *176*

Hradčany (Castle district) 33–73, 75, 84, 94, 140, 169
Hradčany Town Hall 65
Hrzán, Ferdinand 89
Hunger Wall 174
Hus, Jan 73, 123, 124, 135, 136
Hus Monument 123, 126, *124*
Hussite Wars 40, 56, 60, 124, 137, 145, 150, 155, 169, 170

I.P. Master 54, 125
Italian Hospital 82, 84

Jäckel, Matthias 66, 90, 102–4, 105, 133, 155, 167, 174
Jäger, Joseph 79, 86, 90
Janáček, Leoš 152
Jaroš, Tomáš 33
Jesuit colleges 78, 155
Jewish cemetery 111, 112, *112*
Jewish Quarter 111–6, *see also* synagogues
Jewish Town Hall 116
Jirásek, Alois 172
John Nepomuk, St, statues 69, 75, 102, 116, 151, *116*
tomb 44, 45
Josefov 111–6
Joseph, St 75, 95, 155
Joseph II, Emperor 49, 50, 57, 69, 70, 75, 90, 111, 112, 140, 172
Jugendstil 109, 110, 138, 140, 143, 150
Jungmann, Josef 150

Kafka, Franz 54, 126, 133
Kampa Island 86, 89, *87*
Kaňka, František Maximilian 45, 65, 82, 84, 89, 91, 93, 105, 106, 108, 109, 137, 156, 158
Karlštejn Castle 53, 56
Kelley, Edward 161
Kepler, Johannes 93, 108
Kisch, Egon Erwin 143
Klimt, Gustav 62
Koch, Jindřich 124

Kohen, Gershon 112
Kohl, Jeroným 37
Kohl, Johann Friedrich 65, 80, 102
Kohl, J. G. 40
Kokoschka, Oskar 62, *62*
Kolowrat family 66, 77
Kotěra, Jan 150
Kracker, Johann Lukas 80, 82
Kranner, Josef 124, 133
Krocín fountain 167
Kupecký, Jan 38, 54
Kutná Hora 138

Lapidarium *see* museums
Lederer, F.X. 167
Leigh Fermor, Patrick 64
Lenin, V.I. 136, 141, 167
Lesser Town Town Hall 79, 84, 131
libraries:
Philosophical (Strahov) 70–2, *72*
Theological (Strahov) 72
Libuše, Princess 169
Liechtenstein, Karl von 78
Liška, Jan Krystof 54, 105
Liszt, Franz 87, 151, 152
Litoměřice Altar, Master of the 45–7, 53–4
Lobkovic family 63, 65, 86
Lotto, Lorenzo 61
Löw, Rabbi 112, 116
Ludmilla, St 50, 102
Ludvik Jagellon 36
Lurago, Anselmo 36, 49, 69, 70, 80, 138, 143
Lurago, Carlo 56, 82, 86–7, 105, 106, 141, 155, 170
Lurago, J.A. 93

Maisl, Mordechai Markus 115
Malá Strana (Lesser Town) 33, 35, 36, 47, 59–95, 102, 145, 167, 174, *88, 96, 130*
Malá Strana cemetery 175
Maltese convent 87
Mandl, M.B. 99
Mánes, Josef 118, 129

Maria Theresia, Empress 36, 44, 57
Martinitz, Jaroslav von 45, 64
Martinů, Bohuslav 90, 149, 152
Masaryk, Thomáš 136
Mathey, Jean Baptiste 34, 64, 77, 90, 104, 169
Matthias, Emperor 36, 37
Matthias of Arras 38, 40
Maulbertsch, Anton 70, 154
Max, Emanuel 102, 129
Maximilian I, Emperor 61
Maximilian II, Emperor 36, 43, 124
Mayer, J.O. 98, 102, 109
metro stations:
Florenc 177
Hradčanská 170
Malostranská 33, 57, 97
Můstek 143, 145
Muzeum 145, 170
Nádraží Halešovice 165, 169
Vyšehrad 169
Mikuláš of Kadaň 129
Mint 138, *137*
Moravia 56, 70, 111, 112, 113, 115
Mosto, Ottavio 64, 79, 119, 167
Mozart, Wolfgang Amadeus 70, 77, 80, 87, 105, 106, 135, 137, 152, 175
Mucha, Alfons 43, 170, *43*
Munch, Edvard 62
museums:
Bohemian Art 118–9
Czech Literature 73
Decorative Arts 110, 112
Dvořák 156–8, *159*
Ethnographic 135
Ethnographic (Villa Kinsky) 175
Gottwald 136–7, 141
Graphics Collection of National Gallery 124
Historical Museum (Lobkovic Palace) 33, 56–7, 147, 177
Jewish 111, 115
Lapidarium 102, 104, 147, 165–9, *167*

Lenin 141
Military History 64
Mozart 175
Municipal 177
Musical Instruments 87–9, 147
National 57, 77, 145, 147–9, 177, *147, 148*
Police 158
Smetana 104, 105
Myslbek, Josef 44, 147, 152, 170

Nazis 111, 113, 115, 163
Neruda, Jan 77, 170
New Town *see* Nové Město
New Town Hall 155
New Town Waterworks 152
Neumann, P. 65
Nosecký, Siard 72, 73
Nostitz family 137
Novák, I.F. 44
Nové Město (New Town) 50, 145–63, 169

Obecní Dům 140, *139*
Old Town *see* Staré Mesto
Old Town Town Hall 127–31, 177, *127, 128*
Order of the Cross, Master of the 53
Orsi, Giovanni Domenico 72, 155
Oswald, Master 45, 47
Ottakar I 44
Ottakar II 44, 49, 56, 75

Pacassi, Nikolaus 36, 37, 38, 40, 49, *88*
Pachta, Count Jan 106
Palace of Culture 159, 169
palaces:
Adria 150
Archbishop's 60, *63*
Auersperk 94
Belvedere 33–4, 94, 151, *32*
Bretfeld 77
Břetislav 84
Buquoy 89
Caretto-Millesimo 138
Černín (Hradčany) 65, 66, 69

Černín (Malá Strana) 93
Clam-Gallas 54, 109, *109*
Colloredo-Mansfeld 108
Dietrichstein (Hradčany) 65
Fürstenberg 94
Golz-Kinský 123–4, 143, 167
Grand Priory of the Order of the Knights of Malta 87–9
Grömling 79
Hartig 82
Hrzán (Hradčany) 65
Hrzán (Malá Strana) 89
Hrzán (Staré Město) 138
Kaiserstein (Kampa) 89, 90
Kaiserstein (Malá Strana) 79
Kaunic 90
Kinský 141
Kolowrat 94
Kučera 69
Lažan 152
Lažanský 93
Ledebour 94
Liechtenstein (Malá Strana) 78
Little Buquoy 89
Little Černín 94
Lobkovic (Hradčany) 33, 56–7
Lobkovic (Malá Strana) 82–3, 84
Martinitz 64
Morzin 77
Nostitz 86, 90
Oettingen 91
Pachta 105–6
Pötting 108
Salm 60, 75
Schönborn 82, *83*
Schwarzenberg 60, 63–4, 73, *63*
Smiřický 79
Sporck 84
Sternberg (Hradčany) 60–3, 91, *62*
Sternberg (Malá Strana) 79
Sternegg 87
Sweets-Sporck 140
Sylva-Taroucca 143
Thun 91

Thun-Hohenstein (Karmelitská) 84
Thun-Hohenstein (Malá Strana) 77, 82
Toscana 64
Turba 86
Valdštejn 54, 93, 94–5, *74*
Valter 151
Vrtbovský 84
see also Castle
Palach, Jan 110, 147
Palko, Franz Xaver 82
Palliardi, Ignác 70, 80, 82, 94, 174
Palliardi, M.I. 163
Palma Giovane 61
Palma Vecchio 61
Parigi, Abraham 90–1
Parler, Heinrich 47
Parler, Peter 38–40, 41, 43, 45, 47, 64, 98, 131
Parler workshop 44, 49, 50, 53, 104, 126, 167
Pavíček, F. 60
Petřín hill 35, 73, 82, 83, 174
Philippi, Giovanni Maria 36, 38, 70, 79, 84–6
Picasso, Pablo 63
Pieroni, Giovanni 95
Pilsen beer 135, 150
Piombo, Sebastiano del 61
Platzer, Ignác, the Elder 36, 40, 44, 60, 80–2, 90, 105, 124, 126, 138, 141, 143, 151, 167, *37*
Plečnik, J. 38
Polívka, O. 109, 140, 151
Prachner, Richard and Peter 82
Práger, K. 149, 151
Preiss, František 151
Přemyslid dynasty 35, 44, 56, 118, 170
pubs *see* beer halls

Quittainer, A. 65, 69, 70

Raab, Ignác 82
Rauchmuller, Matthias 102
Reiner, Václav 47, 50, 54, 66, 69, 91, 105, 121, 134, 141, 156, 174

Rejsek, Mathias 125, 129, 138–40
Rembrandt 62
restaurants:
    Espreso 49
    Paříž 140
    Pelikán 143
    Three Ostriches 95
    U Bindrů 126
    U Dvou Koček 135
    U Malířů 86
    U Prince 126
    U Schnellů 79, 91
    U zlaté studny 93
    U Zlatého Hada 108–9
    Valdštejnská hospoda 94
    Vikárka 49
Ried, Benedikt 47, 54, *48*
Roder, Pankraz 116
Rodin, Auguste 63
Roland Column 102, 167
Rousseau, Henri 63
Rubens, Peter Paul 38, 62, 91
Rudolf II 36, 37, 45, 50, 57, 61, 93, 115, 124, 126, 161
Ruisdael, Jacob van 62
Ruysdael, Saloman van 62

Šaloun, Ladislav 123, 140, 151
Santini, Giovanni 77, 82, 94, 136
Schiele, Egon 62
Schlanovský, J.G. 158
Schmidt, Anton 90, 161
Schmidthammer, J. 43
Schulz, Josef 110, 147, 151
Schwarzenberg, Cardinal Bedrich 44
Scotti, Bartolomeo 87
Seifert, Jaroslav 54
Sigismund, St 104
Škréta, Karel 54, 82, 87, 126, 141, 156
Slesinger, J. 116
Slovanský Dům 141
Slovanský Ostrov 152
Smetana, Bedřich 105, 126, 152, 156
Soběslav I, Duke 49, 56
Soldati, Tomasso 155
Spazio, Giovanni 34

Spiess, Hans 45, 47
Spranger, Bartholomeus 37
Spytihněv I 38
Spytihněv II 44
squares (náměstí):
    Anenské 106
    Betlémské 134–5
    Charles (Karlovo) 33, 154–5, 156, 161, *157*
    Gorky 141
    Hradčanské (Castle Square) 35, 57, 59–65, 73, 75, 167, *63*
    Jana Palacha 110
    Jungmannovo 150
    Loretánské 65, 69
    Malé (Little Square) 77, 133, 134, *131*
    Malostranské 75, 78–82, 86, 97, 155
    Maltézské 86
    Marianské 109, 131
    Můstek 143, 145, 150
    Na Kampě 90
    Old Town Square 57, 75, 121, 123–33, 143, 167, *122*, *124*
    Pohořelec 69
    Sovětských tankistů 175
    Uhelny trh 135–6, 167
    Václavské (Wenceslas) 123, 143, 145–7, 149, 167, *147*
    Valdštejnské 93
    Velkopřevorské 89
Star Castle 170–2, *172*
Staré Město (Old Town) 36, 56, 77, 97–143, 145, *130*
Steinfels, J.J. 151, 174
Stella, Paolo della 33
Sternberg family 169
streets:
    Betlémská 135
    Břehová 111
    Celetná 137–8, 154, *136*, *137*
    Dlouhá 119
    Dušní 116
    Havelská 136
    Husova 109, 134, 135
    Hybernská 140, 141
    Jánská 84
    Jilskà 134

Jiřská   54, 56
Josefská   90
Kapucínská   66, 69
Karlova   108–9, 134
Karmelitská   84–6
Ke Karlovu   156, 158, 159
Křižovnická   109–110
Lázeňská   86, 89
Letenská   91, 94, 95
Loretánská   64, 65
Melantrichova   126, 143
Mišeňská   95
Mostecká   90, 97
Mozartova   175
Na příkopě   141–3, 150
Na Slupi   159
Národní   150–2
Nerudova   73, 75–7, 79, 82, 90, *76*
New Castle Steps   35
Nový Svět   66, 69, *68*
Old Castle Steps   33, 56, 57
Platnéřská   109–110
Resslova   161, 163
Říční   90
Rytířská   135, 136, 137
Sněmovní   93
Spálená   154
Šporkova   84
Štefánikova   175, 177
Štěpánská   155–6
Thunovská   77, 91, 93
Tomášská   79, 91
Tržiště   82, 84
Týnská   121, 124
U Lužického Semináře   95, 97

U Radnice   131
Úvoz   73, 75
Valdštejnská   33, 94
Vikářská   49
Vlašská   82, 84
Wilsonova   149
Zlatá   134
Stromovka Park   165
Švabinský, Max   47
Symons, Arthur   69
synagogues:
    Altneu   113, 115–6, *114*
    High   115, 116
    Klaus   111–2
    Maisl   113–5, *113*
    Pinkas   112–3, 115
    Spanish   116, *117*

Terezín   111
theatres:
    Magic Lantern   150
    Na Zábradlí   106
    National   33, 35, 102, 147, 149, 151–2, 172, *144, 153*
    Smetana   149, 152
    Rudolfinum   110
    Tyl   137, 175
Theodoric, Master   53, 56
Thirty Years War   57, 93, 95, 116, 167
Tiepolo, Giambattista   61
Tintoretto   38, 61
Titian   38
towers:
    Astronomical   106
    Lesser Town Bridge   90, 95, *98*

Old Town Bridge   98, 104, 167
Powder   138–40, *139*
    see also Castle
Třeboň Altarpiece, Master of the   53, *52*
Trinity Column   78, 86
Týn school   124

U Hybernů   140
Ungelt courtyard   121
Utraquist movement   124

Van Dyck, Anthony   62
Velvet Revolution   64, 109, 123, 136, 147, 151, 156
Ventura, Giovanni   56
Veronese, Paolo   38
Vienna   36, 44, 62, 64, 66, 75, 109, 110, 115, 133, 152, 175
Vischer, Hans   47
Vitus, St   44, 98, 104
Vlach, Augustin   63
Vladislav II, Duke   69
Vladislav II Jagellon   36, 40, 47, 140
Vltava, River   33, 44, 73, 89, 90, 98, 102, 170
Vratislav I   50
Vratislav II   38, 169, 170
Vries, Adriaen de   37, 54, 95, 177
Vyšehrad   135, 147, 167, 169–70
    cemetery   170, *171*
Vyšší Brod Altarpiece, Master of the   53

Wallenstein, General von   93
Weber, Carl Maria von   137
Wenceslas, duke and saint   38, 45, 50, 56, 126, 172
    statues   38, 44, 47, 98, 102, 147, 167, 170
Wenceslas I, King   118
Wenceslas IV, King   36, 44, 45, 104, 140
White Mountain   170, 172–4, *173*
White Mountain, Battle of   36, 44, 56, 57, 60, 75, 78, 79, 123, 129, 137, 161
Willmann, Michael   54
wine bars:
    Klášterní   151
    Makarská   80
    Three Graces   105
    U Kolovrata   94
    U Mecenáše   80
    U Pavouka   121
    U Zlaté Hrušky   66
    U Zlaté Studny   109
Wirch, Johann Joseph   60, 77, 105, 138, 154
Wohlmut, Bonifaz   33, 34, 40, 43, 49, 158
World War I   38
World War II   111, 113, 129, 131, 161, 172
Würth, J.J.   44

Želivský, Jan   150, 155
Zitek, Josef   110, 151
Zizkov   175
Zoo   169